CHILDREN
OF THE DREAM

CHILDREN OF THE DREAM

Why School Integration Works

RUCKER C. JOHNSON

with ALEXANDER NAZARYAN

BASIC BOOKS

Co-published by the Russell Sage Foundation
NEW YORK

Basic Books
Hachette Book Group
1290 Avenue of the Americas, New York, NY 10104
www.basicbooks.com

Printed in the United States of America
First Edition: April 2019
Published by Basic Books, an imprint of Perseus Books, LLC, a subsidiary of Hachette Book Group, Inc. The Basic Books name and logo is a trademark of the Hachette Book Group.
Co-published by the Russell Sage Foundation

The Hachette Speakers Bureau provides a wide range of authors for speaking events. To find out more, go to www.hachettespeakersbureau.com or call (866) 376-6591.

The publisher is not responsible for websites (or their content) that are not owned by the publisher.

Graphics designed by Aaron Reeves
Print book interior design by Linda Mark

The Library of Congress has cataloged the hardcover edition as follows:
  Names: Johnson, Rucker C., author. | Nazaryan, Alexander, author.
  Title: Children of the dream : why school integration works / Rucker C. Johnson, with Alexander Nazaryan.
  Description: First edition. | New York : Basic Books, [2019] | "Co-published by the Russell Sage Foundation." | Includes bibliographical references and index.
  Identifiers: LCCN 2018040106 (print) | LCCN 2018060898 (ebook) | ISBN 9781541672697 (ebook) | ISBN 9781541672703 (hardcover : alk. paper)
  Subjects: LCSH: School integration—United States. | Segregation in education—United States. | Educational equalization—United States.
  Classification: LCC LC214.2 (ebook) | LCC LC214.2 .J64 2019 (print) | DDC 379.2/630973—dc23
  LC record available at https://lccn.loc.gov/2018040106

ISBNs: 978-1-5416-7270-3 (hardcover), 978-1-5416-7269-7 (ebook)

LSC-C

10 9 8 7 6 5 4 3 2 1

In loving memory of my Dad:
my first history teacher

CONTENTS

But my point was that not only I and my children are craving light, the entire colored race is craving light, and the only way to reach the light is to start our children together in their infancy and they come up together.

—Silas Hardrick Fleming, testimony in *Brown et al. v. Board of Education of Topeka*, US District Court of Kansas, 1951

AUTHOR'S NOTE:
RUCKER C. JOHNSON

IT HAPPENED THREE YEARS AGO. I WAS FORTY-TWO YEARS OLD, enjoying my life in the San Francisco Bay Area as an economist, professor, father, amateur musician, and fitness enthusiast. Everything was fine. Actually, everything was great.

One day, I felt a weight on my chest as I walked into the gym. Convinced that it was nothing but a little heartburn, I continued my workout. The pain didn't end, however. I told my wife that I would be okay if I got a good night's rest. But the next morning, she took my blood pressure and looked at me with shock. Based on the reading, I needed immediate medical intervention.

We sped to the emergency room. After excruciating hours of tests, the cardiologist confirmed that I'd had a heart attack; he ordered an ambulance to rush me into emergency cardiac surgery.

I survived to complete this book with new attention to how bodily systems support each other and function interdependently. As I recovered, I considered my life's work on poverty and inequality, specifically on the similarity between the human body's systems and the policy systems of an equitable society. Through my research, I have come to terms with the reality that there is an undeniable interconnectedness among the policies designed to give our children (and their children) the opportunities they deserve to do something meaningful with their lives.

Just as our bodies begin to malfunction when systems fall out of balance, society suffers when we do not address inequality with the holistic strategy it deserves. I write this book as a "health report" on our nation's goal of equal opportunity. I write to charge us individually and collectively to carefully consider the data analysis herein as evidence that we can have superior social outcomes when we design our education, health, housing, justice, and other policies to be connected from inception to implementation—as well as through reformation.

We must tend to the health of those policies through an intentional, sustained effort. If we do it for our individual health, we certainly can do it for the health of the nation.

AUTHOR'S NOTE:
ALEXANDER NAZARYAN

BECAUSE THE SCHOOLS ARE GOOD. THAT WAS WHY MY PARENTS moved our family from Leningrad, in the Soviet Union, to the suburbs north of New York City. There were other reasons, too, that we didn't end up in Kansas or Oregon, but the quality of public education was foremost. In fact, it was a primary reason we moved to the United States instead of moving to Israel, where military service would await at the end of a high school career.

Nobody ever understands how lucky he is. So it was with me. It seemed normal, for example, that I had a full-time language teacher devoted to me and a small scrum of other Russian immigrants. The well-stocked classrooms, the well-compensated teachers, the newest textbooks—that was just how things worked. When my high school was named the sixtieth best in the nation, the news was met with widespread derision by the student body, because we were ungrateful in the way of all teenagers. Most of us had no clue that, just a few miles away, there were children attending schools unfit for the developing world, never mind for the wealthiest and most powerful nation on earth.

It was in high school that I started to understand the vagaries of public education. The way, for example, my own excellent schooling

was funded by the wealthy families with enormous houses sequestered in the wooded hills above town. My own father, meanwhile, a
PhD who had worked in a physics lab in the Soviet Union, delivered
pizza. And there were the inner-city kids who were bused into our
suburban enclave. They were the "benefactors" of a desegregation
plan, though also the victims of long-standing racial inequalities. We
didn't understand that, of course. Those kids, the black kids, stayed
together, moving quietly through the hallways.

Later, after college, I became an educator, working in schools
across Brooklyn, in large part to directly address the inequalities I had
come to understand in the course of my own public education. This
book is a continuation of that effort.

INTRODUCTION:
THE DREAM DEFERRED

M ORE THAN SIXTY YEARS AGO, THE FEDERAL GOVERNMENT EM-
barked upon an experiment of astonishing ambition. It decided
to reverse centuries of racism, discrimination, and forced separation of
the races. The laboratory where this experiment took place is where
we frequently test our grandest ideas about what American society
should be: the public school classroom.

The experiment was called school integration, and it began with
the 1954 Supreme Court decision in *Brown v. Board of Education
of Topeka, Kansas*. The case has become such a mainstay of American culture that we tend to forget just how revolutionary it was for the
nation's highest court to decide that black and white children would
no longer attend separate schools. And, what's more, that the federal
government would exert its fullest power, including that of the military
if need be, to end that separation.

As both proponents and opponents of the decision knew, *Brown*
wasn't just about schools. Kids who went to school together would
also become friends, go to the same swimming pools, eat in the same
restaurants, live in the same neighborhoods. If you struck down segregation in schools, you struck down segregation everywhere. That is

1

what both thrilled and terrified Americans who understood the full scope of the decision. It is no accident, therefore, that *Brown* is often considered the beginning of the civil rights movement.

In spite of all the laws that were passed during the civil rights era and the "War on Poverty" initiatives and all the progress that was made, we find ourselves today groping in the dark, facing many of the same challenges. Looking at schools today, you might think that *Brown v. Board of Education* never happened. True, nobody is foisting "Race Mixing Is Communism" signs, as white protesters did in Little Rock, Arkansas, in 1959. But there are, once again, classrooms in which all the students are white, and other classrooms in which all the students are black. And even in the schools that appear to be diverse overall, students are divided based on perceived ability. Advanced-level courses create a stout wall that overcrowds black students—including gifted ones—into regular or even remedial classes, while white students enjoy enclaves of small class sizes in the advanced courses that provide future academic benefits well into college. Certainly, no one is throwing rocks at school buses carrying black children to white schools anymore. But that's largely because those buses are no longer en route.[1]

Quietly and subtly, the opponents of integration have won. So, at least, it seems, judging by virtually every indicator of American public education, from test scores to social outcomes. The standard narrative is that integration was a failed experiment, one that was noble yet doomed from the very start. We are beyond it now, and if our schools remain grossly imbalanced, we just have to live with that, to make that necessary concession to reality. Our schools were never going to be a rainbow coalition, beacons of equality and racial harmony. It was a nice thought, but, like so much else from the sixties, more dream than achievable goal. Best to let it go.

This book is a counterargument to that defeatism, to that persistent notion that integration failed and must therefore be consigned to the dusty drawer of historical curiosities. What follows is not an impassioned argument about diversity and integration; plenty of those have been made, and they are absolutely essential. Instead, this book uses data to show the power of integration and related efforts. Contrary to popular wisdom, integration has benefited—and continues to benefit—African Americans, whether that benefit is translated into educational attainment, earnings, social stability, or incarceration rates. Whites, meanwhile, lose nothing from opening their classrooms to others. And overall, society benefits from a decrease in the kind of prejudice that, in the past several years, has threatened to tear us apart.

Analyses of those data lead inevitably to a conclusion at once thrilling and frustrating: integration works, but only if we give it a chance—that is, if we implement collaborative policies beginning in the early childhood years and sustain quality investments from prekindergarten through high school graduation and beyond. This book explores the specific ways in which integration showed promise, how that promise has been stifled, and, most important of all, how that promise can be regained and realized.

Now is the time to act. Educational outcomes are stagnant or plummeting for American children, who increasingly lose out to competitors from around the world. Whereas American public education was once a point of national pride, it is today solidly average, on global terms. In part, that is because large swaths of the population have been left behind. Black children are, on average, two grade levels behind white children in terms of academic achievement; and children in the poorest districts are, on average, four grade levels behind those in the wealthiest districts. In the truest sense of the word, these students are no longer "peers." Resegregation patterns prohibit them from attending the same schools and from learning in the same classrooms. This is the affliction of the racial achievement gap—that is, the difference in educational outcomes for white and Asian children, on the one hand, and black and brown children, on the other. The gaps emerge early, during elementary school, and widen over time. The gaps occur, in part, because children enter school with different levels of preparedness: about one-half of the achievement gap observed in third graders already existed on the first day of kindergarten. Contributing to that gap is the fact that black and brown children who attend poorly funded schools have the least experienced teachers and lack access to mentorship opportunities, music, and the arts as well as to the kind of technology that is proving crucial in the knowledge-based economy of the twenty-first century.[2]

We tend to think of the achievement gap as the problem of those who suffer from it. But the problem belongs to us all, making the closure of that gap imperative. And the bigger the gap grows, the greater the harm to the foundation on which our civil society rests.

Our quest is like a search for the cure to cancer—there is no shortage of studies that attempt to find viable solutions and interventions, but there is a paucity of credible ones demonstrating effective, enduring cures for the ailments of schoolchildren who start off behind and are subsequently left behind. But not all research is created equal. Many studies on the effects of school quality are misleading and are rendered useless for policy prescriptions, because they either (a) insufficiently account for childhood family factors, (b) are short-run snapshots of student performance lacking data that follow children over time, or (c) use time-series data analyzed at the state level, giving little consideration to local conditions and trajectories. Like peering through a microscope with the wrong lens, such approaches fail to use the high-resolution tools needed to capture a clear, detailed picture of the problem, which compromises any attempt to identify a solution. These studies measure some correlation between what schools do and how children fare, and they assume that the school conditions fully and exclusively shaped the child's outcomes. Very few of them sufficiently account for the possibility that socioeconomic factors affecting families could play a role in the achievement gap. Nor do they clearly identify effective interventions that could overcome barriers to success regardless of race, income, or family circumstance.

Meanwhile, headlines declare that school spending doesn't matter and that increases in spending mostly lead to waste; that early childhood education programs, such as Head Start, have no lasting effects; and, most damaging of all, that integration was a failed social experiment. As we embarked on our research journey, hanging over our work like a cloud was the deeply held belief by many that ambitious social programs are not worth the sustained investment they require. In broader arguments about the effectiveness of antipoverty programs, much of the public has adopted the sentiment expressed by President Ronald Reagan in 1988: "We waged a war on poverty, and poverty won." This argument has at times prevailed even when there has been ample evidence to the contrary. But why? Our curiosity was piqued. Why did it appear that these policies were not met with the success that inspired the architects of their enactment?[3]

We discovered that many prior studies were biased and had dubious data sources and samples. If we could isolate the causes, we could get that much closer to identifying prescriptions for social change. That's what we've sought to do.

Just as people have intergenerational lineages, so do policies. In the pages that follow, we chronicle key equal-opportunity initiatives through the prism of the generations of children who were directly impacted by these policy changes. We started with the most controversial and ambitious social experiment of the past fifty years—school desegregation—but quickly found that other policies mattered, too, particularly school finance reform and public pre-K investments. Our journey was fueled by a researcher's hunger to solve the achievement gap puzzle and a journalist's nose for on-the-ground reporting. What lessons could we import from history that could inform contemporary policy debates about the best ways to address unequal opportunity in children's lives? Where there was success, what were schools doing right? And so we launched our research expedition: the nation was our lab; schoolchildren, equal education opportunity policies, and schools our subjects. To glean the most useful policy conclusions, quantitative data would give us an aerial view to be matched with some on-the-ground qualitative evidence from discussions with school leaders, teachers, judges, policymakers, and others on the front lines.

We combined original quantitative analyses and qualitative interviews to ensure that our data mirrored the lived experiences of those who were exposed to these landmark reforms. These complementary vantage points of the same narrative bolstered the validity of our argument that, when strategically implemented together with sustained investments over extended periods of time, equal education opportunity policies can and do work. Individually, integration seeks to accomplish the goal by redistributing schoolchildren, school finance reform by redistributing resources, and expansion of pre-K investments by redistributing the timing of school investments back to the earliest years of cognitive development. As we'll see, these policies can each make a difference on their own, but together they enhance one another. In this way, integration is more than a policy, it is the very *approach* to policy. Some advocates have viewed the pursuit of integration as an end in and of itself, but we'll explore how integration is a necessary means to a broader end: equal opportunity.

Haven't all these things been tried? Yes, but not as the kind of holistic cure we prescribe. In most places and times, these policies were advanced one at a time, unevenly and inconsistently, with each policy often framed initially as a panacea. Yet the substantial variation in their timing and implementation across districts is exactly what offers us a rare testing ground for what we call the "first-generation suite" of equal education opportunity policy initiatives.

———

BECAUSE THE ACHIEVEMENT gap has not been closed, marginalized children continue to suffer the repercussions, their lives sometimes snuffed out. It is no accident that many of the late young African American men whom the Black Lives Matter movement has sought to honor and earn justice for had been incredibly ill served by public education as well as by other segments of society. The social integration aspect of diverse schools is an underappreciated aspect that can enhance the quality of schools. Prior research has shown, for example, that greater childhood exposure to individuals of other races can reduce the anxiety and stress experienced in interactions with members of those groups—conclusions our research corroborates. Michael Brown, the high school graduate killed by a police officer in Ferguson, Missouri, in the summer of 2014, attended schools in the starkly segregated suburbs west of St. Louis. The Normandy Schools Collaborative district, from whose schools Brown graduated, lacks accreditation, making a degree like his much less valuable to colleges and potential employers than a degree from an accredited school. Ferguson had become a two-faced city, with prosperous whites living one reality and struggling African Americans living another.[4]

Eric Garner was also killed by a police officer during that tumultuous summer. His death took place in New York City, a thousand miles from the St. Louis suburbs where Brown was killed. But the conditions weren't all that different. Much like Brown, Garner was the product of a heavily segregated education system that sequestered black and brown children in chaotic schools that did more babysitting than teaching. It worsened the life chances of these kids, when it had been charged with improving them.

Garner, who had been born in 1970, graduated from Automotive High School in 1989, a time when the dropout rate in New York City reached as high as 22 percent. The school had proudly graduated generations of mechanics. But over the post–World War II years, the members of white ethnic groups in the surrounding neighborhood, called Williamsburg, had moved away, their white flight taking them to the suburbs of Long Island, New Jersey, and Connecticut. As Latinos and African Americans moved in, the area had suffered from a massive municipal divestment. And no institution suffered quite like its schools. In 1986, when Garner was in high school at Automotive, the *New York Times* reported that a student there "was found with two eight-inch knives and a brass knuckle ring."[5]

Garner went on to work as a mechanic and a horticulturalist and to have children, but by his early forties, he had an arrest record that included driving without a license, drug possession, assault, and grand larceny. He had quit his job and was making his living selling cigarettes on the streets. When officers of the New York Police Department approached him on July 17, 2014, he was living on the margins of society.

Are substandard schools to blame for the lot of Eric Garner, Michael Brown, and so many others? Imagine if Garner had gone to well-funded schools, beginning in preschool and lasting throughout his high school years, where he had been taught by experienced and committed teachers. What if he had been given opportunities to interact productively with whites and members of other races on a regular, daily basis? Or had been counseled by a caring social worker about the life choices that lay ahead? Imagine, also, that the involved police officers had attended truly integrated schools as children, and had developed more diverse friendships. Would they have had more cultural understanding and fluency, making them better able to handle pressurized situations on the job? Would they have responded with peaceful approaches to conflict? It seems likely that, given such opportunities on both sides, Eric Garner might be flourishing today and would not live on only as a symbol of police brutality.

Schools are sometimes the cause of our collective social failure, and sometimes they are the symptom. Sometimes, they are both. But they are almost never the only malefactor. Take, for example, the case of Freddie Gray, who was killed while in the custody of the Baltimore Police Department in 2015 at the age of twenty-five. Gray had grown up in a West Baltimore neighborhood called Sandtown-Winchester. Many of the houses there were tainted with lead, as landlords neglected to make necessary improvements. While federal law banned the use of lead paint in housing built after 1978, lead paint removal was not required in older homes. Because the houses were so rundown, they were cheap enough to be rented by impoverished African American families that, by the 1980s, had seen little of the upward mobility the civil rights movement had promised.

Exposure to lead early in life can have deleterious impacts on a variety of cognitive and behavioral outcomes, and those ailments seemed to be concentrated in Baltimore's African American population. "Nearly 99.9 percent of my clients were black," said one lawyer after Gray's death, referring to his clients in lead-poisoning cases in the city. "That's the sad fact to life in the ghetto, that the only living conditions people can afford will likely poison their kids. If you only have $250 per month, you're going to get a run-down, dilapidated house where the landlord hasn't inspected it the entire time they've owned it."[6]

Gray struggled in school, often getting into trouble. The high school he attended (but from which he did not graduate), Carver Vocational-Technical, has been described as an "apartheid school," because 98 percent of its students were African American. Its low graduation rate and poor academic offerings consigned students like Gray to a life of bleak prospects. At the time of his death, Gray had never had a good job. Before he was even born, Gray was the victim of forces far beyond his control. Those forces kept his parents from living in safe housing in a neighborhood with good schools. They kept him from having a healthy family life. And as a result, he went to schools similar to those attended by Brown, Garner, and many of the other African Americans who were being felled by police violence.[7]

Despite those facts, we will show in this book that segregation is not a black problem, but an American problem. It is not a single loss prospect—it harms whites and blacks alike. And the blockage it creates reverberates throughout the entire body of American society: higher education, the labor market, public health, criminal justice, civic engagement, digital fluency, life expectancy. As for integration, it is not a zero-sum game: whites as well as blacks benefit from it.

Every politician of the modern era pays lip service to the importance of public education, the need to "fix" our schools. Their "fixes" are often a total departure from those of their predecessors. President Lyndon B. Johnson launched a War on Poverty, which included the revolutionary early education program Head Start. Recognizing the importance of money in education, and of education to his Great Society vision, he signed the Elementary and Secondary Education Act of 1965, establishing the stream of federal Title I funds that bolstered impoverished districts. President George W. Bush had No Child Left Behind, and Barack Obama gave us Race to the Top and greater research-based investments in preschool education.

Magnet schools were a craze, then charter schools. The resurgence of technical and vocational schools are on the horizon. We've had regimes of standardized testing and more rigorous teacher evaluations. These have all come and waned. And despite pockets of success (often in districts that eschew this obsession with panaceas), achievement gaps persist, growing with each successive year students are in school.[8]

Even fixing schools will not "fix" all of the problems that American society faces. But those problems will persist unless we fix our schools. The fix outlined in the pages that follow is not some flashy new proposal unlike anything that's come before. As a matter of fact, every idea suggested herein is an old one, but analyzed anew with better data and superior methods to determine the essential ingredients of school quality for all children. Silicon Valley has made innovation the buzzword of our age. In addition to presenting innovative data that spark new insights, the pages that follow point to another word: commitment, and the restoration thereof, to the ideals and ideas that once provided so much hope for the nation's schools.

Rome was not built in a day, and effective social policies do not work overnight. Hope can fuel the perseverance needed to allow policies to reach fruition. But no policy can, and no policymaker should, rely on hope alone. Our conclusions and policy prescriptions rely on something else: research findings that allow for a clear-eyed look at what we've accomplished, where we've come up short, and how we can yet realize the promise of equality of opportunity. Those new findings stand on the extensive, rigorous analyses of the Panel Study of Income Dynamics (PSID), a survey of eighteen thousand Americans begun by the University of Michigan in 1968 and conducted every year since. "America's family tree," as it is affectionately called by researchers, is the longest-running longitudinal household survey in the world, spanning fifty years and encompassing three generations of adult outcomes. The PSID is like an annual exam, one that focuses on various dimensions of well-being, including earnings, income, wealth, education, health, and family structure. It is one of the few nationally representative data sources that, with innovative and vetted analytical tools, can help unearth answers to complicated questions about poverty and inequality and the influence of childhood factors on success in later life. It is considered among the nation's most reliable sources for answering complex questions about intergenerational mobility. With the PSID, it is possible to determine who is moving up that fabled ladder of opportunity—and who isn't.

The analyses that form the foundation of this work overlay data from the PSID onto the landscape of American education in the second half of the twentieth century. We* track life outcomes of cohorts followed from birth to adulthood across several generations, from the children of *Brown* to *Brown*'s grandchildren. One of the most trenchant effects of that Supreme Court decision was the host of desegregation orders it triggered, which peaked in the 1960s and continued, broadly, until the 1980s. The American Communities Project at Brown University compiled a database of every such desegregation order, including when it was implemented and how, making it possible to link generational outcomes from the PSID to the effects of desegregation on the life trajectories of black and white children alike.

To merge the legal data with the PSID, we compiled annual data with information on school district per-pupil spending, racial school segregation, and class size along with public pre-K spending through Head Start for every school district in the nation from the early 1960s through the present. We then combined information about the timing of school desegregation efforts, the timing and type of school finance reforms, and the implementation of and spending on Head Start programs across the country.

The analysis that follows points incontrovertibly to three powerful cures to unequal educational opportunity: (1) integration, (2) equitable school funding, and (3) high-quality preschool investments—all of which were tried before but abandoned, partly out of resistance,

---

* Throughout the book, when describing specific research studies, "we" refers to Rucker Johnson and the economist colleagues with whom I have collaborated, and does not intend to refer to Alexander Nazaryan.

but also out of a lack of collective patience and wholesale integration of the policies themselves. We are a nation that desperately wants to see results; we want immediate returns on our investment. If we aren't winning, what's the point of playing the game? Except that, of course, education is a long game with ever-shifting rules, participants, referees, and rewards. It might take several generations to even see the score.

As these words are being written, the United States has a deplorably low academic standing, according to the Program for International Student Assessment (PISA), which ranks students around the world on math, reading, and science skills. The latest PISA scores, published in late 2016, show the United States near the bottom among thirty-five industrialized nations in math.[9]

The first international test in math occurred in 1964 before integration began in earnest, and at that time, we placed last. Academic performance has been falling in recent years—just as American schools have been rapidly resegregating. Now, about 15 percent of black children, and 14 percent of Hispanic children, attend something like the "apartheid school" that Freddie Gray attended, meaning that the school's white population constitutes less than a single percentage point. White students, by virtue of ethnicity, are not the panacea; but often, white students come from families that bring resources—both human and material. Apartheid schools, in contrast, often lack both. How can low test scores be surprising, given those circumstances? When we fail to educate some Americans, we fail all Americans.[10]

There can be no illusions about the difficulty of the work ahead. But this book is written to propel the reader through the challenges armed with both the conviction and the facts that can spur individual steps toward collective action. Who will join the movement for the children of the dream? Parents, educators, lay readers, researchers, and policymakers alike must combine forces to change policies and improve schools.

The alternative—inaction—is far more terrifying than the task ahead. In his first term as president, Reagan commissioned a panel to write a report on the state of American education. *A Nation at Risk* was published in 1983, and, as the report's title suggests, it wasn't exactly optimistic about our public schools, or about our democratic society. "Our once unchallenged preeminence in commerce, industry, science, and technological innovation is being overtaken by competitors throughout the world," the report warned. "If an unfriendly foreign power had attempted to impose on America the mediocre educational performance that exists today, we might well have viewed it as an act of war."[11]

"History is not kind to idlers," the report's authors declared as they enumerated the educational woes of their time. But *A Nation at Risk* did not account for poverty or segregation, and the problems they uncovered have only become direr in the thirty-five years since those words were written. The question, then, is how much longer will we remain idle? How much longer will we bemoan the state of affairs while lamenting that nothing can be done?

Much can be done. That is the central argument of this book. If mediocre education is a malign force threatening the nation, what follows in these pages is a three-tiered strategy of counterattack: integrated classrooms, high-quality preschool, and school funding that takes the persistent inequalities into account. These are tools that work, our research shows. This is a fight for our collective future that we can and must win.

PART I
FORWARD MARCH

BEFORE *BROWN*—AND BEYOND

We ain't asking for anything that belongs to those white folks. I just mean to get for that little black boy of mine everything that any other South Carolina boy gets. I don't care if he's as white as the drippings of snow.

—THE REVEREND J. W. SEALS, ST. MARK'S AME CHURCH, SUMMERTON, SOUTH CAROLINA, 1953

A WOMAN SITS, HER SHOTGUN PERCHED ON HER LAP, INCHES FROM Dwight and Floyd Armstrong's beds. The brothers, only eleven and ten years old, awaken briefly to the familiar heat of another Alabama summer and the increasingly familiar and reassuring sight of her guarding them. Her presence, and her shotgun, meant they were safe.

"I just rolled right over and went back to sleep," Dwight later recalled, speaking from Louisville—and from the comfortable remove of middle age.[1]

The place was Birmingham, and the year was 1963. Known as the Pittsburgh of the South, the industrious city had come to be at the center of the civil rights struggle. The armed guards stationed nightly at the Armstrong house were what it took for Dwight and his brother to attend school in an integrated setting—that is, as would always be the case, a school that had previously been all white.

Having elected our first African American president, some claim we now have a postracial society. But we forget the grave, life-altering sacrifices that Dwight and other desegregation pioneers made for the greater good of American society. From our comfortable perches many of us see America as a culturally integrated mecca of progressivity, not realizing that the racial makeup and social conditions of our public school classrooms are nearly identical to those of the Jim Crow era. We now know the necessary components of any plan to successfully combat segregation—and now *re*segregation—largely because of what we've learned from *Brown v. Board of Education* and its consequences. And yet accounts of resistance and triumph from the years following *Brown* are sobering reminders that true integration requires collective conviction and intentional, active work. These will be needed in abundance if we are to again forge ahead on the faded path of integration.

The Armstrongs' story was a remarkable one, but it was not so different from what African Americans experienced all over the South as they sought to fulfill the promise of the 1954 *Brown* decision, which struck down the doctrine of separate-but-equal public schooling.

Nine years later, schools all over the South were neither integrated nor equal in the quality of education they provided to black and white students. Nor were many whites especially eager to carry out the mandates of a Supreme Court that, under Chief Justice Earl Warren, had taken a decidedly liberal turn. Then, as now, the rallying cry of "states' rights" was code for the formerly slaveholding states of the South trying to escape the strictures of the North.

Violence, even against children, was seen as an entirely acceptable means of resisting judicial order. "We were potential targets," Armstrong remembered. "Some of our neighbors weren't too happy with our [civil rights activism], and they were grumbling that they didn't want us to be in the neighborhood. So that's when my father set up the protection brigade." The brigade—which included the lady with the shotgun watching over the sleeping brothers—provided nightly protection to the Armstrong household in the Graymont neighborhood in southwestern Birmingham.

This was not out of an abundance of caution. Today it's hard to describe the fierce white response to the court order requiring Birmingham schools to finally comply with *Brown* in 1963. Armstrong remembers that when he and his brother first tried to enter Graymont Elementary, they were greeted by Al Lingo, the notoriously racist chief of the Alabama Department of Public Safety, who was always eager to carry out the orders of the segregationist Alabama governor George Wallace. Armstrong remembered Attorney General Robert F. Kennedy calling his father, James, to assure him that his sons would be allowed to attend Graymont. He did so by promising that federal marshals would be on hand to keep the children safe as they went to and from school.

"Even though we only had to walk a block to school," Armstrong remembered, "they were there every day, twice a day. When we left the house to go to school, those federal marshals escorted us to school. And on the way home every day, they were there along with my father, to make sure we got home safely and there was no other violence, or nobody interrupting us, or confronting us going back and forth from home to school." That's what it took for a black child to safely attend a racially integrated school in Birmingham in 1963. And even those extreme steps nearly proved insufficient.

As the Armstrong brothers persevered, faithfully attending school, protests against their presence at Graymont continued. The nearby home of the civil rights attorney Arthur Shores was firebombed twice. Dwight and Floyd Armstrong had been steeped in nonviolence training, which they had received alongside their father and the civil rights icon Andrew Young, and knew not to react when white students called them "nigger" or "coon." So while those first days were fraught, neither of the Armstrong boys encountered any physical violence. That was, sadly, the best they could expect from a Deep South that had not expelled the pernicious attitudes of Jim Crow from its collective psyche.

And then came the morning of September 15, 1963. It was a Sunday, and the whole city prepared for church. In the basement of the

16th Street Baptist Church, children were changing into their choir robes. They did not know that, several hours before, the Ku Klux Klan had planted a bomb under the church's stairs. The bomb went off at 10:23 a.m., killing four girls: Addie Mae Collins, Carol Denise Mc-Nair, Carole Robertson, and Cynthia Wesley.

"I went to school with three of those girls," Armstrong said. One had a mother who taught at the segregated school he'd gone to before Graymont. "My sister knew all those girls, and she was supposed to have gone to church with them that morning, but she was running late." He remembered that, for some reason, their father allowed them all to stay home from church that morning.

"We were out in the yard, and I heard this enormous *kaboom*. It was almost like a shock wave." Armstrong said his sister told him she'd learned "that the reason why the church was bombed was because they couldn't get to me and my brother." So threatened were some whites by school integration that they were willing to kill.

———

JAMES ARMSTRONG, THE father of the Armstrong boys and their siblings, had been involved in the civil rights movement since the 1950s and had led some of the early efforts to desegregate schools. This made him, and by association, his family, a target. A barber by trade, he had become known as the Barber of Birmingham, a title that reflected his status in the African American community; he was Martin Luther King Jr.'s favorite barber whenever he came to town. Years later, when James had attained a measure of celebrity—he was the subject of a short documentary that was nominated for an Academy Award in 2012—he'd recall how whites would drive slowly past his barbershop in the College Hills section of Birmingham, pointing their fingers at him as if they were holding guns.[2]

That didn't scare Armstrong, who'd fought the Nazis in World War II. Many African Americans who served in that conflict had returned home dismayed to find little gratitude for their service—and more or less the same enmity they'd encountered before the war. But they also returned emboldened to defeat it. As one black corporal from Alabama famously said in 1954, "I spent four years in the Army to free a bunch of Dutchmen and Frenchmen, and I'm hanged if I'm going to let the Alabama version of the Germans kick me around when I get home. No sirree-bob! I went into the Army a nigger; I'm comin' out a *man*."[3]

Armstrong first filed suit against the Birmingham Board of Education in 1957, joining eight other parents in the legal action. In the lawsuit, *Shuttlesworth v. Birmingham Board of Education*, they said the children, who were all African American, could not attend the school nearest to their homes because they had been prevented from doing so "solely on the basis of race or color or resentment by others."[4]

The plaintiffs cited the state's "pupil placement law," whose sole purpose seemed to be to frustrate and forestall the enactment of the edicts of *Brown v. Board of Education*. The state law, which had been passed in 1955, gave school districts immense latitude in how they assigned students to schools. In doing so, it effectively sanctioned segregation. The law's text decreed that "each local Board of Education shall have full and final authority and responsibility for the assignment, transfer and continuance of all pupils among and within the public schools within its jurisdiction, and may prescribe rules and regulations pertaining to those functions." In other words, the local boards could use their own criteria in determining whether to move students in or out of particular schools, including "the psychological effect upon the pupil of attendance at a particular school" and "the possibility of breaches of the peace or ill will or economic retaliation within the community." The implication of the law would have been obvious to everyone: if white schools didn't want to take black students, they wouldn't have to.

Ernest Jackson, a lawyer from Jacksonville, Florida, brought the case on behalf of the Armstrongs and the children from other brave black families and their parents. Attorney Jackson argued that Alabama clearly intended to perpetuate a segregated system without any plan to assign any blacks to white schools. The placement act, Jackson contended, was a device to render the Brown decision "null, void, and of no effect." But the judge disagreed, seeing no direct evidence that the black students had been denied admission simply because they were black. Jackson persevered through six grueling years of motions, rulings, and reversals, and in 1963 the court finally held in favor of the Armstrong children. Dwight and Floyd were in high school by the time the court ruled in their favor.[5]

US District Court Judge Seybourn H. Lynne wrote the decision. A native of Alabama whose roots in the state went back several centuries, Lynne had been on a three-judge panel that heard the case of the Montgomery bus boycott in 1956. Although his two colleagues ruled that the protest was constitutionally valid, he had dissented because, in his conception, "separate but equal" remained the law of the land and had to be followed. But by 1963, Judge Lynne had become more amenable to the cause of integration. In his decision, while chastising Alabama education authorities for using the pupil placement law to further nakedly segregationist ends, he noted the reality of Alabama's education system: "Never at any time has a Negro pupil been assigned or transferred to a school designated 'White' or a white pupil to a school designated 'Negro.' Without exception white instructional personnel have been assigned only to schools designated 'White' and Negro instructional personnel only to schools designated 'Negro.'"[6]

Lynne ultimately gave the Alabama Board of Education one last chance to afford black families their constitutionally guaranteed educational rights, writing that "adequate time remains before the opening of the September, 1963, school term for the processing of applications for assignments or transfers in behalf of interested individuals" and indicating that the district's failure to do so would result in the court developing a desegregation plan to compel justice.[7]

And so that September, James Armstrong took his sons Dwight and Floyd by the hand and led them to their new high school. He'd won, but the victory had taken a remarkably long time: it had been six years since his original suit had been filed—and nine years since the highest court in the land had ruled unambiguously that segregated school systems like the one in Birmingham were plainly unconstitutional.

So what took so long?

To answer that question, we need to look at *Brown v. Board of Education*, which is rightly celebrated, but also widely misunderstood.

———

WE LIKE TO think—we *want* to think—that a light switch was suddenly flipped when the Supreme Court ruled that separate educational facilities could never be equal. Before *Brown v. Board of Education*, we had been living in segregation, allowing African Americans to attend school in wooden shacks, relegating generations to the lowest rungs of society. Then, in 1954, the brilliant African American lawyer Thurgood Marshall convinced an all-white US Supreme Court of the inherent wrongness of this system. Up went the switch, with the court's unanimous decision. Down went the system of separate but equal, not only in education but in the rest of society.

The truth is rather more complicated. "The *Brown* we have today has been formalized and domesticated, limited in its remedial scope, and made palatable for mass consumption," wrote the Yale legal scholar Jack M. Balkin. By treating the decision as a singular, decisive victory against racism, we neglect to see the defeats that preceded it— and those that followed it.[8]

Our cultural memory about *Brown* does get some key points right. The decision was intended to strike at the heart of the degradation and subjugation inherent in segregation. To be sure, there had been *some* progress in race relations by the 1940s. Back in 1918, sixty-four African Americans had been lynched across America, according to records kept at the time. In 1947, there was only one lynching recorded, a significant improvement, though still one too many. But just because whites could no longer murder blacks with impunity across the Deep South didn't mean there was anything like equality ruling the land.

The best that blacks could hope for was a state-sanctioned inferiority in which they would be allowed to languish as partial citizens of states that did not consider them full human beings.[9]

This was true in all aspects of life, from train cars to movie theaters. And it was especially true in schools, making racial separation a primary feature of life for children, both black and white, who would, of course, become adults accustomed to segregation. And the doctrine of separate but equal underpinning the segregationist practices of the Jim Crow states of the Deep South belied an even uglier reality. While some culturally conservative African Americans—including influential figures like the writer Zora Neale Hurston—endorsed the creation of truly *equal* institutions that remained segregated, it was the separate but *not* equal part of segregation that enticed the proponents of segregation to maintain the status quo.

The equality part of "separate but equal" was never more than an illusory promise, and those who made that promise well knew it. After all, the whole point of separation was to keep supposedly superior whites from supposedly inferior blacks. And why would an inferior race deserve facilities as good as those meant for the superior one? Whites essentially said as much in justifying the myriad ways in which African Americans were treated like second-class citizens: "A million years from now, a nigger will still be a nigger in the South," went a popular saying from the time.[10]

Schools across the South in the first half of the twentieth century reflected this ugly sentiment in stark terms. The acclaimed historian James Patterson wrote that in "rural regions" of the South, schools for African American children were still "primitive" before Brown. He described the schooling an African American child might have encountered in Sunflower County, Mississippi, where elementary school teachers "worked primarily as cooks or domestics on the plantations," noting that "most had no more than a fourth-grade education themselves." Some students only attended school in the cold months, when they didn't have to pick cotton to help their families get by. In parts of the Deep South, black poverty was as persistent as the summer heat, and the schools were woefully inadequate, consisting of packed class-rooms taught by teachers who had little to teach because they had not been taught themselves. These conditions were not limited to rural areas. Segregation led to dramatic disparities in the school resources available to black and white children as far back as data are available between, 1900 and 1950. In 1940, for example, black schools in South Carolina had more than forty students per teacher, on average, while white schools had fewer than thirty. In Atlanta during the 1949–1950 school year, the city spent twice as much on white students as it did on African American ones. These differences account for a significant share of the vast racial differences in child literacy and numeracy during the Jim Crow era.[11]

Obviously, there was no intent to provide African Americans with anything approaching equality. Jim Crow was a kind of slavemaster of his own, using the law where his predecessor had used the whip. In both cases, there was only one intent: subjugation.

It was against this subjugation that *Brown v. Board of Education* would strike.

———

"THERE'S A DIFFERENCE between law on the books and the law in action," Charles Hamilton Houston, the chief lawyer for the National Association for the Advancement of Colored People—today known as the NAACP—once said. It was his belief that while segregation itself could not be challenged, the inequality of segregated institutions could be challenged and must be challenged. With Houston at the helm, the NAACP would help guide two decades of strategic litigation that would ultimately culminate in *Brown*.[12]

Certainly, Houston himself had skillfully embraced the "double consciousness" that renowned sociologist W. E. B. Du Bois had described in his landmark 1903 book, *The Souls of Black Folk*: "an American, a Negro; two souls, two thoughts, two unreconciled strivings; two warring ideals in one dark body, whose dogged strength alone keeps it from being torn asunder." This double consciousness is the notion that to survive a society of segregation and subjugation, blacks learn to live in the black community while adapting to the white community. From this double consciousness springs an acute awareness that to allow people of all backgrounds to *authentically* exist requires more than an assimilation that results in a loss of racial and ethnic identity. It requires unity. A common misconception is that to be antiracist means to be color-blind. But integration's power lies in celebrating diversity and reveling in differences of perspective, not conforming to a singular view that makes the majority group more comfortable. One path is harder because it requires genuine community trust between racial groups with a long history of distrust.[13]

Through the lens of double consciousness, Houston understood that part of what makes segregation so hard is that the few blacks who are afforded the social flexibility to interact with whites must split their souls so they might live in two separate worlds. Perhaps this knowledge is part of what drove him to create a society where the fates and souls of blacks and whites were so connected that neither need feel they were in a "separate" society when around the other.

Houston's life experiences had prepared him for the call to desegregation. He had been born in a relatively well-off family in Washington, DC, where he had attended a segregated high school, but then he had gone to Amherst College, the elite Massachusetts school from which he, its only African American student, graduated at the top of his class. He served in World War I in a military that was starkly segregated. "I made up my mind that I would never get caught again without knowing my rights; that if luck was with me, and I got through this war, I would study law and use my time fighting for men who could not strike back," Houston later wrote, reflecting the indignation of many other African American veterans throughout American history, whether they fought in the segregated brigades of the Civil War or wondered what, exactly, they were doing in Vietnam.[14]

Returning home, Houston entered Harvard Law School, becoming its first black *Law Review* editor (it would be another several decades before the *Review* had its first black president: a winsome, ambitious native of Hawaii named Barack Obama). For a while thereafter, he served as dean of the law school at Howard, the prestigious historically black university, before joining the NAACP as a special counsel in 1935.

Houston's target was inequality, and his means of rooting it out was going to be litigation aimed at law schools. There were several reasons for this choice. While parents would be fearful about racial mixing among little children, that wouldn't be a concern with law students. Meanwhile, the NAACP lawyers could reasonably expect white judges to know the difference between a well-maintained law school for whites and the kind of shoddy institution where black students could expect to be marooned.[15]

In 1936 Houston joined *Gaines v. Canada*, a suit by Lloyd Gaines, a black student who had been refused admission by Silas Woodson Canada, the registrar at the University of Missouri School of Law. Although the University of Missouri would pay for him to attend law school in a northern state, it would not allow him to receive an education at its own law school. Gaines made clear that he wanted to be a lawyer in Missouri, which meant that he needed a law degree from a Missouri university.

As was the case with many legal challenges to segregation, the courts issued competing rulings in the years that followed the initial lawsuit. When the US Supreme Court ruled in the case, now called *Missouri ex rel. Gaines v. Canada*, in 1938, it was a victory for Houston and the proponents of equality. Writing for the majority in the 7–2 decision, Chief Justice Charles Evans Hughes decreed that Missouri's unwillingness to educate Gaines violated the equal protection clause of the Fourteenth Amendment. Very simply, that crucial clause, on which so much civil rights law and activism were (and continue to be) based, forbade Missouri from offering something to whites that it did not also offer to blacks. Hughes wrote that "the white resident is afforded legal education within the State; the negro resident having the same qualifications is refused it there, and must go outside the

State to obtain it. That is a denial of the equality of legal right to the enjoyment of the privilege which the State has set up, and the provision for the payment of tuition fees in another State does not remove the discrimination."[16]

Northern states cheered the ruling, while southerners lamented the infringement of federal power on their way of life. Some, like the editors of the *Missouri Student*, the student newspaper at the University of Missouri, understood that change was impossible to forfend. "It is apparent that the state will employ every trick in its hand to maintain its traditional policy of separation of whites and Negroes in schools," the editor wrote. "At the same time it is fighting an uphill battle. . . . The hill is steep, and rugged, and the fight looms as a losing battle."[17]

The Supreme Court ruling was a victory for Houston and the NAACP, but was it a victory for Gaines himself? Missouri decided that to equalize legal education, it would start a law school at Lincoln University, the historically black college from which Gaines had received his undergraduate degree. The new law school would take the building of the Poro Beauty College. But if the facilities were substandard, as they were certain to be, this would prove tragically irrelevant to Gaines. On March 19, 1939, Gaines disappeared in Chicago. To this day, it is unknown what happened to him, but it is widely believed that he was murdered by proponents of segregation as a warning to other African Americans who might challenge the system. In 2006, the University of Missouri School of Law posthumously awarded him an honorary degree, and the state bar association posthumously granted him a license. He would have been ninety-five years old and free to practice law in the State of Missouri.[18]

Houston earned another endorsement of his strategy in the case of Heman Marion Sweatt, an African American mailman from Houston who wanted to become a lawyer. With help from the NAACP, Sweatt petitioned the University of Texas president Theophilus Shickel Painter for admission to the state university's law school. Painter didn't know what to do. As he wrote to the state's attorney general, "This applicant is a citizen of Texas and duly qualified for admission to the Law School at the University of Texas, save and except for the fact that he is a negro."[19]

Sweatt v. Painter went to the Supreme Court in 1950, where it was argued by Thurgood Marshall, who had been a student of Houston's at Howard University. Having passed the baton to Marshall, Houston died that same year at the age of fifty-five. Marshall was a forty-two-year-old lawyer at the time, and he decided to pursue a different strategy from Houston's in his challenges to the separate-but-equal doctrine. Instead of stressing *equal*, he chose to highlight *separate* as the more problematic of the two axiomatic features of segregation.

This would end up being the central strategy of *Brown*: the notion that the separation of the races was injurious to both individuals and society, no matter how equal their facilities. "The modern law school is operated so the student can understand ideas of all stratas of society, so he can go out and be of service to his community, his state and his nation," Marshall had said in arguing the case before a lower court. There could be no equality unless Sweatt was allowed to take part in the "interplay of ideas and exchange of views." In other words, separation necessarily fostered inequality. Separate but equal was a myth. (And if people were inherently equal, why would they need to be separated at all?)[20]

The Supreme Court agreed. Chief Justice Fred M. Vinson wrote the majority opinion, in which he attacked the notion that a law school for African Americans could ever be equal to one that admitted only whites. "The law school for Negroes which was to have opened in February, 1947, would have had no independent faculty or library," he wrote. "The teaching was to be carried on by four members of the University of Texas Law School faculty, who were to maintain their offices at the University of Texas while teaching at both institutions. Few of the 10,000 volumes ordered for the library had arrived, nor was there any full-time librarian." Finally, he pointed out, "the school lacked accreditation."[21]

But there were other considerations, and it is these that would prove key in subsequent years. Even if a law school for African

American students could somehow gain an equality of resources, it would by definition be inferior simply because it was a law school to which African American students *had* to go. That separation, Vinson argued, would be like a shadow that never lifted, an inferiority the black lawyer could never escape. That lawyer would forever feel his or her own inferiority, and so would everyone with whom that lawyer interacted. Without access to the superior institutions of whites, such a lawyer would be relegated to inferior status.

The historian Gary M. Lavergne, who wrote a book about the case, believes that "after *Sweatt*, any judicially acceptable separate equality became a practical impossibility." In fact, as Supreme Court Justice Tom Clark told Lavergne, it was not *Brown* that ended the doctrine of separate but equal, but *Sweatt*.[22]

If *Sweatt* was the crippling blow, *Brown* was the coup de grace.

———

IN 1950, LINDA Brown was seven years old. Near her home in Topeka, Kansas, was a school called Sumner Elementary. When it was time for Linda to attend the third grade, her father, the Reverend Oliver Brown, tried to enroll her there. Like the white parents who would come to resist integration through busing, he wanted his daughter to attend a neighborhood school. He was denied, however, because Linda was black, and Sumner was for whites only. So she instead had to walk across a set of railroad tracks to a bus stop, so that she could be driven to Monroe Elementary, a school two miles away.

"Many were the evenings my father would arrive home to find my mother upset because I had to take a walk, just like she did many years before, and catch a school bus, and be bused some two miles across town," Brown would remember decades later. "I can remember that walk. I could only make half of it some days, because the cold would get too bitter for a small child to bear. I can still remember taking that bitter walk, and the terrible cold that would cause my tears to freeze upon my face."[23]

Monroe was not a one-room shack of the kind one might have encountered in the Deep South. In fact, it was generally considered a good school. That was the entire point. Under Thurgood Marshall, the NAACP strategy had evolved from Houston's earlier push for equality. Now, as in *Sweatt*, instead of trying to prove that the segregated institutions were materially unequal, the goal was to show the harm that separation itself caused. The lawyers now had the poignant cases of children like Linda Brown at their disposal, children who were explicitly prevented from attending certain schools and forced to attend others. If they didn't yet understand the cause of that separation, they would one day. And the knowledge would crush them.[24]

Most people think of *Brown v. Board of Education* as representing a single plaintiff from Topeka, Kansas, but the case actually involved five different plaintiffs from five different states (the case was called *Brown* merely because Oliver Brown's name came first alphabetically in the list of plaintiffs, see Figure 1.1). Despite impressive evidence, there were a series of bruising legal battles before the case reached the US Supreme Court. But even as the lower courts sided with the separate-but-equal doctrine that was in place in Topeka, the NAACP had reason to hope for an ultimate victory. While the federal district court in Kansas held *against* the NAACP, Judge Walter Huxman wrote in his findings of fact that "segregation of white and colored children in public schools has a detrimental effect upon the colored children. The impact is greater when it has the sanction of the law." Even if southern states believed they had a legal right to maintain a segregated social structure, the courts were coming to recognize that segregation caused a profound psychological harm that no appeal to constitutional precedent could justify.[25]

The Supreme Court first heard the desegregation cases that would come to be known as *Brown v. Board of Education* in late 1952. However, they were dilatory in ruling on the case, aware of how sensitive the topic was and how enormous the social repercussions would be, regardless of how they ruled. This prolonged deliberation had an unexpected effect that likely ensured the NAACP's success, however inadvertently. On September 8, 1953, Chief Justice Vinson died of a heart attack at the age of sixty-three. To replace him, President Dwight D. Eisenhower appointed Earl Warren as the new chief justice. This would soon prove a very fortuitous development for the proponents of integration.

Warren had already served as the governor of California, but he was not known as either an especially promising politician or a brilliant legal mind. During World War II, he had endorsed the internment of Japanese Americans in camps across California and the West—a decision he would later come to regret, and which has rightly been regarded as one of the most shameful abrogations of civil rights in American history. At the same time, in 1947, Mexican Americans emerged in the national desegregation debate when the District Court of California ruled, and the US Court of Appeals for the Ninth Circuit affirmed, that segregating Mexican Americans from whites in schools was unconstitutional. According to the ruling, "the equal protection of the laws pertaining to the public school system in California is not provided by furnishing in separate schools the same technical facilities, textbooks and courses of instruction to children of Mexican ancestry that are available to the other public school children regardless of their ancestry." Soon thereafter, the California State Legislature followed suit. It passed, and Governor Warren signed, a bill repealing the remaining segregationist laws that acted against other races, making California the first state to outlaw school segregation.[26]

Eisenhower would come to regret appointing Warren, whom he had not expected to become a wellspring of judicial liberalism. But why, if Warren had already signed desegregation into law in California six years prior, did Eisenhower nominate him to the Supreme Court? One potential explanation is that Eisenhower didn't think a legal challenge to segregation would come before the Court. This view is bolstered by the fact that Eisenhower attempted to dissuade the outcome of *Brown* and tried to coax Warren against holding for the plaintiffs in the case. At a White House dinner in 1954, "over coffee," according to a journalist for *The Atlantic*, "Eisenhower took Warren by the arm and

FIGURE 1.1

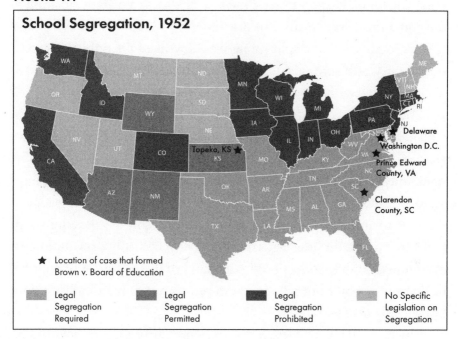

School Segregation, 1952

★ Location of case that formed Brown v. Board of Education

■ Legal Segregation Required

■ Legal Segregation Permitted

■ Legal Segregation Prohibited

■ No Specific Legislation on Segregation

asked him to consider the perspective of white parents in the Deep South. 'These are not bad people,' the president said. 'All they are concerned about is to see that their sweet little girls are not required to sit in school alongside some big black bucks.'"[27]

"It was a big mistake," Eisenhower complained later of the nomination. Indeed, Warren would become anathema to conservatives, who saw his Supreme Court as foisting a new liberal order on the land. In time, "Save our republic, impeach Earl Warren" started to appear on highway signs across the South. That was largely because of the decision the chief justice announced on May 17, 1954.[28]

Warren's initial effect on the Court was to lighten its mood as he attempted to present himself as a nonthreatening newcomer. "He believed in the old adage that he was Chief among equals," Justice William Brennan later recalled. "He fought like the devil against increasing the disparity between what he got paid as Chief and what the Associate Justices received." That approach helped immensely when, within months of his confirmation, Warren took on the challenge of trying to persuade his colleagues to see *Brown* as he did, as a blatant violation of the equal protection clause. In due time, with Warren's lobbying, and clear recognition that a split ruling would weaken the public's perception of the Court's moral authority, his eight colleagues came around to his point of view, making the decision a unanimous triumph.[29]

Warren wrote the decision in *Brown* himself. And he wrote it in a plain and clear style, without any of the grandiosity that might have attended such a momentous case. No grandiosity was necessary. The unanimity of the decision gave it immense power. As for the ruling's main argument, the assertion seems so obvious today that it is almost difficult to imagine that the nation's highest court was required to make it. But six decades ago, racial equality was still a revolutionary, even transgressive, concept in many parts of the nation. And so it fell to Warren to point out why integration was not only morally correct, but socially necessary.

"In these days, it is doubtful that any child may reasonably be expected to succeed in life if he is denied the opportunity of an education," Warren wrote. "Such an opportunity, where the state has undertaken to provide it, is a right which must be made available to all on equal terms." Proof that Thurgood Marshall's strategy of focusing on the ill effects of inequality was evident throughout Warren's ruling, but nowhere more so than in Footnote 11, in what may be the most famous annotation in legal American history. The footnote came after Warren quoted the earlier Kansas court ruling that had been in favor of the Board of Education, but which nevertheless affirmed Marshall's central argument that a "sense of inferiority affects the motivation of a child to learn."[30]

In the dry language that marks the entire ruling, Warren wrote that "this finding is amply supported by modern authority." Then comes the famous footnote:

K. B. Clark, Effect of Prejudice and Discrimination on Personality Development (Mid-century White House Conference on

Children and Youth, 1950); Witmer and Kotinsky, Personality in the Making (1952), c. VI; Deutscher and Chein, The Psychological Effects of Enforced Segregation A Survey of Social Science Opinion, 26 J.Psychol. 259 (1948); Chein, What are the Psychological Effects of Segregation Under Conditions of Equal Facilities?, 3 Int.J.Opinion and Attitude Res. 229 (1949); Brameld, Educational Costs, in Discrimination and National Welfare (MacIver, ed., 1949), 44–48; Frazier, The Negro in the United States (1949), 674–681. *And see generally* Myrdal, An American Dilemma (1944).[31]

This seems an ordinary footnote—in fact, a footnote so ordinary, it shouldn't merit much attention at all. To the contrary, Footnote 11 has engendered a body of scholarship all its own, and that is largely because Warren did here what had not been done before. Instead of only citing legal precedent, he also cited social science. In doing so, he knowingly—and brilliantly—violated the way jurists were supposed to interpret the US Constitution. It led to what the Cornell legal scholar Michael Heise has called "the empiricization of the equal educational opportunity doctrine," meaning that empirical evidence (i.e., evidence gleaned from science) would now inform how we understood, in this case, the equal protection clause. Long an abstract legal concept, "equal protection" would now become a scientific one.[32]

Footnote 11 augured a new type of judicial thinking that acknowledged a modern reality that could prove to be at odds with established legal principles. In later years—up to and including today—when political conservatives complained about "judicial activism," they would have in mind precisely what Warren did, using up-to-date research to supplement decades of precedent. "Judicial restraint," to conservatives, involves an exclusively "originalist" interpretation of the Constitution—one that asks simply "What did the Framers of the Constitution mean when they wrote each provision," absent any intrusion of modernity, of changing social mores, and of social science.[33]

In his famous footnote, Warren alluded to research on the socio-economic and psychological effects of segregation. The final citation, for example, is to Gunnar Myrdal's 1944 *An American Dilemma: The Negro Problem and Modern Democracy*. A Swedish economist and sociologist who would go on to win a Nobel Prize, Myrdal had been commissioned to write the book by the Carnegie Corporation to try to understand, as the book's title suggests, the central problem of American civic life: race. What he found was not encouraging. "The Negro problem in America represents a moral lag in the development of the nation and a study of it must record nearly everything which is bad and wrong in America," Myrdal warned. "The reading of this book must be somewhat of an ordeal to the good citizen." Warren's allusion to Myrdal's work was as an extraordinary departure from the historically conservative temperament of the Supreme Court.[34]

But it is the first citation in the note that is the most famous—and controversial. Kenneth Clark had worked with Myrdal on *An American Dilemma*, but he was more famous for a study he and his wife, Mamie, published in 1950. Titled "Racial Identification and Preference in Negro Children," that work is more commonly known today as "the doll study." For all that has been written about it, for all the ferocious debates it has engendered, the Clarks' experiment was remarkably simple: "The subjects were presented with four dolls, identical in every respect save skin color." They were then asked, in a series of questions, which doll they liked the best, and also to determine the race of each doll. The subjects were 253 African American children, about half of whom went to segregated schools in Arkansas. The others went to an integrated school in Massachusetts. They were all between three and seven years of age.[35]

The Clarks found that the children had "a clearly established knowledge of a 'racial difference' . . . and some awareness of the relation between the physical characteristic of skin color and the racial concepts of 'white' and 'colored.'" But their awareness was deeper than that. The Clarks' most astonishing finding was couched in a one-paragraph section titled "Preferences and Skin Color," which included the crucial observation that "there is a tendency for the majority of these children, in spite of their own skin color, to prefer the white doll and to negate the brown doll."[36]

The doll study also found that "the crucial period in the formation and patterning of racial attitudes begins at around four and five years." After that, racial attitudes would irrevocably harden in ways that led to lifelong feelings of inferiority among African Americans that no redress could remove. "That's a nigger. I'm a nigger," said one of Clark's young subjects as he picked out the doll that resembled him most in skin color. No evidentiary data set could be as brutally convincing as those simple words.[37]

———

AT THE FEDERAL level, with the doll study and related social science evidence, Thurgood Marshall had the proof he needed to convincingly argue that segregation fostered a feeling of inferiority that no equalization of resources could cure. Throughout the legal wars they waged, Charles Hamilton Houston and Thurgood Marshall used social science evidence to undergird their arguments. And in Earl Warren, they found a surprisingly liberal judge willing to use his powers to fundamentally reshape American society. The drawbacks of that approach would soon become evident, but on the spring day in 1954 when Warren read the landmark decision, there was plenty to celebrate.

"It is not too much to speak of the Court's decision as a new birth of freedom," joyously editorialized the *Washington Post*. "America is rid of an incubus which impeded and embarrassed it in all its relations with the world. Abroad as well as at home, this decision will engender a renewal of faith in democratic institutions and ideals." The reference to the reception abroad had to do with the way the United States was perceived by the Soviet Union and its allies. To the communist nations of Eastern Europe, segregation was the symptom of a profound sickness within the free-market capitalist West. The communists reasoned that because they didn't have racial discrimination, their economic system was superior (although such gloating neglected the fact that there was plenty of discrimination behind the Iron Curtain, in particular against homosexuals, the Roma, Muslims, Jews, and others).[38]

Not everyone was celebrating the *Brown* ruling, of course. James Eastland, a segregationist senator from Mississippi, said the South would "take whatever steps are necessary to retain segregation in education." Invoking the doctrine of states' rights that remains popular in the South to this day, he declared that Dixie "will not abide by nor obey this legislative decision by a political court."[39]

These words would prove prescient soon enough.

———

BY 1957, THE year James Armstrong filed his lawsuit in Birmingham, little progress had been made in fulfilling the promise of *Brown v. Board of Education*. That's because while the Court struck down segregation, it did not say how its opposite—integration—should be enacted. *Brown* diagnosed the illness but did not prescribe the cure. It sketched the vision of a racially just society but left the details for someone else to fill in.

In 1955, as the nation grappled with the implications of *Brown*, the Supreme Court issued a ruling that has come to be known as *Brown II*. But this was not the thundering, unambiguous mandate integration required either. There was nothing in the ruling about how specific districts were to be compelled into desegregation; nor was there an exact definition of what it would mean to have a desegregated school, or a deadline by which every district in the Jim Crow South would have to show itself in compliance with the ruling. But it did say that desegregation must take place "with all deliberate speed." Those words from *Brown II* are probably the most famous to have come from the two *Brown* cases.[40]

The vagueness of the ruling still gave southern states the space to resist the order to desegregate, just as Eastland promised they would. What did "deliberate speed" mean? And who would enforce that standard? The lack of answers to such questions quickly curdled the initial enthusiasm over *Brown*. The ruling had been immensely powerful in countering segregation, but it was far less effective in prescribing a means of integration. Inadvertently, it left plenty of crevices in which a weakened Jim Crow could hide, nurturing himself back to strength. Its failure to articulate the penalties that might befall would-be segregators yielded an unsurprising outcome: little integration occurred without the subsequent force of judicial rulings in local federal courts (or threat of litigation). The pace of desegregation after the *Brown* rulings was aptly described by legal scholar Walter Gellhorn as one of an "extraordinarily arthritic snail."[41]

And when African Americans (or their white allies) did try to integrate schools, they were met with such fury by the proponents of segregation that it surely made others wonder if such efforts were worth the trouble. Watching what happened in Little Rock, Arkansas, one could dispiritingly conclude that perhaps it was not.

What happened there, very simply, was this: nine African American students were slated to attend Central High School in that city. But Arkansas governor Orval Faubus inveighed against what he called "the forcible integration of the schools of Little Rock," which he claimed would "bring about widespread disorder and violence." He said that there had been "an unusually large number of weapons" sold in Little Rock prior to the start of school, "mostly to Negro youths."[42]

"One store reported that a gang of Negro youths came as a group, and every one of its members purchased knives," Faubus said, cynically playing on the fears of the city's white citizens.[43]

To keep the Little Rock Nine from attending Central High—and to ensure that his own favorability with segregationist Arkansans remained high—Faubus used the National Guard to block entrance to the school. Even more frightening must have been the mobs of racists who tried to assail the students, shouting imprecations like "Nigger go home." It took an intervention of 1,100 US Army troops, ordered to Little Rock by President Eisenhower, to ensure that the Little Rock Nine could simply attend class. This outcome had plainly not been what Earl Warren had in mind.

One of the Little Rock Nine, Melba Pattillo Beals, later wrote a memoir of school integration, *Warriors Don't Cry*. She remembered how even some older African Americans thought asking for school integration was too much, too soon. "We're just getting settled on the front of the bus," a friend of her grandmother's said in reference to the Montgomery bus boycott.[44]

But another disagreed. "White folks ain't never given us nothing," she said. "You just move right long, girl, you hear me. You integrate, now!"

That's what they did—in Little Rock, in Nashville, and in Birmingham, where Floyd Armstrong kept going to Graymont Elementary even as the taunts and threats continued and his neighbors mourned the four little girls killed at 16th Street Baptist Church. They understood that the segregated school was the bulwark of the Jim Crow South. Do away with separate classrooms, and the whole system would crumble.

The parallel here between the NAACP's litigation strategy that led to *Brown* and the research strategy taken in this book, to document the impacts of *Brown*, is that both arguments summon the power of a collection of evidence. It is evidence that derives from multiple districts and municipalities, rather than statistics from a single place, whose implications could easily be dismissed. And it is evidence for contemporary policy writ large. Our goal, as was theirs, is to use the research from this collective evidence to help stimulate and revive a new, national consensus on education and race and to enact remedies for inequality in this country.

THE INTEGRATED CLASSROOM

Desegregation of schools does not automatically transform them into better schools. It is only a step. The larger goal is to see that the education of our youth is not merely deseg-regated, but that it is excellent.

—ROBERT KENNEDY, MAY 20, 1964

THIS BOOK AIMS TO ANSWER A BASIC QUESTION: DOES INTEGRA-tion work? Thus far, we can say that integration was hard fought—a product of brave families and tireless attorneys who, against all odds, won a long and strategic battle to dismantle the legal structure of "separate but equal." Their endurance was an acknowledgment that segregation is not only about separation of people, but it is segrega-tion—hoarding, in fact—of opportunity. And we can say that integra-tion was slow and uneven. With Chief Justice Warren's decree that integration must happen "with all deliberate speed," segregationists throughout the country buttressed the status quo, intransigent against anything shy of the combined might of the Supreme Court and local court decisions, which did not spring up in every place and all at once, but rather trickled into the American experience, creating new obliga-tions to integrate one district at a time.

The slow and uneven pace of integration provides a convenient clue into whether integration works. While some black students born in 1960 may have experienced integration for all twelve years of their schooling, other black students born in the same year but from different school districts may not have experienced even one year of integration. And while some black students born in 1950 may have turned seventeen before integration came to their school districts, their younger siblings may have experienced several years of the policy simply because of when they were born. The ability to compare the outcomes of otherwise similar children who differed in how many years of integration they experienced is precisely the insight we, as social scientists, needed to answer our burning question. Our research shows integration does work. But to fully appreciate why, and how, we have to understand how integration spread and explore the experiences of those who lived it.

Thus, before reviewing the analytical tools used to answer our question and presenting the findings of our research, we will survey the historical progression of desegregation and detail the lived experiences of two individuals—one black, one white—who provide a glimpse into how desegregation impacted real lives.

———

THE GAVEL SOUNDED, and through it, Chief Justice Earl Warren decreed that schools and teachers around the country were required to teach a racially diverse set of students. But deeply rooted belief systems do not magically crumble from the reverberations of a wooden sound block. In the nine years that followed *Brown II*, 1955 to 1964, almost no integration occurred. Then President Lyndon Baines Johnson signed the Civil Rights Act of 1964, creating new avenues for parents and federal agencies to press for enforcement. Title IV of the act authorized the federal government to file school desegregation cases, and Title VI prohibited discrimination in public schools and hospitals receiving federal financial assistance. This prohibition became potent with the passage of the Elementary and Secondary Education Act in 1965, which dramatically raised the amount of federal aid to education from a few million dollars to more than $1 billion a year. For the first time, the threat of withholding federal funds became a powerful inducement for school districts to comply with integration mandates.[1]

Still, change was slow. By 1968, only 6 percent of the districts that would eventually undergo court-ordered integration had implemented significant desegregation plans. Courts were partially stymied by uncertainty regarding what steps they should compel a district to undergo to undo generations of separation. Then, in 1968, the Supreme Court decided *Green v. County School Board of New Kent County* and sketched a blueprint for desegregation plans. The Court ruled that the provision of equitable, desegregated schools was not just a matter of "the composition of student bodies," or the provision of a free choice for blacks to attend white schools. Instead, it extended "to every facet of school operations"—to ensuring black students had access to integrated schools with "faculty, staff, transportation, extra-curricular activities and facilities" of sufficient quality to dismantle the legacy of segregation—the separation and the degradation. The six "*Green* factors," as they came to be known, established the prototype that would define, across the country, district compliance with desegregation mandates. The significance of this ruling is nowhere more evident than in a note Justice Earl Warren wrote to Justice William Brennan, "When this opinion is handed down, the traffic light will have changed from *Brown* to *Green*. Amen!"[2]

Following the ruling, desegregation efforts accelerated, particularly in the South, and by 1972 integration plans had been implemented in 56 percent of the districts that would eventually undergo court-ordered desegregation. That year, schools in Dixie became more integrated than those in the rest of the county. But while the South evolved, schools in other regions of the country remained segregated. This was partly because the roots of segregation in the South were largely "de jure," meaning codified in law, making it easier for courts to determine which districts had segregated and order them to mend their ways. In non-southern cities, such as Denver, however, segregation was largely "de facto," a result of policies that subtly ensured segregation without relying on actual statutes. Courts were unable to attack this kind of separation—that is, until 1973, when the Supreme Court decided *Keyes v. School District No. 1, Denver*.[3]

In *Keyes*, the Court explained that evidence of de facto segregation, if uncontested, could give courts cause to issue desegregation orders. It was the first Supreme Court case involving school desegregation from a major non-southern city, and it ushered in a period of desegregation efforts in both the North and the South, regardless of whether the segregation resulted from a legal mandate or residential segregation patterns.[4]

As desegregation expanded its reach, court orders began to expand to new, explicit goals beyond racial integration. Segregationists took this new challenge head on, arguing that segregation plans could not require compensatory or remedial educational programs or investments. But in *Milliken v. Bradley* (1974), the second in that line of cases, the Court held that desegregation orders could, in fact, include mandates for compensatory spending on educational programs to reduce class size and increase per-pupil spending. The case sanctioned a more comprehensive approach to undoing the legacy of separation—one that was adopted by many districts.[5]

By 1977, the courts of the nation had completed essentially all of the work they would do, and they decided precious few new desegregation cases at any point thereafter. But in those two decades, beginning with the issuance of *Brown*, and continuing with the subsequent desegregation of the District of Columbia schools in 1954, and then through the mid-1970s, which saw desegregation orders in Baltimore, Cleveland, and Los Angeles, select communities throughout the nation experienced a radical transformation.[6]

So, too, did the heart of the nation, with southern opinions changing more slowly than non-southern ones. In 1942, 40 percent of non-southerners and just 2 percent of southerners believed that whites and blacks should attend the same schools. By 1956, 61 percent of non-southerners and 14 percent of southerners favored integration.

On the eve of the passage of the Civil Rights Act of 1964, 73 percent of northerners and 34 percent of southerners opined that schools should be desegregated. And by 1970, 84 percent of non-southerners and 46 percent of southerners supported integration. The slow shift in opinions toward integration, and the persistence of those who opposed it both north and south of the Mason Dixon line, suggest that those who experienced integration in their communities had powerful, and often distinct, experiences. To truly understand how integration operated, we must hear their stories.[7]

———

"I'M THE CHUBBY white kid down here," Dr. Paul Goren says, pointing to a childhood photograph that, a half-century later, continues to define who he is and what he believes, where he comes from and why he returned to his Chicago-area roots. The photo is from room 306 at the Avalon Park Elementary School, taken in the fall of 1968. Goren, now a crisply dressed fifty-nine-year-old, was then eight—and also crisply dressed, in a short-sleeved shirt and skinny tie. Seated in the front row, he smiles at the camera. There are three rows of children behind him, their own smiles remarkably unforced. Except for Goren and two other children, all the other children in the composite are black.[8]

The photo from 1968 sits in a frame that hangs on the wall in Goren's office at the central office for Evanston/Skokie School District 65, outside of Chicago, where he is the superintendent of schools. Below that photograph are two others, both also from Avalon Park. The first is from 1964, when Goren was in kindergarten, and it shows a class that is about half white and half black; three years later, in 1967, the third-grade class is almost entirely black, as it is in the photograph from 1968.

The journalist Edward McClelland once quipped that integration is "the period between the arrival of the first black and the departure of the first white." Indeed, many of Goren's neighbors did depart the

Kindergarten class in comparison with third- and fourth-grade class photos highlight how fast white flight occurred in response to school integration. *(Photo credit: Wilfred Ortiz)*

(Above) First integrated kindergarten class, 1964, Avalon Park Elementary (Chicago Public Schools; Paul Goren smiling in middle of third row).

(Below) Third-grade class, 1967, Avalon Park Elementary (Paul Goren smiling in far left of third row).

Fourth-grade class, 1968, Avalon Park Elementary (Paul Goren smiling in far right of front row).

South Side of Chicago, in large part because they didn't want their children's school photographs to look like Goren's. That movement—usually called white flight—contributed at least as much to segregated education as the explicit racism of the Deep South did. It was a cruel irony that many African Americans left the states haunted by Jim Crow and the legacy of bondage expecting better opportunities for their children—if not for themselves—in the cities of the North and West. These pilgrims did not yet know that Boston was as eager to avoid integration as Birmingham, that Manhattan secretly harbored the very same animosities as Montgomery, so much so that they would travel hundreds of miles only to end up where they had always been.[9]

And few places resisted integration as eagerly as Chicago, whose identity as a center of industry was fostered and celebrated by the city's working-class whites, particularly Catholics who had come from Ireland, Poland, and Ukraine. This was their city, or so they thought. Then, by the middle decades of the twentieth century, some half a million African Americans arrived on the shores of Lake Michigan, expecting freedom and looking for work. The city's whites—and particularly the middle-class whites whose neighborhoods were becoming integrated—felt like they were under siege, a sentiment that was stoked by malefactors within the real estate industry. Fear proved a terrific motivator, driving many to sell their homes in Chicago and move to the newly constructed suburbs outside the city, which Chicagoans could reach by that great innovation of postwar America: the freeway.[10]

Goren's was that rare family that stayed, refusing to move even as the neighborhood became more populated with African Americans and the pressure to leave grew ever greater. For his part, Goren would come to understand that "better schools" was just code for "schools without blacks." "They're really moving because African Americans are moving into town," he recalls thinking. So even as others left, the Gorens remained in Marynook, watching as African American families moved in. When real estate agents called their house, Goren's father would shout at them and hang up the phone. His parents "hated the real estate crap," which is what they called it. More importantly, his parents liked where they lived and saw no reason for leaving, since the claims about crime and incipient urban decay were, it seemed to them, so obviously untrue. A few others grasped this, too. "I never knew Negroes could be such nice people," a Marynook resident named Anthony Blazevitch admitted. "The Negroes moving in here are far better caliber than most of the people I've known, black or white." Such enlightened insights, however, were preciously rare in the era of white flight.[11]

As whites gave into fear, Marynook changed. For each black family that moved in, it seemed, ten white families moved out. By the late 1960s, Goren recalled, fewer than half a dozen of the families in Marynook were white, out of a total of about four hundred, although the neighborhood had recently been entirely white. That mattered little to the Gorens, however, and Paul would live in Marynook, and attend its integrated schools, all the way until he graduated from high school.

In 1976, he became a freshman at Williams College, a prestigious liberal arts school in Massachusetts. His parents remained in the

Marynook house for fifty-eight years altogether. Their impression was that the threats of "urban decay" were little more than marketing for suburban housing, and they proved right. They suffered one break-in during those nearly six decades—but nobody was hurt, and nothing was taken. Paul Goren sold the house only a few years ago, after his father passed away. He talks about the old abode not just as a home, but as a place where lives were forged in meaningful experience.

"It was a sad day when we finally sold," he says.

———

INTEGRATION WAS THE force that brought Paul Goren and Forrest Jones together. They attended the same integrated high school, they knew each other's families well, and both went on to attend Williams College, though not in the same year. Each later returned to Chicago to engage in their professions as leaders in education and medicine, respectively. As a black man, Dr. Jones had a different vantage point from which to view Chicago's integration—one that complicates conventional wisdom.

"We weren't prepared for integration," he now says, speaking like the doctor that he is, confronted with having to explain a complex diagnosis. It is a diagnosis rooted in his own experience as well as in his family's history. Before moving to an integrated neighborhood, Jones lived in Robbins, a neighborhood that bore the strain of segregation but was also strangely idyllic, at least in Jones's telling. He waxes romantic about the schools. "It was all black students, all black teachers. Black male teachers."[12]

His seventh-grade teacher was Charles Evers, a brother of the early civil rights leader Medgar Evers. He remembers Mr. Evers announcing that his brother had been killed. "All of a sudden, history was really real." Segregation was, in the doctor's nuanced conception, a negative pressure that produced some positive results. "In segregation, you had these much closer connections to people," Jones says. "That's missing today." And segregation also produced "the whole concept of 'You gotta be twice as good,'" which had provided Jones and his peers with a powerful motivating force.

In November 1963, the same week President John F. Kennedy was assassinated, Jones and his family moved to the Avalon Park neighborhood in Chicago. In 1964, the year LBJ signed the Civil Rights Act, he attended Hirsch High School, a mostly black school. But the Civil Rights Act and the Elementary and Secondary Education Act empowered desegregation decrees, and so, just as Jones was "settling in, getting comfortable in high school," Chicago enacted a school integration plan. In the middle of his sophomore year, he joined the wave of students around the country being shuttled into integration, transferring to South Shore High School. The school was heavily Jewish, "which was new to me," Jones remembers. The fault lines of whiteness were difficult to navigate. Growing up in Robbins, Jones hadn't had much opportunity to ponder the Holocaust, for example. Now, he was attending school among the descendants of that catastrophe. Curiosity about the Jewish experience, as well as its similarities to the African American one, would remain with him for years to come.

"I'd never really been among whites like that," Jones recalls. "You start to think about and care about the heritage of races outside your own." Some think that such empathic identification is one of the main benefits of integration.

But while Jones quickly adjusted to the social aspects of his new school, the academics were another matter. The schooling at Robbins would have prepared him for Hirsch, but he found himself floundering at South Shore. He "went into regular English," where he found himself "making Cs." "I gotta get to the top," Jones thought. He did, eventually, returning to advanced English, among other achievements, and becoming vice president of the student body. When it came time to apply to college, he took the advice of a pastor at his integrated church. The pastor had gone to Williams, in Massachusetts, and though it was not a place known for its diversity, the pastor urged Jones to apply. He did, and was admitted (he was among the first African Americans to graduate from the institution four years later).

If Paul Goren's experience was atypical because his family opted to stay in what became an integrated community, the rarity of Forrest Jones's experience comes down to the fact that his family had the opportunity to join one. His hard work there landed him a spot at one of the nation's most prestigious colleges. But most other African American children in Chicago were not so fortunate.

———

Did Dr. Jones believe integration worked? What would his childhood classmate and friend Dr. Goren's answer be? Both of them responded with an emphatic "yes."

For all that, Goren doesn't remember any of the urban depredations we've come to associate with the decline of the American city in the second half of the twentieth century. "What do I remember? That families were families, and neighbors were neighbors," he says. He remembers that Mrs. Jones, in particular, was like a mother to him. When Dr. Martin Luther King Jr. was assassinated in the spring of 1968, and students from the Chicago Vocational High School took out their rage on local businesses, Mrs. Jones called Mrs. Goren. "Don't go out on Eighty-Seventh Street," she warned, referring to a major commercial thoroughfare in Marynook. "I'll get your groceries for you. Stay inside."

———

Forrest Jones went on to become one of the first African American doctors to integrate Chicago-area hospitals and has been a leader in medicine and outreach to underserved minority and poor communities. All of his children graduated from flagship colleges and universities.

Paul Goren went on to earn a doctorate from Stanford in education, commencing a career in public schools that eventually led him back to Chicago. In 2014, he was appointed superintendent of the

Evanston/Skokie schools. All three of his children have gone through Evanston's public schools, which are regarded as some of the best in the country.[13]

Goren wants to replicate the best of what Avalon Park Elementary had to offer and fulfilling the unrealized promises of school integration continue to animate him to this day. Yet he must do so in a relatively affluent suburban district where parents will expect their kids not only to attend college, but to attend the kind of college whose name they can proudly wield on a car decal or sweatshirt.

Goren believes this is an achievable goal. "Equity and excellence can live together," he says. More importantly, he puts this belief into everyday practice. He recently noticed, for example, that middle schools in his district were offering two identical math courses. The only difference was that Algebra 1 was billed as an advanced, high-school-level course, while Algebra 8 was offered to eighth graders who were on the standard track. Because of the way students are sorted—and sort themselves—Algebra 1 ended up with mostly white kids, while Algebra 8 ended up with mostly black ones. This was precisely the kind of segregation Goren wanted to avoid, so he combined the classes, believing that students who needed help would get it from advanced students, while those advanced students would not be academically harmed by no longer being in a class of their own (they could even benefit from helping peers who were not as advanced as they were).

Statistics bolster Goren's convictions about the potential coexistence of equity and excellence, but it is not statistics he must fight against. The much more formidable foe is the perception among parents that their children can only realize their potential in educational environments that lack "struggling" students. Many people move to places like Evanston—or Walnut Creek, in California, or Scarsdale, in the suburbs of New York City—because of the schools. That is what Goren's white neighbors did fifty years ago, and that is what people have done ever since. They do so with the expectation that their property taxes will fund great schools, and those great schools will shuttle their children to prestigious colleges. And after that: comfort, security, and prosperity. Who wouldn't want that for their children?

Goren wants access to excellence for all the students who attend his schools, not just the savvy or those persistent enough to get into Algebra 1. He wants to remind parents, even those with "liberal tendencies," as he puts it, that education is not a "private commodity" but a "public good." Moreover, that good is expressed in complex ways that test scores and college admissions cannot possibly express.

In these and in other one-on-one, in-depth interviews we conducted with the early pioneers of integration, from Chicago, Birmingham, Charlotte, Memphis, and Evanston, our subjects spoke a more universal message: "The process is painful, but the change is priceless." "The greatest motivator of change is pain." "Pain ignites change." One of the take-home messages from their stories was that integration is like a surgery performed on a school system—it hurts, but it cures. Segregation (and white flight) is like a painkiller, providing instant relief for families looking to avoid diversity, but also plaguing them with long-term side effects. True integration has the redemptive power to heal divisions. It can serve as an incubator of ideas, provide catalytic effects, and exert a gravitational pull to bring people together across racial lines. The power of desegregation can be felt in the words of California senator Kamala Harris: "Two decades after Brown v. Board, I was only the second class to integrate at Berkeley public schools. Without that decision, I likely would not have become a lawyer and eventually be elected a Senator from California. That's the power a Supreme Court Justice holds." And that power irreversibly altered the life courses of select families around the country. Unfortunately, it also showed us there are no shortcuts. But without continual advancement, our current pattern of historical amnesia is destined to repeat its cycles. We must reckon with our racist past and present in the service of an inclusive future.[14]

———

PAUL GOREN AND Forrest Jones experienced integration in a city that resisted it, at a time of assassinations and riots and in a manner that unsettled their communities. And yet both were unwavering in their conviction that it worked—so well, in fact, that one has devoted his life to expanding it. And in our conversations, theirs was the common view. Why, amid this chorus of support from those on the ground, have we all but abandoned the policy? Much of the challenge traces back to the difficulty of assessing whether integration works. Had we stopped at conducting interviews, it would be possible for us to believe that the experiences of Goren, Jones, and the others with whom we spoke were atypical, and that, on the whole, the strife endured by integrated communities was all for naught. We needed a methodology that would allow us to determine the long-term effects of integration from experiences nationwide.

Finding such a methodology is trickier than it may seem. You might say, "Why not simply compare the educational and life outcomes of people who were exposed to desegregated schools against those who weren't?" And that is what many prior researchers have done. But this approach falls far short of assessing whether integration *causes* certain outcomes, because the family backgrounds of the children who attended integrated schools may differ in important ways from the family backgrounds of those who did not. In other words, we can't be sure that we are comparing "apples to apples" if we simply compare those from integrated schools to those from segregated ones. To determine whether integration in fact causes *anything*, what is really needed is a source of randomization that assigns some children into integrated schools and other, similarly situated students into segregated ones.

This language may sound familiar. Since the 1950s, when the first clinical trials of new drugs and other medical therapies were conducted, many researchers have emphasized "randomized controlled trials," or RCTs, as the preferred way to evaluate not only health interventions but also policy reforms in schools and elsewhere. The acronym may sound lofty, but most people have heard of it via the clinical study that has two groups: one receives the treatment, the other receives a placebo. RCTs are considered the gold standard in research design because they allow researchers to accurately discover what causes what.

Of course, it is neither ethical nor practical to randomize children to attend integrated schools. But fortunately we can follow the same *logic* of an RCT by using naturally occurring policy changes. RCTs randomly subdivide all subjects into "treatment" and "control," but the desegregation orders that were sprinkled into districts sporadically throughout the country between 1954 and 1977 also subdivided students into "treatment" and "control." The orders were enacted in ways that enabled some children to obtain better educational opportunities while leaving other, similar children in their previous substandard school contexts. And the choice of who was in the "treatment" group (integrated schools) and who was in the "control" group (segregated schools) was essentially random. Because of the importance of legal precedence, the NAACP pursued a legal strategy to bring suits first and foremost where and when they had the greatest chances of winning, which was not necessarily where blacks would benefit most. A win would establish a precedent that could be applied to achieve integration elsewhere more quickly. They well recognized the importance of minimizing the risk of a loss, which could have far-reaching, cascading consequences that could derail future efforts. Thus, the timing was driven largely by a number of chance factors, not systematic differences in families or neighborhood conditions that may have independently affected children's outcomes. Figure 2.1 shows the timing of desegregation court orders, and Figure 2.2 presents the rising proportion of school-age years in which children were exposed to court-ordered desegregation for successive cohorts born between 1950 and 1975.[15]

To discern which group each student was in, we obtained a comprehensive inventory of every judicially enforced desegregation case in the nation from 1954 to 2013, including detailed information about the school district, the year the court order was enacted, and the type of desegregation plan implemented. There were, in all, 868 such

FIGURE 2.1

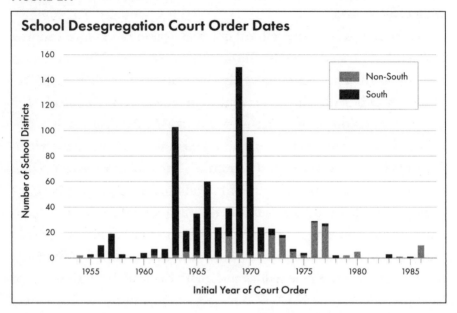

FIGURE 2.2

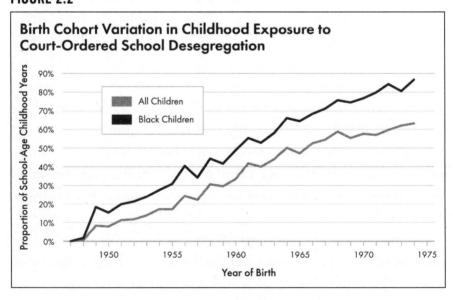

orders enacted between 1954 and 1980, with the result that by 1988, the nation reached the high point of integration.[16]

Next, we needed to combine information about our cause (desegregation) with data about potential effects. We therefore integrated two other data sources. The first was data from school districts containing markers of school quality. The second was a nationally representative longitudinal data set regarding a host of life outcomes for tens of thousands of children born between 1945 and 1970.

Using the three together, we were able to develop a methodology akin to creating virtual twins, in a statistical sense, where all other childhood factors were similar on average. Our design created a "parallel universe" where we could witness the outcomes that would have prevailed for these children in the absence of desegregation. Our approach effectively eliminated bias, and our estimates were cleansed of the influence of childhood family factors that would have otherwise obscured our ability to isolate the role of school quality on student outcomes. These statistical methods are the empirical gymnastics that enable us to land the triple back flip and land gracefully and solidly on two feet to provide a definitive answer on the effects of desegregation. The results of that trial can be simply put: the medicine called integration works.

———

WHEN WE SAY "integration works," let's be clear: our argument is not predicated on the false notion that poor and minority children can't learn in schools without white and non-poor children. Likewise, any assessment of a school's quality based solely on the racial composition of its students would be woefully incomplete. So what makes integration "work"? It's in part the resultant impacts of integration on both school resources and school practices.

Thus, in order to evaluate the impacts of desegregation, we must understand how integration impacted access to school resources. Desegregation required not only the integration of schoolchildren but the integration of teachers, facilities, curricular offerings, after-school

FIGURE 2.3

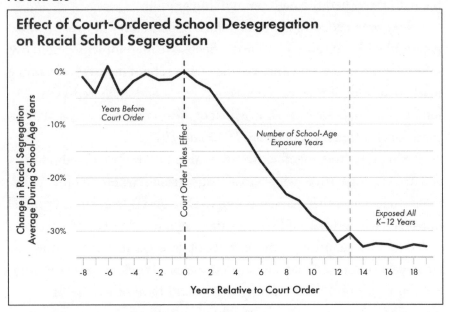

Effect of Court-Ordered School Desegregation on Racial School Segregation

programs, public summer school enrichment activities, and the like. The resultant change in school resources is often underappreciated.

Reviewing our data, we first saw some obvious and immediate effects. Almost as soon as desegregation plans were enacted, there were not only substantial reductions in racial segregation, among both students and teachers, but also sharp increases in per-pupil spending (by an average of 22.5 percent) and significant reductions in the average class sizes experienced by black children (as shown in Figures 2.3–2.5). In other words, the mere act of desegregation had an immediate impact on the quality of the education black children received. But the more important question, the question at the heart of this research, was whether those changes led to lasting impacts for children's subsequent educational and life outcomes.

We can answer this question by looking at whether cohorts who experienced more integration fared better than cohorts in the same district who did not. In other words, if a school district integrated in 1968, did students in those schools who had been born in 1962 (who

FIGURE 2.4

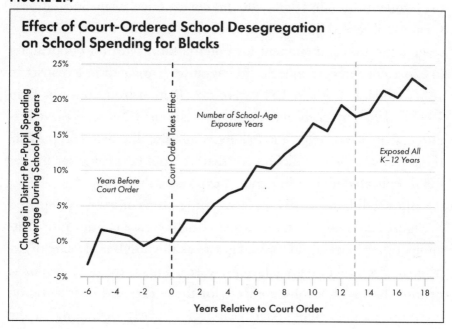

Effect of Court-Ordered School Desegregation on School Spending for Blacks

FIGURE 2.5

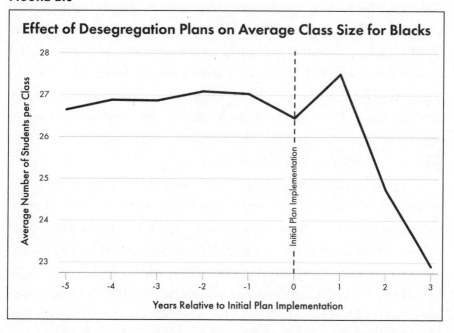

Effect of Desegregation Plans on Average Class Size for Blacks

therefore experienced twelve years of integrated schools) fare better than students born in 1950 (who did not experience any integration)? First, we observed that, as expected, there were no differences in average educational attainment for cohorts born with no opportunity to experience integration. So if integration happened in a district in 1968, students born in 1950 were no different from those born in 1949 or 1948, in terms of educational attainment, because, as we surmised, they had no exposure to integration. But did this trend persist? If integration made no difference, then we would expect to see the flat trend replicated in post-integration exposed cohorts.

But we didn't see this. In fact, quite to the contrary, as depicted in Figures 2.6 and 2.7, there is a striking increase in educational attainment for black children that grows as the number of years of exposure to school desegregation increases. This is the dose-response relationship, with stronger effects for those exposed to integration for more of their school-age years, particularly beginning in the elementary school years and in places in which desegregation resulted in larger increases in school resources. Compared to black children who were not exposed to integration, black children who *were* exposed throughout their K-12 years had significantly higher educational attainment, including greater college attendance and completion rates, not to mention attendance at more selective colleges. Specifically, black children exposed to desegregated schools throughout K-12 completed more than a full additional year of education than comparable black children confined to segregated schools throughout their school-age years.[17]

To put the magnitude of these findings into perspective, note that as late as 1960, only 20 percent of black men were high school graduates, compared to about 50 percent of white men; and that only 3 percent of black men had college degrees, compared to 13 percent of white men. However, by the late 1970s and early 1980s, college enrollment for black eighteen- to nineteen-year-olds rose to rates similar to those for white students. Our work shows that desegregation played a dominant role in explaining this convergence. The estimated

FIGURE 2.6

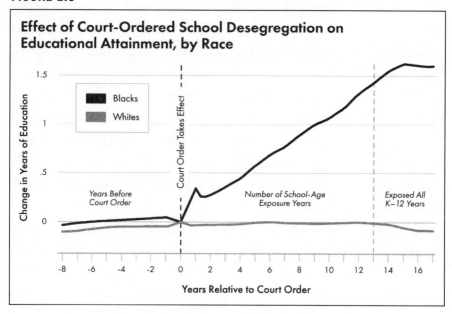

Effect of Court-Ordered School Desegregation on Educational Attainment, by Race

FIGURE 2.7

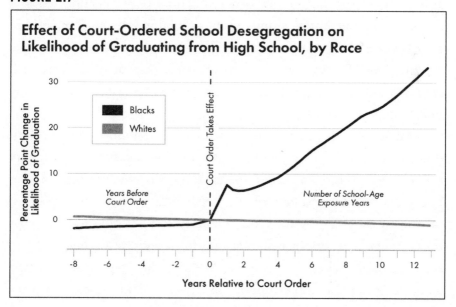

Effect of Court-Ordered School Desegregation on Likelihood of Graduating from High School, by Race

effect of desegregation exposure throughout all twelve school-age years for black children proved large enough to eliminate the black-white educational attainment gap, which has flummoxed education reformers for decades. It turns out that the solution was right before us all along.[18]

It is important to note that bridging the black-white gap did not involve making performance by whites worse. As the flat light gray line in Figure 2.6 shows, for whites, exposure to integration neither helped nor hindered their overall education attainment. The Gorens, it seems, were right—fears that integration would harm educational attainment were overblown.

The beneficial effects of integration for blacks continued in the decades to come. We discovered that the average effects of a five-year exposure to court-ordered school desegregation led to about a 15 percent increase in wages and an increase in annual worktime by roughly 165 hours, which combined to result in a 30 percent increase in annual earnings (Figure 2.8). Furthermore, the average effects of a five-year exposure to court-ordered school desegregation led to a decline of 11 percentage points in the annual incidence of poverty in adulthood and about a 25 percent increase in annual family income (Figure 2.9). We saw significant increases in marital stability as well, which could explain a significant part of the increase in adult family income among blacks.[19]

Our results also demonstrate that one of the most effective antidotes to criminal involvement in adulthood is access to high-quality schools as a youth. Too often, the early antecedents of crime are delinquency and poor schooling outcomes. We see that the school-to-prison pipeline can be in close proximity to a school-to-life success one. For African Americans, exposure to desegregation beginning in the elementary school years, instead of attending segregated schools alone, led to a reduction of 3 percentage points in the annual incidence of incarceration and a decline of 22 percentage points in the probability of adult incarceration (Figure 2.10).[20]

FIGURE 2.8

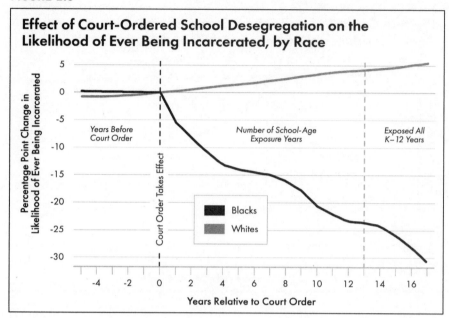

Effect of Court-Ordered School Desegregation on the Likelihood of Ever Being Incarcerated, by Race

FIGURE 2.9

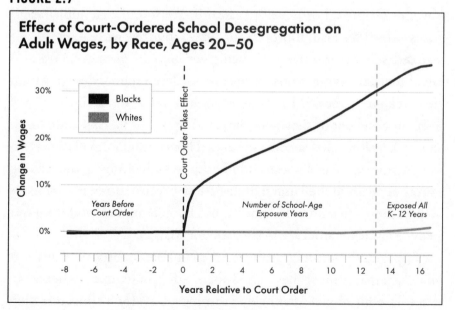

Effect of Court-Ordered School Desegregation on Adult Wages, by Race, Ages 20–50

FIGURE 2.10

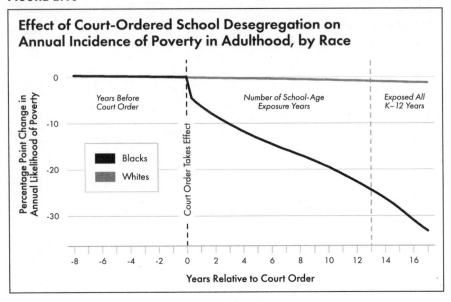

It has often been said that the currency of inequality is best measured in differences in life expectancy and quality of life—and in this way, the reciprocal of poverty is health. We found that adult health status outcomes also improved for black children with access to integrated schools (on par with being seven years younger). We also found that a five-year exposure to court-ordered school desegregation yielded an increase of 11 percentage points in the annual incidence of being in excellent or very good health (Figure 2.11). Exposure to integrated, well-funded schools predicted lower adult rates of hypertension, cardiovascular disease, and obesity (which is among the leading causes of death in the United States). The precise causal mechanisms behind these specific outcomes cannot be fully understood from our analysis alone (as we'll see in subsequent chapters).[21]

Importantly, we once again see the consistent absence of any significant impacts on whites across these adult outcomes—whether in terms of educational attainment, earnings, poverty, or incarceration rates. This finding flies in the face of the fears that many whites held

FIGURE 2.11

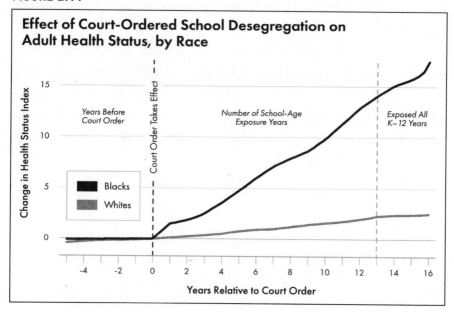

Effect of Court-Ordered School Desegregation on Adult Health Status, by Race

about integration as they predicted it would have negative effects for white children. Those negative effects simply never occurred.

Conversely, our results show that confinement to segregated, poorly funded schools interferes with children's life chances. Not only that, but children in these schools struggle to develop the ability to empathize with others, to appreciate the validity of other cultures, and to experience "the art of thinking individually together," as Malcolm Forbes, of *Forbes* magazine, aptly described diversity. The challenge is to decipher how we, through policy, can leverage the tools of integration to achieve positive outcomes now and in the long run.

In sum, these findings tell us a simple thing: integration, when implemented in a holistic fashion, has the power to break the cycle of poverty and can benefit all groups, regardless of race and ethnicity. Like the vaccines that have saved millions of lives in the medical field since they first appeared on the scene, integration is an unmitigated good. Goren's argument—and, in many ways, the argument of this book—is that integration is a kind of success of its own, one in which all of society can share, and one that shows up later in life in surprising ways. But the work of integration requires patience, a resistance to giving in to fear.

Integration alone is insufficient to achieve the kind of educational equality Thurgood Marshall and his allies sought. There could be no cure without it, but it was not the full cure itself. Instead, a whole apparatus of educational equity had to be constructed around the integrated classroom, a kind of scaffolding that protects the work done in the wake of the *Brown* ruling.

EQUALITY PROMISED,
EQUALITY DENIED

The white race deems itself to be the dominant race in this country. And so it is, in prestige, in achievements, in education, in wealth, and in power. So, I doubt not, it will continue to be for all time, if it remains true to its great heritage and holds fast to the principles of constitutional liberty. But in the view of the Constitution, in the eye of the law, there is in this country no superior, dominant, ruling class of citizens. There is no caste here.

—SUPREME COURT JUSTICE JOHN MARSHALL HARLAN, DISSENTING
OPINION, *PLESSY V. FERGUSON*, MAY 18, 1896

F EDERAL COURTS WERE CENTRAL TO THE FIGHT FOR DESEGREGA- tion. The judicial landmarks of the school desegregation cases also provided part of the basis for the movement toward school finance reform litigation and debates about the constitutionality of local finance systems. But what the courts did in *Brown* they were unable, or unwilling, to do in the fight to expand school funding equalization, another powerful method of ensuring educational opportunities for all. As we will see, despite hard-fought battles, the nation never realized the kind of progressive funding policies that many countries around the world currently enjoy, leaving the work of equalizing school funding to states, and sometimes districts. The uneven implementation that ensued provides evidence we can exploit to answer another critical and perennial question in education: Does funding matter? And when we say "matter," we do not mean simply for test scores—we mean for people's lives. To fully appreciate school funding reform, we must first understand the status quo and the efforts to undo it.[1]

——

JOHN SERRANO JR. was born into an East Los Angeles working-class family in 1937. He got married, went to school for sociology, and had three children. Two of them were attending Eastman Avenue Elementary School when Serrano asked the principal what he could do for his precocious older son. The principal gave a simple but astonishing answer: "You've got a couple of very bright kids—get them out of East L.A. schools if you want to give them a chance."[2]

It was a blunt assessment, but not an inaccurate one. East Los Angeles was then—and remains to this day—a hardscrabble area of immigrants who have little political leverage. Their children were the most in need of good schools, but also the least likely to have access to a high-quality public education. That lay on the other side of the I-5 freeway, in expensive, exclusive West Side neighborhoods like Santa Monica and Westwood.

Serrano followed the honest principal's advice, moving his family out of East Los Angeles into the presumably superior school districts of Whittier and Hacienda Heights, near the suburban eastern edge of Los Angeles County. It was sometime after this move that a lawyer from the Western Center on Law and Poverty, having heard Serrano's story at a party, decided to turn it into a legal crusade that would challenge California's reliance on local property tax wealth as the sole determinant of school funding. Under that system—prevalent across the nation—a child in Beverly Hills attended far superior schools than a child in East Los Angeles simply because the houses in Beverly Hills were of much higher value.

The case, *Serrano v. Priest*, was filed in 1968, with Ivy Baker Priest, the California state treasurer, named as the defendant. That's because, as the lawsuit argued, the state's funding formula was creating the very kind of "inherently unequal" schooling opportunities that *Brown v. Board of Education* had struck down fourteen years before. The lawsuit charged that "the quality of education for school age children in California" was "a function of the wealth of the children's parents and neighbors, as measured by the tax base of the school district in which said children reside," as well as of "the geographical accident of the school district in which said children reside."[3]

The case was led by Jack Coons, who had previously investigated schooling disparities in Chicago as part of the early research team that would later produce the famous Coleman Report (*Equality of Educational Opportunity*), the first large-scale national study of racial gaps in student achievement, under the leadership of the sociologist James Coleman. In the Los Angeles case, Coons was joined by his protégé Stephen Sugarman, who had completed his graduate degree at Northwestern University under Coons's mentorship. Sugarman, who eventually also followed Coons to the University of California, Berkeley, and remains on the law school faculty there to this day, remembers that he and Coons believed the case could be argued as one of "wealth discrimination," with children from more affluent districts effectively receiving access to higher quality schools than children from lower-income areas merely by virtue of being raised in wealthier neighborhoods.[4]

"The hook for legal purposes had to be discrimination on the basis of wealth," Sugarman says. "What you had to do was eliminate wealth advantages somehow. And we offered several possible ways you could think about how to try to let the court know that we're not saying that you *have* to do *X*, but stop doing *this*. Here are alternative ways they could potentially eliminate wealth discrimination by funding schools differently.

"We were trying to be conservative, because we didn't think the court wanted to be too aggressive. . . . It was a big thing to get into.

The other lawyers may have been more ambitious than us, but they were ambitious with things we thought were not officially practicable."

Coons and Serrano decided to use wealth discrimination as the central argument of the case only after other legal avenues had been explored. Another lawyer had drafted documents using ten different legal theories to argue Serrano's case when the notion of wealth discrimination came up. "We didn't think any of [those theories were] going to make it," Coons now says. It was the eleventh theory, wealth discrimination, which Coons and Serrano added, that ended up being the deciding factor.

The complaint used the example of Beverly Hills, a municipality of wealthy whites, and Baldwin Park, a middle-class community on the East Side of Los Angeles. Baldwin Park had property taxes that were twice as high as a percentage of assessed value as those of Beverly Hills, but the houses in Beverly Hills, home to Hollywood elites, were much more valuable. So while Beverly Hills could spend $1,232 per student, Baldwin Park could only afford $577. Circling back to the powerful argument of *Brown*, *Serrano v. Priest* made the case that the equal opportunity clause of the US Constitution promised to all children was being undermined by school financing formulas relying on local property taxes. They also argued that California's state constitution provided the same right, which would prove critical later on.[5]

"We found it unbelievable, the relentless intentional discrimination," Sugarman recalls. The complaint reflected the plaintiffs' outrage at the status quo—at the disparities that had become intrinsic in American life. "A disproportionate number of school children who are black children, children with Spanish surnames, children belonging to other minority groups reside in school districts in which a relatively inferior educational opportunity is provided," the lawsuit declared.[6]

Serrano v. Priest was filed when Lyndon B. Johnson was still president, though by 1968 his Great Society promises had been compromised by the nation's bloody involvement in Vietnam. By the time the case was decided by the Supreme Court of California, Richard

Nixon—a native of California who had attended the public schools in Whittier—was the president; meanwhile, the California governor, Ronald Reagan, was remaking the state's welfare program (or at least claiming to). The social contract that had been in place since the New Deal was about to be diminished, if not quite demolished.

Coons explains how much of a factor race did—and didn't—play in the case. "We looked as hard as we could for discrimination by race, but we couldn't find it," he remembers. "It was always hovering there somewhere, but we just could not find it for California in the way race had been so starkly a factor in our 1960s analyses of schools in Chicago."

The 1971 ruling by the state's highest court in *Serrano v. Priest* was a bold assertion of fairness at a time when "fiscal prudence" was increasingly the order of the day. Writing for the majority of the court, Justice Raymond L. Sullivan decreed that "the right to an education in our public schools is a fundamental interest which cannot be conditioned on wealth," and that he and his fellow jurists could "discern no compelling state purpose necessitating the present method of financing." As a result, "we have concluded . . . that such a system cannot withstand constitutional challenge and must fall before the equal protection clause."[7]

The Fourteenth Amendment had won the day—but only in California. Soon enough, Texas would also have its say.

———

EDGEWOOD IS ON the western edge of San Antonio, an area of single-story houses covered in vinyl siding and ringed by chain-link fences. And although it is part of the River City, Edgewood maintains its own schools. Among those who sent their children there in the 1960s was Demetrio P. Rodriguez, a sheet-metal worker who had not graduated from high school. He had five children, all in Edgewood public schools.

The schools were not good, and everyone in his predominantly Latino community knew it. In 1968, they decided to do something about it. Many years later, the *New York Times* described what had happened on a "balmy March day":

> Students at Edgewood High School here decided they deserved better than tattered textbooks, busted typewriters and tin cans used as beakers in science labs.
>
> Four hundred students, about a third of the school's enrollment, walked out of classes after lunch. They marched several blocks, carrying placards and chanting for better schools, to the school district administration building where they presented their grievances.[8]

Sixteen families therefore joined in filing a lawsuit against the school district alleging a fundamental unfairness in public education. Their case eventually went to the US Supreme Court as *San Antonio Independent School District v. Rodriguez*, decided in 1973. And although, like *Serrano*, it bore a single family's name, it also, like *Serrano*, did not represent a particular grievance confined to a single individual. It was a broader complaint about how American society was structured, how the fundamental fairness promised by the US Constitution was frequently subverted in practice.

Among those who testified on behalf of the plaintiffs, starting at the level of the US District Court for the Western District of Texas in 1971, was Jose Cardenas, the superintendent of the Englewood Public School District. He depicted a scenario strikingly similar to the one *Serrano v. Priest* had described in Los Angeles. That case had highlighted the disparities between Beverly Hills and Baldwin Park; Cardenas contrasted Edgewood with the neighboring North East Independent School District.

Edgewood was at such an inherent disadvantage, Cardenas said, that even the district's relatively high rate of taxation could not allow it to catch up to North East, where the per pupil spending was $310 higher in 1968 (that would have been a difference of $2,140 in 2016, when adjusted for inflation). Students in North East had every advantage they could want: more space, more books. Its dropout rate was one-quarter of Edgewood's. There was nothing Edgewood could do on its own to close these gaps. The kids there needed help.

Rodriguez sought the same thing as *Serrano*: a recognition that basing funding on property taxes was fundamentally unfair because it tended to reward wealthy, landowning whites at the expense of less-well-off minority groups. At the same time, the proposed remedy—redistribution—brought the unwelcome specter of socialism to mind for many whites at a time when the Cold War was still going strong. One account said that Cardenas's deposition before the trial "ended abruptly" when "Cardenas advocated an egalitarian model for school financing": "The Assistant Attorney General replied somewhat dramatically: 'There is a name for that. I have no further questions.'"[9]

At the district court level, *Rodriguez* was decided in favor of the plaintiffs—that is, the Edgewood parents—by a three-judge panel. The judges concluded that the way Texas funded its schools made "education a function of the local property tax base," and that this method had "adverse effects" that had been "vividly demonstrated at trial." In the opinion of the court, this was a "defect." In its ruling, the court cited both *Serrano v. Priest* and the equal protection clause of the Fourteenth Amendment to the US Constitution, which had also been the foundation of *Brown*.[10]

The victory, however, was not a lasting one. The decision was appealed to the US Supreme Court, where the defendants won in 1973. The majority opinion was read by Justice Lewis F. Powell Jr., whom Nixon had recently appointed to the Court. Although he would in time become a centrist on a rightward-moving court, Powell had been born in Virginia, and his roots were in the segregated South of the early twentieth century. He had been "shocked" by the 1954 *Brown* decision, writing, "I am not in favor of, and will never favor compulsory integration."[11]

In the Supreme Court's *Rodriguez* decision, Powell showed his conservative side, writing that "the Texas system [did] not operate to the peculiar disadvantage of any suspect class," because poverty of the kind that infected Edgewood did not explicitly demand govern-mental redress. "The Constitution does not provide judicial remedies for every social and economic ill," Powell wrote. And, although edu-cation was important, the court held, it was not a fundamental right: "Though education is one of the most important services performed by the State, it is not within the limited category of rights recognized by this Court as guaranteed by the Constitution."[12]

Sugarman remembers how *Rodriguez* dashed his hopes of a wider school funding reform movement. "We had a vision that we could win not only in California but that we could win everywhere," he remem-bers thinking after the *Serrano* victory. But that would not be the case.

"Later on," Sugarman says, "we learned it was sort of hopeless from the start."

And so the journey from *Serrano* to *Rodriguez* would live on to represent the failed fight for a federal constitutional right to education unencumbered by wealth disparities.

———

GIVEN THE STRIKINGLY different outcomes of *Rodriguez* and *Serrano*, one might expect that California spends much more than Texas on education. Somewhat startlingly, that is not the case. Texas is, indeed, one of the lowest-spending states in the nation, thirty-eighth by one measure. But even more astonishing is California's rank, which is forty-sixth in one ranking and forty-first in another. (Other rankings put California in the mid-twenties; the disparity is a reflection of how hard it is to determine student spending in a way that makes sense for every state and takes account of differing definitions for seemingly straightforward words like "spending" and "resources.")

On the face it, this makes no sense whatsoever. California has the fifth-largest economy *in the entire world*, and is powered by Silicon Val-ley, the fertile plains of the Central Valley, and, of course, Hollywood. As of 2015, it had the ninth-highest average income of any state, at $64,500. That same year, WalletHub ranked the relative wealth of American cities, finding that nine of the top ten were in the Golden State. There are more billionaires in California (131) than there are in any other nation on earth (except for the United States, of course, and China).

Not only that, but it is probably the country's most socially progressive state, closer in outlook (if not weather) to Scandinavia than to South Carolina. On issues like gun ownership and LGBTQ protections, California is well to the left of the rest of the nation. It is not only a progressive state but an educated one. The University of California is a jewel of American higher education, with Berkeley deemed by many as the finest public university in the world. In other words, the state has the money, the human capital, and the political inclination to foster great public schools.

And yet the public schools are a "lesson in mediocrity" (*The Economist*) if not "among the worst" in the nation (*LA Weekly*), tough judgments backed up by sound statistics.[13]

So what happened?

In short, the answer is Proposition 13, the "taxpayers' revolt" that Californians voted into law in 1978. The ballot measure effectively capped property taxes, cutting off the stream of funds that flowed to schools. School spending would now be centralized in the state capital, Sacramento, and would have to draw from additional forms of revenue rather than relying on property taxes alone.[14]

Prop 13 was, in part, a reaction to climbing taxes—and the way those taxes were being distributed because of decisions like *Serrano v. Priest*. The mastermind behind the initiative, Howard Jarvis, explained his rationale thusly: "The most important thing in this country is not the school system, nor the police department, nor the fire department. The right to preserve, the right to have property in this country, the right to have a home in this country—that's important." The idea was pitched as a kind of populist statement of values, a principled stand by taxpayers against rapacious tax collectors. It was a starkly individualist sentiment, with which 64.8 percent of voting Californians agreed.[15]

What they probably didn't realize was that most of the benefits of Prop 13 would redound to businesses, while most of its ill effects would fall on the infrastructure of public life. Education was an obvious victim, losing one-third of its $9 billion in state funds, which had, in turn, come from taxes. Prop 13 may have padded some bank accounts, but that wasn't going to do much for schools. Quality has suffered, too. According to *Education Week*, which issues an annual report card on school quality in each state, California gets a C– for the quality of its schools. Texas has exactly the same grade.[16]

But does school funding even matter? California's fall from grace since the passage of Prop 13 would seem like suggestive evidence that it does, but ironically, this is precisely the type of simple analysis of aggregate trends that we show can be highly misleading. Some believe that the role of money in education has been exaggerated. They point to a number of allegedly failed school funding reforms of the late 1980s and early 1990s as the main evidence for their argument. To them, more money spent on schools is more money wasted.[17]

Since the release of the Coleman Report more than half a century ago, researchers have questioned whether increased school spending actually improves student outcomes. Published in 1966, James Coleman's groundbreaking report painted a dire portrait of the racial disparities in American public education:

> For most minority groups, then, and most particularly the Negro, schools provide little opportunity for them to overcome this initial deficiency; in fact, they fall farther behind the white majority in the development of several skills which are critical to making a living and participating fully in modern society. Whatever may be the combination of non-school factors—poverty, community attitudes, low educational level of parents—which put minority children at a disadvantage in verbal and nonverbal skills when they enter the first grade, the fact is the schools have not overcome it.[18]

Notably, school spending was found to be unrelated to student achievement. But did the interpretation of these findings paint an accurate portrait in its broad-brush conclusions that money doesn't matter? In the decades following the release of the Coleman Report, the effect of school spending on student academic performance has been studied extensively, and Coleman's conclusion has been widely upheld.

Stanford economist Eric Hanushek, a leading education scholar, is among the foremost proponents of the view that increases in school spending over the past two decades have not been an effective cure. In 2009, he authored an influential paper that looks at court decisions that, like *Serrano*, declared that school funding formulas were unfair. The most notable of these was the 1989 decision by the Supreme Court of Kentucky in *Rose v. Council for Better Education*. Rose was John A. Rose, the president of the Kentucky Senate, and the Council for Better Education was a group started in 1984—and still at work in 2017—advocating for better public education in one of the nation's poorest states.[19]

Rose was an unequivocal victory for the proponents of school funding reform. Chief Justice Robert F. Stephens wrote the majority opinion for the Kentucky court, in which he sharply criticized the state's political leaders for failing the state's children, saying, "It is crystal clear that the General Assembly has fallen short of its duty to enact legislation to provide for an efficient system of common schools throughout the state. In a word, the present system of common schools in Kentucky is not an 'efficient' one in our view of the clear mandate of Section 183. The common school system in Kentucky is constitutionally deficient."[20]

The *Rose* ruling became the blueprint for plaintiffs around the country seeking to attack unequal funding schemes in their local contexts. The decision "heralded in the golden age of successful adequacy litigation, lasting from 1990 to 2004," as Hanushek and his coauthor, Alfred Lindseth, wrote in their 2009 analysis. According to their calculation, "over twenty states" participated in the push to equalize school funding formulas, as *Serrano v. Priest* had done in California many years before. The authors did not cheer these reforms, for, in their estimation, "the plaudits showered on the Kentucky remedy relate mostly to the structural changes it brought about and not to success in improving the achievement of students." In other words, they believe these were merely cosmetic changes that did not fundamentally ame- liorate the inequalities at work in Kentucky's education system. They found, for example, that between 1992 and 2007, although the test scores of white students in Kentucky improved, they remained below the national average, and the scores of black students did not improve. To them, this was an obvious sign of failure.[21]

Hanushek and Lindseth also looked at Wyoming's school funding reform, which they said had been "perhaps the most dramatic court intervention" in the nation to date. In 1995, that state's Supreme Court "decreed that the legislature provide whatever funds necessary to make education in the state the 'best,'" in the authors' words. There, too, Hanushek and Lindseth saw little evidence to suggest the money made much of a difference in educational outcomes, at least as those were measured by test scores. "Despite these unprecedented increases in school funding," they wrote, "the achievement of Wyoming's stu- dents has largely failed to keep up with the nation or even with its much lower-funded, although demographically similar, neighboring states."[22]

New Jersey left them similarly unimpressed. Only in Massachu- setts did they see evidence of school funding reform doing what it was intended to. "Simply spending more on the existing system, whether brought about by court order or legislative action, has not yielded re- sults," they wrote in the conclusion of the study.[23]

To some, this conclusion makes visceral sense, in particular older Americans who went to public schools without cutting-edge com- puter labs or science teachers with degrees from the Massachusetts Institute of Technology. During the Cold War, the American public school system was the pride of the world, this argument goes (con- veniently ignoring segregation and other ills). Now, we spend a col- lective $634 billion on education, *more than the entire gross domestic product of Argentina.* And yet, on a recent Programme for Interna- tional Student Assessment (PISA) test, American fifteen-year-olds placed thirty-eighth out of seventy-one test-taking nations in math and twenty-fourth on science. This, from the nation that cured polio and placed a human being on the moon. Something must be wrong.[24]

———

ONE OF THE themes of this book is patience. Education reform often proceeds by a kind of punctuated equilibrium. We implement some new whiz-bang reform, let it run its course for a little while, but then become impatient because things haven't improved as much we wanted them to: test scores haven't jumped, for example. Studies are published to confirm that, yes, indeed, X reform failed to achieve Y effect. The studies suggest a new reform, one that in large part reverses the previous one. New fixes are tried, reversed, and then new fixes are tried again.

And so we continue on. What is often confirmed, however, is not the futility of public education but the lack of the kind of perseverance this work requires if it is to be done properly. Too often, we take the pan out of the oven far too early, only to find the result woefully undercooked.

In 2015, we published a study that examined the long-term impacts of school spending induced by school finance reforms in this country. Others, like Hanushek and Lindseth, had taken snapshots of school funding reform efforts. Those snapshots may have provided some clarity, but only about a strictly limited period of time. Our study sought to take something closer to a time-lapsed video, looking at the effect of school funding reform over decades.[25]

We did so by avoiding the easy allure of relying on test scores, since they are imperfect measures of learning and may be rather weakly linked to adult earnings and success in life. Indeed, recent studies have documented that effects on long-term outcomes may go undetected by test scores. We decided to focus instead on the effect of school spending on life outcomes such as educational attainment and earnings.

To investigate whether the first wave of school funding reforms worked, we focused on children born between 1955 and 1985, whose school-age years straddled the period in which reforms were implemented. We assembled data that detailed exactly where court-ordered educational reform had taken place and how such decisions had altered school funding formulas. We used "geodata" from the University of Michigan's Panel Study of Income Dynamics (PSID)—the vast life outcome database that is a gold mine for social scientists—to compare such outcomes for students who did and did not experience the increased spending resulting from school funding reforms. If education is the work of generations, this approach would allow us to determine whether there were long-term benefits to school funding reform that had not been visible before in more blinkered analyses.

School finance reforms have sprung up in pockets around the country over the past several decades, but their timing and the exact types of reform implemented have been uneven across states and districts. This uneven spread may seem familiar—it is exactly what we exploited to study the effects of desegregation (and it is how we will examine the effects of Head Start spending in the next chapter). But it is these very geographic differences in the timing of reforms that we will use to assess the impact of school finance reforms. Although others have tried to answer this question before us, we think they got it wrong—methods matter.

To reach our conclusions, we analyzed data that surveyed 15,353 people (two-thirds of them from disadvantaged backgrounds) for a total of 93,022 data points about their lives. The research encompassed 1,409 school districts in 1,031 counties in every state in the land. It accounted for other differences in school environment and family background in such a way that any change to per-student spending the respondents faced had to have come from court-ordered reform, not some other source. The study then compared the outcomes for exposed and unexposed children, along with the spending dosage of court-ordered reform.[26]

In contrast to Hanushek and Lindseth (and other funding-reform skeptics), we did not look at test scores, but at what happens long after tests are taken. It helped that we had valid wage observations for about 95 percent of the sample.

We found that there were small effects for children from affluent families. However, for low-income children, a 10 percent increase in per-pupil spending each year for all twelve years of public schooling was associated with 0.46 additional years of completed education, 9.6 percent higher earnings, and a reduction of 6.1 percentage points in the annual incidence of adult poverty. Perhaps most important of all, our study found that a 25 percent increase in per-pupil spending throughout one's school years could eliminate the average attainment gaps between children from low-income and non-poor families.

Overall, there is a clear pattern of improved outcomes for cohorts of students exposed to greater "doses" of spending. Indeed, the longer students are treated for the symptoms of poorly funded education, and the higher the doses of school funding reform they are administered, the better their outcomes are bound to be.

The results suggest that a significant portion of this improvement took place because increased funding led to reductions in class sizes and went to hiring better teachers. For example, when a district increases school spending by $100 due to reforms, spending on instruction increases by about $70, spending on support services increases by roughly $40, and spending on school buildings increases by about $10, on average, while at the same time there are reductions in other kinds of school spending. Instructional spending makes up about 60 percent of all spending and accounts for about 70 percent of the marginal increase. In other words, superior instruction leads to superior adult outcomes. This conclusion agrees with other studies that have highlighted the importance of good teaching.

We also found that schools in these districts had fewer students per school counselor and fewer students per administrator, factors that have also been found to improve student outcomes. Overall, these positive effects are driven, at least in part, by some combination of reductions in class size, improvements in adult-to-student ratios, increases in instructional time, and increases in teacher salaries, which can help to attract and retain a more highly qualified teaching workforce.

School funding reform does not happen in a vacuum. If anything, external social stimuli explain why there isn't an even greater benefit from increased spending in public education. Some of the countervailing forces include persistent residential segregation, the crack epidemic of the mid-1980s, and the mass incarceration of young men of color, which had frequently left families without fathers. It is therefore likely that any positive school spending effects were offset by deteriorating conditions for low-income children in other dimensions.[27]

Something was wrong—in other words, *is wrong*. But it isn't because we've "wasted money" on making our schools more fair. Our findings indicate that state school finance reform policies can improve student outcomes and help reduce the intergenerational transmission of poverty. It stops the spread of the virus called inequality.

Money alone may not be sufficient, but provision of adequate funding may be a necessary condition. And *how* the money is spent is especially important. As such, to be most effective spending increases should be coupled with systems that help to ensure that the money is allocated toward the most productive uses.[28]

———

THE DESCRIPTION OF Spring Garden School is painful and poignant: "The school lacks central air conditioning, and the electrical circuit is not able to support multiple window AC units running simultaneously. . . . There is no auditorium that can seat all students. . . . The school does not have working bathrooms on every floor. . . . [T]here is no music teacher, only an itinerant string teacher who comes to the school for a half-day every other week. The school has only a half-time librarian."[29]

Those words come from a lawsuit, *William Penn School District v. Pennsylvania Department of Education*, that was originally filed in

2014 and is still wending its way through the courts today on behalf of Pennsylvania parents who say the state unfairly allocates funds for public schools. The suit powerfully echoes *Serrano v. Priest* and *San Antonio Independent School District v. Rodriguez*. In doing so, it harkens back—as do those two lawsuits—to *Brown*, and to two crucial words in the Fourteenth Amendment: "equal protection."

Pennsylvania had the largest spending disparities between rich and poor districts of any state in 2012. As shown in Figure 3.1, per-pupil spending in the poorest school districts is 33 percent lower than per-pupil spending in the wealthiest school districts in Pennsylvania.

The Pennsylvania lawsuit charges that "rather than equip children to meet [state academic standards] and participate meaningfully in the economic, civic, and social life of their communities," state and municipal education officials had "adopted an irrational and inequitable school financing arrangement that . . . discriminates against children on the basis of the taxable property and household incomes in their districts."[30]

This is the same argument that has been made about Los Angeles, San Antonio, and so many other places across the nation: the more prestigious your zip code, the better your schools are bound to be. If it is your poor luck to have been born in a destitute district, you can expect subpar schools that will, in all likelihood, keep you in the state of poverty into which you have been born.

Pennsylvania is especially egregious in this respect. It has what the *Washington Post* called in 2015, after the *William Penn* suit was filed, "the nation's most inequitable" schools, with a wealthy district like Bryn Athyn spending $26,675 per student and a poor one like Mount Carmel spending about a third of that ($8,860).[31]

Pennsylvania, at the time the suit was brought to court, was one of three states in the country without a school funding formula that would at the very least attempt to equalize such disparities. As the state's Education Law Center wrote in 2013, "most states use data-driven, cost-based education funding formulas to meet these goals. Most of these formulas use accurate student data, account for differences among

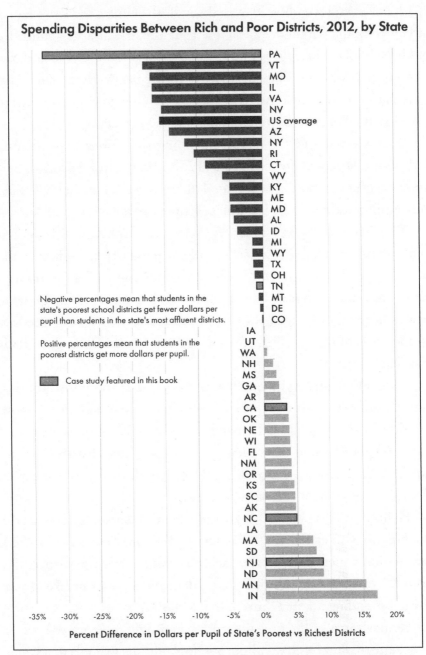

Figure 3.1. The figure shows funding differences between school districts for each state in 2012 based on state and local funds. National Center for Education Statistics, https://nces.ed.gov/edfin/Fy11_12_tables.asp.

school districts, direct funding to address those differences, and do so with a goal of ensuring all students have adequate funding to meet state standards."[32]

Pennsylvania's lawmakers declined to put such a system in place. Its schools would continue to be grossly unfair even as they operated on a premise of fairness and equality. "Pennsylvania has become a national outlier," the Education Law Center grimly declared, pointing out a little later that the state "does not currently use an education funding formula, and its leaders cannot guarantee that state education dollars are being distributed accurately, fairly, or transparently." The report additionally noted that Pennsylvania is "near the bottom in the percentage of state funding for local schools—only 9 states contribute a lower percentage of state education funding than Pennsylvania."[33]

The Millers fully grasped this reality. The solidly middle-class African American family lived in Upper Moreland, a wealthy white suburb of Philadelphia, the kind of place people move for the schools. But as the Miller family grew—a son, in addition to three older daughters—they needed a bigger house. For that, Jamella and Bryant Miller moved their family from Upper Moreland closer to the core of Philadelphia, where their children would attend the William Penn district schools.

William Penn spends $2,600 less per student than Upper Moreland. Jamella and Bryant described the William Penn schools in a 2016 op-ed for the *Philadelphia Inquirer*, which began as follows:

> Our 13-year-old daughter is just starting eighth grade at Penn Wood Middle School in the William Penn School District near our home in Delaware County. Her favorite subjects are science and math. But her school cannot support 21st-century science and math programs. In past school years, there were no textbooks for students to take home, so she would bring home worksheets that were not very challenging. There were no fancy robotics or technology programs. And the average size of her classes ranged from 28 to 35 students.[34]

The difference was especially noticeable to Jameira Miller, the oldest of the Miller children, who was in high school at the time of the move. She told National Public Radio how students would race to Spanish class in her new school in order to secure a blanket, so cold was the room where they were supposed to be learning a foreign language. Of the divide between rich and poor districts, Jameira said, "It's never going to be fair. They're always going to be a step ahead of us. They'll have more money than us, and they'll get better jobs than us, always."[35]

Her parents were unwilling to accept defeat, especially since they have three younger children they don't want to see racing for classroom blankets. So they joined the lawsuit over the way Pennsylvania funds its schools, hoping to force the state to acknowledge the vast inequalities it allows to fester.

Meanwhile, the state's Democratic governor, Tom Wolf, has made his own push to equalize school funding. In the summer of 2016, the first-term governor signed into law the Basic Education Funding formula, which was expected to add $100 million to school funding this year. But as the formula was being implemented, Wolf warned that, "while Pennsylvania is no longer one of the only states without a fair funding formula, our commonwealth's schools remain the most inequitable in the nation." (His promise is complicated by the intransigence of Republicans in the state capital of Harrisburg and their unwillingness to spend more money on education.)[36]

Then, in the fall of 2016, the Millers and other plaintiffs won a major court victory when a state court ruled that *William Penn School District v. Pennsylvania Department of Education* could move forward. "The court did not compel the state Legislature to redistribute money—not yet," cautioned one news report. "It simply said the judiciary can consider whether legislators have satisfied clauses in the state Constitution that require Pennsylvania to provide equal protection under the law and a 'thorough and efficient system of public education.'" The news report noted that the decision "opens the door for a breakthrough challenge to the state's educational funding system. If that challenge succeeds, Pennsylvania school districts could see dramatic changes in state aid."[37]

That may not seem like victory, as such, but remember that *Brown v. Board of Education* was not a straightforward case, either. Few landmark decisions are. Rather, they move haltingly, seemingly fueled by little more than the conviction of those who believe themselves to be on the side of justice.[38]

The Millers saw another victory in the fall of 2017, at the Supreme Court of Pennsylvania. "It is settled beyond peradventure that constitutional promises must be kept," wrote Justice David N. Wecht, in a sign that the decision that followed would be friendly to the plaintiffs—for the Commonwealth of Pennsylvania plainly promised equal education to those who dwelt within its borders. Much of the decision dealt with the complexities of Pennsylvania's constitutional law. But the premise embraced by the justices was also beguilingly simple. Although they did not rule in favor of the Millers, they ruled that *William Penn School District v. Pennsylvania Department of Education* should proceed on its merits. They agreed with the plaintiffs' central assertion, which Wecht described as follows: "Notwithstanding the General Assembly's partial mitigation of the differences in resources produced by school districts' heavy reliance upon highly variable local tax policies and tax bases, plaintiffs argued that the legislative formula was insufficient to satisfy the Education Clause's mandate."[39]

In other words, what has been done has not been enough. And so the Millers wait for justice as their challenge to Pennsylvania's school funding continues. And even though Jameira is now off to college—Villanova—millions of children around the nation remain trapped in eddies of educational poverty from which they cannot escape. And it will continue without end until we retire the model of a single-subject policy and cast a new, three-dimensional mold that reflects the intersectional nature of integration, preschool investments, and K-12 school spending.

GETTING AHEAD WITH HEAD START

This program this year means that 30 million man-years—
the combined life span of these youngsters—will be spent
productively and rewardingly, rather than wasted in
tax-supported institutions or in welfare-supported lethargy.
I believe that this is one of the most constructive, and one
of the most sensible, and also one of the most exciting programs that this Nation has ever undertaken.

—President Lyndon B. Johnson, announcing the creation of
Head Start, May 18, 1965

A WOMAN WENT FROM HOUSE TO HOUSE KNOCKING ON THE DOORS of shotgun shacks in the black part of Ames, Texas. It was the spring of 1965, and the air was laden with humidity and the screeching of cicadas. This section of the Lone Star State had more in common with the Deep South than with the rolling Hill Country to the west.

Darren Walker remembers the young woman coming to the door of the house where he lived with his mother and three sisters. The woman told Walker's mother about "a new federal program called Head Start." "My mother didn't know what that was," Walker says many years later, sitting in the Manhattan offices of the Ford Foundation, the philanthropic organization he has directed since 2013.[1]

President Lyndon B. Johnson had recently announced the Head Start program as part of the Great Society legislation Congress engineered to patch up the social safety net it had first created some three decades before, under Franklin Delano Roosevelt in the New Deal. The federally funded early childhood education program, established in 1964, began as a summer program in 1965, but by 1968 it ran during the school year as well. Head Start, with a curriculum that aims to improve literacy, numeracy, reasoning, problem-solving, and decision-making skills, provides indigent three- and four-year-olds with the kind of learning opportunities they might otherwise lack, and it does so with the knowledge that lacking such opportunities in young childhood results in a host of costly social ills. To orchestrate a prelude to a better life, it targets the whole child, with nutritious meals, development screenings, and medical, dental, and mental health referrals factored in.[2]

Head Start teaches early literacy skills and tries to instill a basic sense of curiosity about the world. It lets children play—which enhances social, emotional, and motor development as well as cognitive skills. It feeds and nurtures the children and tends to their health needs. At its best (although there have been places and times in which Head Start was not at its best), Head Start puts children into the hands of adults who care for them and who capably promote learning and growth.

Educators and the general public often refer to the years from kindergarten to high school graduation using the shorthand "K-12." We know, however, that education begins much earlier than age five, when children enter kindergarten. Some child development experts think certain aspects of rudimentary language acquisition begin in the womb, although we won't concern ourselves with prenatal matters here. The proponents of school integration and racial equality in the years following *Brown v. Board of Education* understood that, even if schools were integrated, many black children would enter those schools well behind their white peers, in large part because many of them would come from socioeconomically disadvantaged home situations where the foundations of learning had not been set. In order to make integrated schooling successful, quality *preschool* was a necessary ingredient. Indeed, as we will see, high-quality preschooling enhances subsequent investments in education, because otherwise the investments will come too late. Preschool is that important.[3]

More than half a century after its founding, Head Start remains the prototype of what a multidimensional, high-quality preschool program should look like. Darren Walker, for one, credits the program with nudging him ever so gently out of Ames, Texas, and the existence of poverty that would have portended. Without Head Start, there would have been no University of Texas in his future, no law school to follow his undergraduate degree. Nor would he have had his years in banking, followed by a shift to public service, or the opportunity to oversee an $11 billion endowment at the Ford Foundation, or a *New Yorker* profile. It all began with his neighbor's knock on the door.[4]

Like many black children in the South in the 1960s, Walker came from a low-education background. His mother had great hopes for him, but she could do little to provide him with the kind of enrichment necessary to see those goals fulfilled. Like many poor people, both then and now, she understood the value of education but didn't have the tools to extract that value for her own children. She couldn't simply send her child to the prestigious Phillips Academy in Andover, Massachusetts, from which George W. Bush had graduated the year before. That level of privilege was simply inaccessible to her. In fact, even Head Start must have seemed surprising, an odd but reassuring sign that the black folk of Ames had not been forgotten by the power brokers of Washington.

"In many ways, my life has come full circle," Walker wrote in 2015. "The Yale University researchers who helped design Head Start were supported by none other than the Ford Foundation, the institution I am privileged to lead."[5]

Walker began attending Head Start in the summer of 1965 at a local Catholic school. While he already had a budding interest in books, Head Start was where he began to learn to read. There, Walker recalls, he "started to construct sentences and understand formal English as opposed to the vernacular way in which we rural, poor blacks spoke.

And to see how through reading, I could in some ways escape my world."[6]

Walker had been, he now says, "considered by many of my relatives and neighbors a persistent and lovable nuisance": with an insatiable curiosity, he often proved exasperating to the adults around him. "Reading allowed me to channel a lot of that energy" in a constructive way, he says, especially after his mother invested in a set of encyclopedias from a door-to-door salesman, who came around every Friday to collect payment. His grandmother, a maid for a wealthy white family in Houston, brought home books that one of the boys in that family no longer wanted.

"I loved the art books," he recalls. "I loved the Richie Rich cartoons and Johnny Quest." He even remembers the name of the white boy to whom those books had once belonged, and who likely had no idea he was nurturing the intellect of someone whom he would never encounter face to face.

Head Start not only enriched Walker's early cognitive development but also helped to compensate for the limited enrichment opportunities in his home life. And although it is important to note that Walker's experience is not necessarily representative of the program as a whole, which has faced various challenges over the years, his experience is nevertheless instructive, a symbol of how good the program can be when it is given the resources to thrive.

By the third grade, Walker was making puppets for a production of William Shakespeare's *Macbeth*. The love of reading and learning eventually propelled him to the University of Texas, where he received his undergraduate and law degrees. (Attending college would have been impossible for Walker without another federal program the Johnson administration created: the Pell Grant.) Walker subsequently moved to Manhattan, where he worked as a corporate lawyer. But in the spring of 1991, he was struck by an *Economist* cover showing two black boys drinking soda on what appeared to be a desolate city street. "America's wasted blacks," the text on the cover said. The jarring image led him to become involved in social causes, which in turn led to his eventual appointment at the Ford Foundation.[7]

Now in his mid-fifties, Walker is just a little older than Head Start itself, which celebrated its fiftieth birthday in 2015. "If we want to secure lasting, measurable gains for our most vulnerable young people, the answer is not to give up, but to follow through," Walker said on that occasion. "We must continue investing in poor students—early, often, and throughout their entire lives."[8]

But whereas leaders like Walker see Head Start as a sound downpayment on the nation's finest natural resource—its young people— others disagree, disparaging Head Start as government waste. Yet our evidence suggests that the human cost of losing Head Start would be substantial.

———

IN HIS LATER years, Lyndon Baines Johnson would fondly remember the red-brick Welhausen School in Cotulla, Texas, where he had taught and served as principal in 1928–1929. West of San Antonio, Cotulla is a ranching community with a heavy Hispanic population. That was as true ninety years ago as it is today. Johnson himself had been educated in a one-room schoolhouse, where "Miss Katie Deadrich taught eight grades at one and the same time." Johnson was dismayed by the lack of opportunity he knew society would afford his young charges at Welhausen. He understood that what we today call "savage inequalities" would invisibly but inexorably govern their lives, like a high-pressure weather system that never lifts to let sunlight through.[9]

Nearly four decades later, as president of the United States, Johnson recalled his formative year as a teacher in the Texas scrublands. "I shall never forget the faces of the boys and the girls in that little Welhausen Mexican School," he said, "and I remember even yet the pain of realizing and knowing then that college was closed to practically every one of those children because they were too poor. And I think it was then that I made up my mind that this Nation could never rest while the door to knowledge remained closed to any American."[10]

Johnson was speaking at the time in San Marcos, Texas, where he had gone to college at Texas State. He was there to sign the 1965 Higher Education Act, which was intended to make it easier for American children outside the northeastern corridors of power—that is, the ones who could not use family connections to earn dubious admission to Andover and Yale, as Bush did—to attend college. The Higher Education Act, too, was part of Johnson's ambitious Great Society program, which renewed FDR's concern for the poor but with a new focus on race, in particular the plight of African Americans living under segregation in the South.

The early education portion of Johnson's Great Society was not an entirely new idea—it had some precedent going back to Roosevelt. The New Deal's primary task had been to address the plight of 15 million out-of-work Americans during the Great Depression. By 1938, an estimated 372,000 women were able to work because of FDR's Works Progress Administration, and that, for the first time, introduced the problem of child care into American society for households with two working parents. FDR's solution was the creation of "emergency public nursery schools" through the Federal Emergency Relief Administration. There was further investment in early childhood education during World War II, when some 350,000 women served in the military and nearly 3 million women worked in military factories, in accordance with the popular Rosie the Riveter image. A provision of the Community Facilities Act of 1940, also known as the Lanham Act, provided federal funds for child-care centers for these working mothers. "You cannot have a contented mother working in a war factory," one legislator noted, "if she is worrying about her children[,] and you cannot have children running wild in the streets without a bad effect on the coming generations."[11]

It wasn't just a matter of getting the kids out of the way while the war with Hitler raged. Social scientists were beginning to gain a deeper

understanding of the early life factors that influenced child development. For most of human history, it had been assumed that an individual's intelligence was innate, inherited, and constant: you were as smart
at birth as you were ever going to be, and there was little society could
do to change that fact. A researcher at the University of Iowa's Child
Welfare Research Station, Bird T. Baldwin, along with his colleagues
J. McVicker Hunt and Benjamin S. Bloom, realized that the childhood
brain was remarkably pliant—though also remarkably vulnerable.
Their work made clear that a lack of attention to early childhood development could set children up for subsequent failure.[12]

The social justification was provided in part by the "Gray Areas"
research of the very same Ford Foundation that Walker heads today.
This research, focusing on neighborhoods that were "becoming
black," "sought to address the bricks-and-mortar and human aspects
of poverty." In doing so, the private philanthropy provided a blueprint
for the public-sector reformers in the Johnson administration.[13]

Among these was Sargent Shriver, one of the many JFK holdovers
in the LBJ administration. Shriver was married to one of Kennedy's
sisters, Eunice. Another sister, Rosemary Kennedy, had been institu-
tionalized with severe mental disabilities, and her plight gave Shriver
an acute interest in what we today call *neuroplasticity*, the ability of
the brain to adapt, evolve, and overcome—if it is trained correctly to
do those things. He was especially impressed by a teachers' program
in Tennessee designed by Susan Gray, an authority on early childhood education. "If you intervene effectively and intelligently, at, let's
say three, four, or five years of age, you can actually change the IQ of
mentally retarded children," Shriver observed. But what interested
Shriver even more was that Gray's research showed that you could
intervene on behalf of children whose brains had been starved by
poverty and hardship.[14]

Johnson, who had been influenced by Shriver's interest in this
work, introduced Head Start in a Rose Garden ceremony on May
18, 1965. He spoke in the kind of visionary tones that seem especially remarkable today, when politics has become incremental and

idealism of any kind sets one up for mockery and suspicion about motivations.[15]

Johnson made his own motives perfectly clear: "I believe this response reflects a realistic and a wholesome awakening in America," he said, demonstrating an ability to grasp both the practical and idealistic aspects of politics. "It shows that we are recognizing that poverty perpetuates itself. Five- and six-year-old children are inheritors of poverty's curse and not its creators. Unless we act these children will pass it on to the next generation, like a family birthmark." He proposed opening eleven thousand childhood centers around the nation, "serving as many as possibly a half million children." They would not only receive an education, as Walker did, but also medical and dental care as well as nutritional services (long before First Lady Michelle Obama planted a vegetable garden on the White House grounds).[16]

"We have taken up the age-old challenge of poverty and we don't intend to lose generations of our children to this enemy of the human race," Johnson said as Head Start became a reality. Volunteers started canvassing the nation, looking to enroll children like Darren Walker in the new program.[17]

———

HEAD START WAS, from the outset, an extremely ambitious program, one whose founders perhaps didn't understand the scope of what they were putting in place. Some hubris may have been at work, too, in this administration full of the best and the brightest, who thought they could usher in an "abundance and liberty for all," as LBJ said in his speech introducing the Great Society.[18]

Head Start was targeted at preschool age children (three through five), and the vast majority of Head Start enrollees were four years old at enrollment during the first fifteen years of the program. At each center, at least 90 percent of enrollees had to be from families whose income was below the federal poverty line, and at least 10 percent of the children had to have a disability. Between 1965 and 1970, most of the enrollment in

Head Start was in summer-only programs. However, from 1972 to the present, most of the enrollment has been in the full-year Head Start. As such, the early rollout of Head Start represented both increases in Head Start participation and enhancements in the programs themselves. The likelihood of Head Start enrollment among poor children reached 86 percent for income-eligible cohorts entering kindergarten in 1969, fell in the early 1970s, and stabilized at around 63 percent by 1990.

But there were challenges from the start. The primary one was staffing—that is, finding teachers capable of putting LBJ's ambitious vision into practice at the levels of pay being offered. "We may have paid too little attention to the educational component," Edward Zigler, one of the program's founders, later reflected. James L. Hymes Jr., another of the program's founders, recalled a cavalier "anyone can teach young kids" attitude that clashed with the seriousness of Head Start's mission.[19]

At the same time, the program—which now seems exceptionally revolutionary for 1965, when the study of childhood development was in its infancy—attracted a level of skeptical scrutiny it could not quite withstand, and from which it has never really recovered. Zigler and another social scientist, Jeanette Valentine, reflected on this point, writing, "Particularly detrimental to the program has been the coterie of psychologists, early childhood educators, and social analysts who have regularly, albeit erroneously, proclaimed the failure of Head Start."[20]

Indeed, given the headwinds of prevailing suspicion, it is remarkable that Head Start has survived for more than half a century. And it is not just because of valid professional inquiry of the sort Zigler and Valentine described, from people who generally believed in early childhood education but may have disagreed about means and methods. Like many other aspects of Johnson's Great Society programs, Head Start has been under sustained assault from conservatives, for whom the government's helping hand is also the creeping claw of socialism. While the Voting Rights Act has been gutted by the Supreme Court, many of Johnson's antipoverty programs have been under systematic attack: some of them are either no more or have been diminished beyond recognition and utility.[21]

And yet Head Start continues to fulfill the mission Johnson outlined for it in 1965. It is estimated that in the past fifty-two years, the program has served 32 million children. Today it operates more than 58,385 classrooms across the nation serving more than 900,000 children—771,479 in "traditional" Head Start (i.e., three- and four-year-olds), and 149,986 in Early Head Start, the program for infants. Current Head Start expenditures average about $8,700 per enrolled child (in 2015 dollars). This level of per-pupil spending is much lower than those at model preschool programs such as Perry Preschool or Abecedarian. By comparison, average public K-12 per-pupil spending is currently about $11,000 (also in 2015 dollars).[22]

Longevity, of course, is not necessarily a marker of success. Neither is size. But the rapidity with which Head Start was deemed a failure is astonishing. Predictable broadsides from the right notwithstanding, it speaks to a kind of fundamental impatience in the American spirit. That collective impatience has sometimes led to incredible achievement by restless men and women eager to disrupt the status quo, but it can also prevent us from engaging in the kind of sustained work a program like Head Start requires. Head Start is not the work of weeks and months, but of years and decades, even of generations. In failing to recognize that, we consign Head Start to failure.

"The preschool program for disadvantaged children is not worth the cost in its present form and ought to be radically revised," declared a 1969 report in the *New York Times*, describing the results of a study on Head Start conducted at a time when it was not yet five years old. The "poor children who participated," the *Times* said, "were not appreciably better off than equally disadvantaged children who did not."[23]

The *Times* article is notable because it set the tone of coverage, which pundits have dutifully followed ever since. "Head Start simply does not work," crowed the columnist Joe Klein in *Time* magazine in 2011, making an argument nearly identical to the one that had appeared in the *Times* forty-two years before. Without offering concrete evidence, Klein charged that Head Start programs were "far more adept at dispensing make-work jobs than mastering the subtle nuances of early education." In essence, he called Head Start a scam. "Even Government Agrees Head Start Is a Failure," said a headline on the conservative website Townhall.com four years later.[24]

That's not to say that critics use what is today called "alternative facts" in leveling their criticisms against Head Start. Some of the criticisms go back to the very founding of the program, starting with a White House Task Force on Early Childhood Education that, as early as 1966, was sounding alarms about the effectiveness of the initiative, which was rooted in years of research but had been implemented with haste. Another report, from 1969, "A Report on Evaluation Studies of Project Head Start," acknowledged that "Head Start may have been oversold or may not be the success that we hope." It said that Head Start was a valuable program, but one that needed bolstering. "Sustained gains are still being sought," the report warned.[25]

Today, critics can point to reports like the one issued in 2010 by the Government Accountability Office, which found that "the system is vulnerable to fraud," in the words of one investigator, who detailed troubling abuses, including the theft of $23,000 from one Head Start location in New Jersey. But vulnerability to fraud, while obviously troubling, cannot be the sole criterion by which we judge institutions. For if it were, the nation's banking system would have been dismantled after the Great Recession of 2008.[26]

There is only one question about Head Start that is worth asking, and it is one that, until now, has not been sufficiently answered with the right data, using appropriate methods gleaned from the right places: *Does it help children?* Have the sustainable gains sought in 1965 been accomplished?

———

As WE'VE SEEN, education research is inherently tricky. Our research subjects are not lab mice but children, often vulnerable ones. You can't subject them to adverse conditions to test a hypothesis about, say, teacher quality or standardized testing. Nor are the effects of interventions immediately observable the way they would be if you injected a mouse with some powerful new drug of questionable but potentially powerful benefit. A certain revolutionary method of teaching math to third graders could prove disastrous—but that might only become apparent when they reach the eighth grade.

Because of the challenges of trying to apply the rigors of social science to human beings living within complex tangles of difficult-to-isolate conditions, in our research we used longitudinal data from the Panel Study of Income Dynamics (PSID) matched with detailed information on county Head Start spending. We sought to provide fresh evidence to determine the efficacy of Head Start with special attention to teasing out its impacts on children's later-life success. Working with economist C. Kirabo Jackson of Northwestern University, we conducted an analysis of forty years of findings from the PSID, combined with another data set we assembled on Head Start and K-12 public school spending. Our goal was to find out whether early childhood human-capital investments are complementary to those made later in life. Basically, we wanted to know if Head Start (and other programs like it) worked.

Differences between individuals from more- and less-advantaged backgrounds manifest early in childhood and tend to grow as children age. Accordingly, correcting the effects of childhood poverty may require early—and sustained—investments. In our research, we sought to discover just how potent a "fuel" Head Start could be—and how much fuel would have to be added in ensuing years to maintain that early progress. Our study was motivated by the hypothesis that: (1) early-life interventions such as Head Start can realize their potential long-run returns *only* if they are followed up by quality investments during the school-age years; and (2) the potential benefits of many important social and economic policies may be missed unless other long-term outcomes, beyond test scores, are also evaluated.[27]

To see if this two-pronged hypothesis was sound, we first compiled data on Head Start spending for every county in the United States. We looked at Head Start spending per poor four-year-old for each year from 1965, the inaugural year of the program, through 2000, as well as district K-12 spending per pupil across the entire country for each year between 1967 and 2000. This sample includes 15,232 individuals born between 1950 and 1976 and follows them from birth to adulthood. They come from 4,990 childhood families, 1,427 school districts, and 1,120 counties across all 50 states. They are, in other words, America.

Our study takes advantage of the variation in spending on Head Start that occurred because the program was rolled out incrementally. There was also significant geographic variation in the timing of Head Start's arrival in different communities. That variation allowed for the same kind of design—mimicking a randomized controlled trial—that we applied to desegregation and school finance reform, as described in the preceding chapters.

We also looked at the variation in funding for K-12 education that occurred because of the court-ordered school finance reforms that took place in 28 states between 1971 and 2010. Before the 1970s, most public school spending was funded with local property taxes, meaning that wealthier neighborhoods could spend more per pupil on education than poor ones. School finance reforms altered formulas for school spending such that poorer districts were sometimes graced with an influx of funds (as we noted in the discussion of school funding reform in the previous chapter).

As with Head Start, these funding changes occurred at different times in different places, allowing us to examine the effect of spending levels. Looking at the two sets of data (implementation of Head Start and school funding reform), we were able to compare the adult outcomes of individuals who were from the same childhood county but exposed to different levels of Head Start spending, because some of them were four years old when Head Start spending levels were low (or nonexistent), while others were four years old when Head Start spending levels were much higher.[28]

In terms of school funding reform, we were interested in how the reforms sometimes added funding to the very same indigent school districts that were relying heavily on Head Start. Again, as with integration, our research was aided by the fact that such reforms were applied unevenly across both space and time. Some districts experienced increases in school funding when Head Start was available in the district, while others experienced similar funding increases when Head Start was not available. Moreover, Head Start was rolled out in different counties at different times, both before and after the local school districts experienced increases in spending from reform efforts. These discrepancies allow one to test whether K-12 spending increases have produced more results with Head Start investments or without them. And in addition, it allows for a test of Head Start's effectiveness when it occurs in areas with and without increased school funding.[29]

In our statistical analyses we discovered significant positive synergistic effects between policies promoting early childhood education and policies aiming to improve public K-12 school quality, such as the school funding reforms. The effects of Head Start are small when public K-12 spending levels are low. This phenomenon can explain the fadeout effects in prior studies, which has led to much of the criticism of Head Start that has become something like conventional wisdom.

At the same time, we found that K-12 spending is more effective at improving the outcomes of low-income children when it is preceded by a well-funded Head Start program. For poor children, both Head Start spending increases and K-12 spending increases lead to significant improvements in educational and economic outcomes as well as reductions in the likelihood of incarceration. Importantly, the long-run effects of increases in Head Start spending are amplified when

FIGURE 4.1

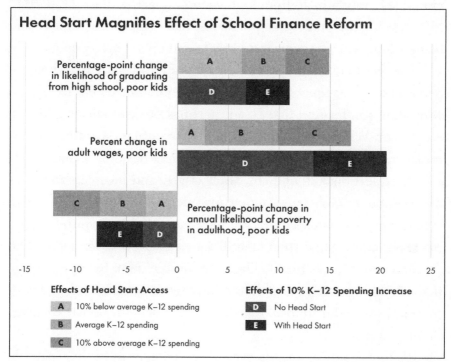

children subsequently attend schools with greater K-12 per-pupil spending induced by school funding reforms.[30]

Across all the outcomes, the marginal effect of the same increase in Head Start spending was *more than twice as large* for students from K-12 school districts spending at the 75th percentile of the distribution than for those from K-12 school districts spending at the 25th percentile. Similarly, the benefits of K-12 school-spending increases on adult outcomes were larger among poor children who were exposed to higher levels of Head Start spending during their preschool years (Figure 4.1). For poor children, the combined benefits of growing up in districts with both greater Head Start spending and greater K-12 per-pupil spending were significantly greater than the sum of the independent effects of the two investments in isolation.

For example, among poor children exposed to a 10 percent increase in K-12 spending, exposure to a typical Head Start center leads to 0.6 additional years of education, being 14.8 percentage points more likely to graduate from high school, wages that are 17 percent higher, being 4.7 percentage points less likely to be incarcerated, and being 12 percentage points less likely to end up in poverty as an adult.

The fact that the long-term benefits of Head Start spending depend on the subsequent level of K-12 spending may help to explain why some studies find that Head Start has positive effects and others do not. When it is not preceded by Head Start spending, an increase in public K-12 spending of 10 percent has only a small effect on the educational attainment, adult wages, and incarceration rates of low-income children. Among low-income children exposed to Head Start, that same 10 percent increase in K-12 per-pupil spending raises educational attainment 0.4 years, boosts earnings by 20.6 percent, and reduces the likelihood of incarceration by 8 percentage points. Among non-poor children, increasing K-12 spending by 10 percent raises educational attainment 0.2 years and boosts earnings by 11.7 percent.

We found similar results even when comparing sibling pairs in which the younger sibling was exposed to Head Start while the older one was not, because Head Start only became available after the older sibling was beyond the age of four. Head Start, in other words, is a force multiplier whose power can ripple through the teenage years. In fact, it could be more powerful than fixes attempted later on, after the achievement gap has already widened. At average K-12 and Head Start funding levels in the 1970s, the marginal dollar spent on Head Start was much more efficient in terms of improving long-run outcomes than the same expenditure on K-12 schooling.

What does this mean for future policy design? It is important for policymakers to consider preschool and K-12 spending as complementary efforts, rather than viewing educational spending as a zero-sum game in which spending on any one program reduces available funding for others. Instead, the total combined effect is greater than the sum of the investments in isolation. Because of the complementary nature of these investments, redistributing spending from well-funded K-12 schools to Head Start or preschool programs for poor children would improve both the efficiency and the equity of the system. As policymakers across the country consider state investments in pre-K programs, our work provides new evidence about the effectiveness of these programs. Past studies on pre-K spending showing inconsistent evidence on the long-term effects may not be truly reflective of the effectiveness of the pre-K programs. Instead, the data indicate the wasted potential that occurs when children who received a quality pre-K education go on to attend underfunded K-12 schools.[31]

Our findings point to the critical role that investments in early childhood can play in narrowing long-term gaps in well-being. They also highlight the importance of making sustained investments in the skills of disadvantaged youth. These results are the first to show that early and sustained complementary investments in the skills of low-income children can be a cost-effective strategy to break the cycle of poverty—and to turn poor children of color into their own versions of Darren Walker.

———

HEAD START ISN'T just about school. "The major fear was that we would end up with one large reading program and no concern for the whole child," said D. Keith Osborn, one of the founders of Head Start. In keeping with Osborn's whole-child approach, in a revolutionary program to alleviate hunger the children in Head Start were served both breakfast and lunch. Head Start continues to feed children today, helping to solve the perennial problem of hunger in America's schools (an estimated thirteen million children still go to school hungry each day).[32]

In their book *The Hidden History of Head Start*, Edward Zigler and Sally J. Styfco argued that "Head Start has never received sufficient credit for improvements in children's physical health." According to a 1968 report, in the first two years of Head Start's operation "98,000 children had eye defects diagnosed and treated, 900,000 dental problems were discovered with an average of five cavities per child, and immunizations were given to 740,000 children who had not previously been vaccinated against polio and to 1 million children who had not previously been vaccinated against measles." And, as our research highlights here and in the next chapter, healthier children are better learners.[33]

The public health benefits of Head Start remain evident today even as a more recent epidemic makes inroads. The nation's obesity rate is climbing—and with it, the health-care costs of unhealthy living. Educating young children about food choices is one of the surest methods of keeping them from becoming overweight, a precursor to diabetes and other ills. A 2015 study found that "preschool-aged children with an unhealthy weight status who participated in Head Start had a significantly healthier [body mass index] by kindergarten entry age than comparison children in a primary care health system." The authors concluded that "Head Start participants were less obese, less overweight, and less underweight at follow-up than children in the comparison groups."[34]

Another study, conducted in 2016, concluded that Head Start "has been successful in its goals to promote the healthy development of low-income children." The researchers asserted that Head Start "could be an important avenue for improving health and nutrition outcomes among low-income children, which would be particularly consequential given [their] poorer health status."[35]

Like the educational gains that Head Start students made, the health benefits offered a sturdy foundation on which to rest future gains and achievements.

———

NEUROSCIENCE BARELY EXISTED when Lyndon Johnson created Head Start in 1964. That year, in fact, the University of California at

Irvine did something no other university in the land had ever done before: it opened an entire neuroscience department. It would be another forty years before functional magnetic resonance imaging (fMRI) provided researchers with a clearer idea of what was actually happening within the body's most mysterious organ.

Despite the nascent state of neuroscience at the time, President Johnson's convictions and his War on Poverty reforms proved prescient—and correct. We know today that putting off rigorous educational intervention until kindergarten (or even later) is like letting a fire burn on an airplane until it hits cruising altitude. By that time, it is far more costly and difficult to remediate the problem than if it had been addressed at the outset.

The inherent cuteness of babies belies a sobering fact: their brains are developing at astonishing speed, forming about one million new neural connections *each second* in the first several years of life. By the age of three, a child's brain weighs 90 percent of what it will weigh in adulthood. What's most vexing is how much poverty can affect neurologic development, condemning a child to a life of underachievement before he or she has even learned to walk. By the age of eighteen months, a child with college-educated parents will begin to show significant linguistic gains as compared to a child whose parents are poor. In another eighteen months, the child with college-educated parents will have *double* the vocabulary of his or her indigent peer. These are, very simply, gaps that are far more difficult to close in later years if neglected in the earlier years.[36]

A host of studies show that early-life poverty produces higher risks of impaired social and cognitive development as well as greater sensitivity to stress. Nurturing, interpersonal interactions and play-based educational enrichment in the preschool years can release a cascade of neurotransmitter development and synapse growth in the young developing brain. Like a vaccine, they offer protection well into the future. And, as with some vaccines, booster shots are needed to ensure sustainable impacts through high school. The prescribed nurturing environment lowers cortisol levels, and therefore stress. It bolsters the immune system, sends feel-good hormones surging through the bloodstream, and promotes healthy development that will support future learning.[37]

Access to high-quality schools beginning in one's preschool years creates a human-capital force field against disease and decline. It is, in fact, a propeller of upward mobility. Nurturing interpersonal interactions in early life turn on a light bulb of learning that stimulates social competency and executive function while helping to regulate emotion and impulse control. Fostering learning across differences may be further enhanced as children are exposed to racial and socioeconomic diversity.[38]

A punitive environment engenders much the opposite. African American children constitute 18 percent of preschoolers but make up nearly one-half of preschoolers ever suspended. That statistical calamity is the beginning of the school-to-prison pipeline. Research has shown that roughly half of the achievement gap between poor and non-poor children apparent at third grade already existed at by the time the children started kindergarten. Head Start sought to address these shortcomings and to close the gap that poor children would experience from the moment they entered kindergarten. If the investments in early childhood that Head Start provided could improve school readiness, they could facilitate better learning in the K-12 system. The program wasn't just an investment in knowledge, but an investment in the cognitive ability to acquire *future* knowledge.[39]

In addition to cognitive development, policymakers should consider the fact that infants are socially discerning beings—even when it comes to recognizing race. Research has shown that an infant prefers faces that are phenotypically similar to theirs by the age of three months. By two years of age, a child uses race as a factor to understand human behavior. By the time another year has passed, race plays a role in picking playmates. Children's expression of prejudice peaks at around age four or five, with their attitudes often mirroring those of the adults around them. That is when white children begin to demonstrate a strong preference for other whites—though black and Hispanic children do not demonstrate a preference toward members of their own group.[40]

For fear of creating bias or soiling innocence, adults often avoid having culturally sensitive, healthy discussions around race with the children in their care. This approach is misguided. Instead, as with intellectual skills, an appreciation of racial difference is best instilled at an early age. Our legislative bodies, schoolhouses, and individual households should design opportunities for cross-cultural interactions and dialogue that intentionally foster positive attitudes about diversity. "Silence about race reinforces racism" has become a key phrase in the movement to foster improvements in this area from an early age. Open discussion disarms fear and helps build a foundation for prosperous interpersonal relations. Trying to make up for lost time in high school, or later, in contrast, is expensive and inefficient. In so many ways, early childhood offers the simplest and best opportunities for progress in this area.[41]

——

ALTHOUGH THE PERRY Preschool Project is not nearly as well known—or as expansive—as Head Start, it, too, makes a powerful case for early childhood education. The Perry Preschool Project began in 1962, three years before Head Start, with the aim of providing early childhood education to children in Ypsilanti, Michigan, a small community between Ann Arbor and Detroit. The sixty-four children enrolled in the study were all from poor African American families, and they were all three or four years old. They spent either one or two years in the program, which included an "active learning" curriculum and weekly home visits by the teachers. This model program and others like it—including Abecedarian, Chicago's Child-Parent Centers, and the like—spend much more per enrolled child than the typical Head Start program. Throughout the course of the Perry project, the children were studied by the HighScope Educational Research Foundation. Their outcomes were then compared to those of sixty-four otherwise similar children who had not gone through an intensive early childhood education program like Perry's.

Despite the small size of the study, HighScope was able to reach definitive conclusions about the efficacy of early childhood education. Their conclusions echo the ones we reached about the nationwide Head Start program: it works. And while targeted high-quality pre-K programs come at a cost, both our study and HighScope's show that they more than pay for themselves in the long run from a societal benefit-cost perspective, especially when they are accompanied by the right levels of K-12 spending. HighScope caught up with its subjects when they were twenty-seven years old and found that those who had gone through Perry stayed in school longer than their peers who had not gone to preschool and were more likely to graduate from high school. They were less likely to have committed a crime than their non-preschool peers, and the girls were less likely to have become pregnant as teenagers.

HighScope revisited its initial subjects again another thirteen years later, when they were forty. Remarkably, the researchers were able to interview 97 percent of the original participants. Yet again, the power of early intervention shone through. A full thirty-six years after they had attended preschool, those who had passed through Perry's doors "had higher earnings, committed fewer crimes [and] were more likely to hold a job."[42]

Employment, familial stability, economic productivity, lack of criminality: these are social outcomes that both conservatives and liberals—indeed, all Americans—should want for themselves and their fellow citizens. So why are so many people resistant to Head Start? In part, one has to suspect, because it is a program that suggests, to some, the excesses of a federal government reaching almost into the cradle.

Even as Head Start continues to serve as a target of conservatives critical of safety-net programs, many municipalities, including some GOP-controlled state legislatures, have enacted their own versions of early childhood education. Their approval of these institutions has been fueled by burgeoning new evidence of their long-term impacts, by education advocacy, and by grassroots organizations that have spread the word about the most promising ways to close achievement gaps. In effect, these are Head Start by any other name, and while they have their critics, they do not carry the taint of midcentury Great Society liberalism, a philosophy which to many Americans continues to seem, even after all these years, like a dangerous flirtation with communism.

In 2016, the National Institute for Early Education Research at Rutgers University published a definitive study, called "State(s) of Head Start," examining how the program was being implemented in all fifty states. It found wide disparities across the nation, so that, for example, while only 7 percent of eligible low-income four-year-olds were enrolled in Head Start in Nevada, in Mississippi the share that attended was 52 percent. Moreover, in some states Head Start was plagued by "low-quality instruction and insufficient hours." Overall, the report found that "less than 40 percent of the 3- and 4-year-olds in poverty" were attending Head Start. That's simply insufficient to make the kind of social impact LBJ envisioned more than half a century ago. The report's authors wrote, "Simply put, the program is not funded at a level that would make it possible to provide child development services of sufficient quality and duration to achieve its goals."[43]

The report concluded that fully funding Head Start to serve every one of America's 3.9 million indigent children would cost $20 billion; today, the program receives about $9 billion. No increase in funding—and certainly not one of $11 billion—is going to come from the federal government in the administration of Donald Trump, whose proponents tend to conflate all government spending with government waste. Indeed, a budget proposal released by the White House in May 2017 wanted to reduce funding for Head Start by $85 million.[44]

When we choose not to make the requisite investments in all of our children—not just those from privileged backgrounds—we pay for it down the road in other ways, both measurable and immeasurable. Consider the societal costs of crime, and the excess health-care costs due to preventable illnesses. The State of California spends more on its criminal justice system and incarceration than it does on higher education.

The most ambitious early childhood program in the nation was enacted in New York City by Bill de Blasio in 2014. The city's universal prekindergarten (UPK) program now educates 71,337 children across the five boroughs at no cost to parents. And although some of the wealthier parents elect to send their children to private preschools, the city's prekindergarten is truly "universal," open to all comers. Thus far, NYC UPK, as it's sometimes known, has been judged a success. Writing about NYC UPK in the *New York Times*, David Kirp, a public policy professor and education scholar at the University of California, Berkeley, described the ingredients that made it a model program: "A full-day program, staffed by well-trained teachers, supported by experienced coaches and social workers, who know how to talk with, not at, youngsters; a teacher for every 10 or fewer children; a challenging curriculum backed by evidence; and parental involvement."[45]

New York is hardly alone in these efforts. Tennessee has devoted $84 million to a statewide pre-K program that remains an ambitious and intelligent investment in the state's youngest citizens, though it has struggled with quality issues. Memphis, one of the poorest cities in the nation, with a childhood poverty rate of 43 percent, has 122 pre-K classrooms in its greater metropolitan area. Boston has also shown success with its pre-K initiative, as have Charlotte, Baltimore, and Los Angeles.

But we know that the potential positive benefits of preschool programs will dissipate if they are not followed up by quality investments in the K-12 years. High K-12 spending, with progressive state funding formulas (as in the case of Massachusetts), as opposed to relatively low K-12 spending, with regressive state formulas (as in the case of Tennessee and North Carolina), may determine the eventual success of the programs, as their long-term impact is influenced in large measure by whether high-quality investments are sustained.

True early childhood education would begin even earlier than prekindergarten, in recognition of the crucial neurological development that takes place in the first three years of life—and the enormous costs society will incur (in the areas of criminal justice and social welfare) if that developmental opportunity is squandered.

Geoffrey Canada, the education visionary who founded the Harlem Children's Zone network of charter schools, invites parents and children to something he calls The Baby College®, a family induction into a multifaceted support system that escorts students from the womb to a college degree. To help jump-start students' success, parents are educated about the many aspects and phases of child well-being—starting even before the child is born.[46]

These are wise public investments in our future that more than pay for themselves in the long run. Indeed, the societal returns to these pre-K investments far exceed the returns received by the individuals who participate in them. As our work highlights, the societal benefits include monetary savings from the lower educational remediation costs down the road, from the reduced likelihood of public assistance, from the averted costs of crime, and from the reductions in health-care costs, as well as the boon received from increased tax revenues from working-age adults who are more productive because of the individual gains they made as youths. When we elect to forgo these critical early-life public investments in disadvantaged children, we pay for it dearly down the road in the form of reduced national and state tax revenues, greater strains on the state and federal budgets, increased crime, poorer health, reduced political participation, and reduced intergenerational mobility—that is, the chance of moving up the social ladder among the members of a younger generation, to make gains that were not possible for their parents. We are all inextricably linked together when it comes to what it will take to succeed.

PUTTING THE PIECES TOGETHER

> In short, money matters, resources that cost money matter, and a more equitable distribution of school funding can improve outcomes. Policymakers would be well-advised to rely on high-quality research to guide the critical choices they make regarding school finance.
>
> —BRUCE D. BAKER, PROFESSOR, GRADUATE SCHOOL OF EDUCATION, RUTGERS UNIVERSITY, 2016

WHETHER IT BE CHARLES HAMILTON HOUSTON AND HIS COL-leagues at the NAACP, or Paul Goren and his Chicago school staff, those in the vanguard of desegregation have always been painfully aware of how much resources matter. Based on the available evidence from social science and their own lived experiences, they know that what makes segregation so deleterious is that it combines multiple forms of disadvantage. It is a matter of separation, of constrained budgets, of absent early investments, of lagging teacher quality, and on and on. Together, these problems are greater than the sum of their individual parts.

But, as we have shown, it is possible to disentangle and address the effects of segregation. Desegregation efforts alone have, on the whole, made a huge difference, and so, too, have investments in pre-K programs and school funding reform. But, most notably, we have shown that at least one synergistic solution—combining investments in pre-K with school funding reform—has, where employed, shaken the foundations of segregation. As the award-winning *New York Times* writer David Shipler has explained in writing about poverty, "every problem magnifies the impact of the others, and all are so tightly interlocked that one reversal can produce a chain reaction with results far distant from the original cause." In short, "if problems are interlocking, then so must solutions be." The same is true regarding our schools. Extant efforts at solving our educational woes detach health from education, early education from K-12 schooling, and so on. Current policy designs are as divided as our segregated classrooms—and must be combatted just as vigorously. This chapter shifts the paradigm from a singular approach chasing after illusory silver bullets to an integrated solution.[1]

Up to this point, the combination of pre-K programs and school funding reform have often occurred coincidentally, as a result of districts trying two (among many) policies in parallel. The results have been incredible, though often those who have implemented them did not understand why. The question is, Can we employ this synergistic solution intentionally? To answer it, we must look at New Jersey.

———

DURING THE COLONIAL era, education in cosmopolitan New Jersey was much like education in the nation's hinterlands: a largely freewheeling affair. Whereas today, every single state has a state constitution providing students at least some guarantee to a state-funded education, in 1776 in New Jersey, "the state constitution . . . did not even mention education," according to a scholarly historical account. Instead, "education was left to local community or private prerogatives."[2]

Enter Friends of Education, a collection of high-minded intellectuals dedicated to improving educational opportunity in the Garden State. One of the men who became involved was John Maclean Jr., vice president and then president of the College of New Jersey, which would later become Princeton University. As America sought to define and refine its new society following independence from British rule, the Friends of Education pushed for a formalized and universal education system in their state. They scored a major victory in 1829, when state legislators agreed to create public schools. But there was a catch: funding would go only to counties that also provided part of the funding themselves through local taxation. Thus, the less affluent townships that opted not to tax local citizens would not receive the funding.[3]

The imposition of this regressive funding system would set in motion a battle that endures to this day. It foreshadowed the kind of zip-code inequality that continues to exist across the nation. Districts with citizens who were wealthy enough to pay a tax had their educational funds bolstered by the states, whereas districts in which the citizens could not afford to pay an extra tax received no help for their schools. So while the 1829 law was a start, it was not an especially satisfactory one. Even at its inception, critics would inveigh that "the system we have now is worse than none, and our legislators have [merely] quieted their consciences that something has been done." Such critiques would continue, but Friends of Education and others would need to anchor New Jersey's nascent and fragile state education system before focusing on equalizing funding within districts. In 1844, they did just that, spurring New Jersey to become the first state in the country to include a constitutional amendment guaranteeing permanent state funding for education. But what precisely constituted "education" in New Jersey? An early, and critical, answer would come in 1875.[4]

That year, the state amended its constitution to declare that "the legislature shall provide for the maintenance and support of a *thorough and efficient* system of free public schools for the instruction of all the children in this state between the ages of five and eighteen." Beginning then and continuing for over a century, various interpretations of "thorough and efficient" would come to define the battle for the soul of the state's education system. But even in 1875, one thing was clear:

the new amendment required the state to provide *some* level of education to *all* students, and it potentially called into question the constitutionality of the antiquated, regressive school funding system in New Jersey. To critics, this was just another instance of good schools for some of the state's children and poor ones for others.[5]

Legal language rarely renders speedy social change. It would take another hundred years for New Jersey courts to even begin to confront the glaring funding inequities in the state's education system. And by then, patience among New Jersey's black residents had all but run out.

———

IN THE SUMMER of 1967, Newark burned in a paroxysm of civil unrest, spurred in large part by what African Americans perceived—fairly—to be unjust treatment by the police, as well as a greater feeling that the black community had been abandoned by state institutions. What began as the needlessly violent arrest of an African American cab driver soon turned into an all-out war. The *New York Times* reported that "two Negro women were killed in clashes between snipers and the National Guard and the police, and a looter was killed as he ran from a store. Terrorists ranged outside the ghetto and gunfire—including bursts from machine guns—resounded in downtown Newark. There was a renewed outbreak of arson. A guardsman was critically wounded." And that was just one night of the riots, which lasted for six days, claiming twenty-six lives and inflicting $75 million in damage to an already struggling city.[6]

The nation—and President Lyndon B. Johnson—watched a city set ablaze, wondering if it was a rebuke to the Great Society that Johnson had envisioned after his landslide 1964 election. Newark, and other burning cities across the land, suggested that his bevy of social programs had failed to resolve the knots of unease lodged within the body politic. If anything, the knots were getting tighter. Johnson, an idealist, was mounting a reelection campaign, and he was both flummoxed about the riots and motivated to get to the bottom of what had sparked them. He wanted to know what his administration could do to quell the unrest.

And so, amid the heat of the infamous summer of '67, the National Advisory Commission on Civil Disorders, or Kerner Commission, was born, chaired by Governor Otto Kerner Jr. of Illinois. It was given the remit to study and find solutions to the problems affecting urban centers throughout the country. Also on the commission was John Lindsay, the forty-three-year-old mayor of New York City. Lindsay was a Republican with remarkably progressive views on race, and he had obvious political ambitions beyond City Hall.[7]

After seven months of intensive study, the commission published its revolutionary report, replete with a kind of fiery rhetoric that is unusual in government reports. On the first page, the authors provided a grim warning: "Our Nation is moving toward two societies, one black, one white—separate and unequal." It went on: "Discrimination and segregation have long permeated much of American life; they now threaten the future of every American."[8]

The report found that a lack of education had contributed to the explosions of civil unrest. "Social and economic conditions in the riot cities constituted a clear pattern of severe disadvantage for Negroes compared with whites, whether the Negroes lived in the area where the riot took place or outside it. Negroes had completed fewer years of education and fewer had attended high school," the commissioners wrote. They concluded that this lack of education stemmed from a paucity of good, even decent, educational facilities. In a section devoted to education, the commission praised the American public school system in general, but observed that conditions in "the ghetto" were bleak: "The schools have failed to provide the educational experience which could overcome the effects of discrimination and deprivation. This failure is one of the persistent sources of grievance and resentment within the Negro community. The hostility of Negro parents and students toward the school system is generating increasing conflict and causing disruption within many city school districts."[9]

The commission's solution was to spend more money. Among the report's recommendations to ameliorate conditions in segregated inner-city schools was "sharply increased efforts to eliminate de facto segregation in our schools through substantial federal aid to school systems seeking to desegregate either within the system or in cooperation with neighboring school systems."[10]

The report was a clarion call. If New Jersey's school districts—or the districts of any other state, for that matter—were to avoid riots on their streets, they needed to address the educational inequities stemming from their antiquated and regressive school funding policies, which, in the case of New Jersey, among others, had barely evolved since their incarnations in the 1800s. Under the New Jersey policy, the state provided only a meager, minimum level of funding to each district, leaving the bulk of school funding to come from local taxes. Poorer districts, like Newark, which could not hope to tax their largely working-class citizens to increase funding, were essentially guaranteed substandard funding levels.

In 1970, the problem made its way into the New Jersey Superior Court, with the plaintiffs in *Robinson v. Cahill* filing a complaint arguing precisely that. Their claim hinged on the "thorough and efficient" clause that had been inserted into the state constitution almost a century before, and they argued that the clause created an affirmative obligation by the state to fairly fund a system that was available to all children—rich and poor alike. By 1973, the case had predictably wound its way up to the Supreme Court of New Jersey. There, Chief Justice Joseph Weintraub sided with the plaintiffs and made clear that, in the court's view, money matters. He wrote, "It is agreed there is a disparity in the number of dollars spent per pupil, depending upon the district of residence. . . . It is . . . clear that there is a significant connection between the sums expended and the quality of the educational opportunity. . . . Hence we accept the proposition that the quality of educational opportunity does depend in substantial measure upon the number of dollars invested."[11]

In other words, it was incumbent upon the New Jersey Legislature to pass a budget that would ensure adequate funding for every school district. Two years later, the legislators took their first bite at the apple, passing the Public School Education Act of 1975. The law promised to "establish a funding structure which will ensure that adequate financial resources shall be available to enable a system of free public schools to operate throughout the State." It also provided clues regarding why such funding was necessary: "to provide to all children in New Jersey, regardless of socioeconomic status or geographic location, the educational opportunity which will prepare them to function politically, economically and socially in a democratic society."[12]

But high-minded language is one thing; turning that language into material reality is quite another. Attempts to pass an income tax failed—six times in all—effectively making it impossible to achieve the promises outlined in the 1975 law. Frustrated with lawmakers' intransigence, the New Jersey Supreme Court shut down the state's schools, leaving one hundred thousand summer school students with nowhere to go for classes.

Legislators eventually got the message and passed an income tax to address the funding inequities. But school funding overall continued to rely heavily on the local property tax base, so income taxes were insufficient to help poor areas where property values were low. Nor can they alone correct historical deprivations. And so, despite the new tax, schooling in New Jersey remained a fundamentally unequal enterprise.

That was, until *Abbott*.

———

It was not hard for the Education Law Center, an educational justice advocacy group based in New Jersey, to find families willing to take on the state's school funding system. Beginning with Raymond Abbott and his mother, Frances Abbott Cherry, the filing in *Abbott v. Burke* listed nineteen families that were fed up with a long-lived status quo.

Their suit contended that because the state provided only part of the funding school districts needed, the schools were inherently unequal, with property taxes remaining inordinately influential in dictating how much money each district had to spend on schools. The suit effectively argued that the promises of the Public School Education Act of 1975—to provide to *all* of New Jersey's children with educational opportunity—had gone unfulfilled.[13]

In 1985, Justice Alan Handler on the New Jersey Supreme Court issued the decision in *Abbott I*—the first of a long line of cases. In a thorough, thirty-five-page opinion, he acknowledged that it remained unclear what the state's constitutional obligation to every child *was*—and that determining the nature of that obligation was a constitutional matter for the courts. Although he remanded the case to the lower, administrative court for a final decision, Handler's clarification of the obligation seemed almost like a note under the table to the plaintiffs, suggesting that, on remand, they should come armed with evidence that owing to funding discrepancies, "disadvantaged children will not be able to compete in, and contribute to, the society entered by the relatively advantaged children," and that unevenness in the "financing scheme engenders more inequality" than could be justified by other state interests. And they did.[14]

But their fight would be a long and draining one. In 1988, the administrative body would hold for the defendants. The plaintiffs would immediately appeal to the New Jersey Supreme Court. The state, and thousands of schoolchildren, could only wait and watch as the duo of governmental bodies grappled with their rights. On January 9, 1990, at his final State of the State Address, New Jersey governor Thomas H. Kean said, "Our taxpayers now spend more money per child in school than any other taxpayers in the United States. And yet our state monies are distributed by a formula that is outdated and unjust. Now we are waiting for the courts to tell us what to do. That's wrong."[15]

Abbott II came later that year—a full five years after *Abbott I*, and fifteen years after the New Jersey Senate passed the Public School

Education Act at the heart of the decision. In *Abbott II*, Chief Justice Robert Wilentz wrote for a New Jersey Supreme Court that sided fully, and unambiguously, with the plaintiffs: "We find that under the present system the evidence compels but one conclusion: the poorer the district and the greater its need, the less the money available, and the worse the education. That system is neither thorough nor efficient. We hold the [Public School Education Act of 1975] unconstitutional as applied to poorer urban school districts. Education has failed there, for both the students and the State."[16]

The decision ordered that the 1975 law be amended "to assure funding of education in poorer urban districts at the level of property-rich districts," to forbid that such funding "depend on the ability of local school districts to tax," and to affirm "that such funding . . . be guaranteed and mandated by the State." This wasn't just a victory—it was a rout. The state then created twenty-eight "Abbott districts," as they came to be known, which would receive restitution from the state.[17]

"We documented the disparity and the unfairness so precisely and so ostensibly, it was really hard to argue with," remembers Gary Stein, who was then a judge on the New Jersey Supreme Court. "We wanted the state to spend money rehabilitating urban schools because they were so torn down and in disrepair. So we really issued a comprehensive remedy."[18]

Judge Stein did not mince words in describing just how much power New Jersey courts wielded to shift the funding system.

It was a very muscular court. And we weren't afraid to assert ourselves. Everybody moved out of the cities into the suburbs and left the cities' tax bases in shambles and never lifted a finger. So we were indignant. We were angry. You know, the legislature and the executive branch didn't have a hell of a lot to say, because they had screwed up royally for four decades. So, it was really time to do something. And the reason that we were able to do it was that we had a court composed of seven people who weren't afraid to assert ourselves and to order this terrible injustice be corrected.[19]

While the case was a critical victory for the twenty-eight Abbott districts—including Newark, Camden, and Trenton—that would receive extra aid, the remedies it required would fail to touch hundreds of other struggling New Jersey school districts. And even the chosen twenty-eight would experience setbacks before their ultimate victory. In 1990, partly in an attempt to comply with the judicial decree, the state passed the Quality Education Act, which would have bolstered aid to schools via a $2.8 billion tax increase. But just a year later, Governor Jim Florio clawed $360 million back for property tax relief, and three years after that, the courts deemed the law an unconstitutionally inadequate remedy to funding inequities. Back to the drawing board. After two years of toil, in 1996 the legislature passed the Comprehensive Educational Improvement and Financing Act (CEIFA), another challenge followed, and the courts *again* ruled this new funding formula unconstitutional, moving the legislature to allocate an additional $246 million to the Abbott districts. "A very muscular court," indeed—and one unwilling to settle for anything less than a fairly funded system.[20]

Along the way, the court sharpened the state's constitutional obligation, creating the nation's first—and so far only—intentionally synergistic education policies. A year before his retirement, and thirteen years after penning the decision in *Abbott I*, Justice Alan Handler finished what he had started thirteen years prior—this time, in *Abbott V*. Reflecting on the long battle behind the court on the matter, he wrote, for a unanimous court, "This decision should be the last major judicial involvement in the long and tortuous history of the State's extraordinary effort to bring a thorough and efficient education to the children in its poorest school districts." The court held that the state's constitutional obligation to fund a "thorough and efficient" system of schools required nearly a dozen unique investments, including funding "full-day kindergarten and a half-day pre-school program for three- and four-year-olds as expeditiously as possible," and thus giving New Jersey its own version of Head Start.[21]

And so, after a battle lasting nearly two centuries, New Jersey went from a haphazard education system to one that, in twenty-eight lucky districts, combined two effective policies—pre-K and K-12 education funding reform. "That was the beginning of a breakthrough," recalls Deborah Poritz, the chief justice of the New Jersey Supreme Court at that time and the first woman to hold that title. "There was beginning, then, a discussion of the substantive needs of urban schoolchildren to make up for the deficits that they were experiencing in their lives. I mean, how does a child come to school with a toothache that's overwhelming and study when the family doesn't have health care and can't take the kid to a dentist? How does a kid survive in school if the kid isn't eating proper meals? And so that came in with extensive hearings in *Abbott V*." *Abbott V* demonstrated that, indeed, we can intentionally create synergistic policies—although the road to creating them can be a long and winding one.[22]

———

So did the funding reforms work? We saw in Chapter 3 that school finance reforms result in increased resources to less wealthy districts and enhanced achievement for students residing in those districts both during their academic careers and in their subsequent labor-market outcomes. We have already shown from our national study that the synergistic combination of pre-K programs and school finance reform worked, meaning that the policies, together, had greater positive impacts on schooling and later life outcomes than the sum of the effects of the individual policies in isolation. In other words, the effects of pre-K and K-12 spending should not be viewed in additive terms; rather, the combined effects are multiplicative, and potentially exponential, owing to their synergistic qualities.[23]

Important questions remained. While our prior work demonstrated the long-term beneficial impacts of school finance reforms in earlier eras, would the magnitude of those impacts be as large for more recent cohorts following *Abbott*? That is, did the pre-K and K-12 funding reforms work in New Jersey, specifically? More generally, have more recent school finance reforms had different effects on student learning?

Were the successes of earlier reforms a relic of the past, or might similar educational investments, if enacted today, yield similar returns?

A 2018 paper examining the effects of school finance equalization efforts across the nation enacted since 1990 found significant positive impacts on test scores. The study was conducted by Julien Lafortune, Jesse Rothstein, and Diane Whitmore Schanzenbach, and I asked my University of California, Berkeley, colleagues Rothstein and Lafortune to share their results for the outcomes in New Jersey with me. Neighboring Pennsylvania provided useful data as well as a comparison state, as it had a similar demographic composition along race and class lines, had experienced similar labor-market conditions over this period, had a similar industrial base, and so on. But Pennsylvania and New Jersey were on opposite ends of the spectrum when it came to the progressivity of their school funding formulas. The most recent wave of finance reforms—"adequacy"-based finance reforms, as they are commonly called among education scholars—are designed to ensure that low-income schools have adequate funding to achieve desired outcomes. Lafortune, Rothstein, and Schanzenbach used student-level data to identify the effects of reform-induced changes in spending by comparing the achievement of students in high- and low-income school districts both before and after reforms were implemented.[24]

In New Jersey and Pennsylvania—and nationwide, in fact—the authors documented per-pupil revenue between the highest-income districts and the lowest-income districts (i.e., the top income quintile versus the bottom income quintile). At the beginning of the "adequacy" era in 1990, for example, for every dollar spent on high-income districts in Pennsylvania, the low-income districts received $1.62; that number increased moderately over the years, reaching $2.53 by 2011. In New Jersey, for every dollar spent on high-income districts, low-income districts received $3.05 in 1990, and that figure more than doubled, to $6.61, by 2011 as a result of the *Abbott* rulings. The gap the other way around used to be vast in New Jersey: 1990 had the highest-income-quintile districts receiving $3,000 more per pupil than districts in the lowest-income quintile. By 2010, because of all the *Abbott* suits and subsequent efforts, this disparity was not only eliminated but, in fact, had been reversed. Now, districts in the lowest-income quintile were able to spend roughly $3,000 more than the highest-income quintile. This discrepancy allowed the poorer districts to spend in a way that compensated for historical inequalities. (They also had more special-needs students, English-language learners, and concentrated poverty, which made their per-pupil costs higher.)[25]

These spending increases would have meant little if they had not been followed by educational gains. But they were. The average test-score gap between students from the highest-income-quintile districts and the lowest-income-quintile districts in New Jersey narrowed significantly as a result of the reform-induced school-spending changes that took place following the *Abbott* decisions. (The test in question was the National Assessment of Educational Progress—commonly viewed as the nation's report card. The study looked at fourth- and eighth-grade reading and math scores.) On average, they found that the magnitude of the effects of the New Jersey finance reforms were large enough to close about 20 percent of the achievement gap between high- and low-income districts during the period in question. In contrast, in Pennsylvania, where these redistributive school finance reforms did not occur, achievement gaps grew substantially.

All of this is to say that the pre-K and K-12 funding reforms worked in New Jersey. But could the state have done more? Judge Stein lamented that while New Jersey during his years on the Supreme Court made significant progress on pre-K access and school funding issues, the prevailing high levels of school segregation persisted. In our interview, he speculated that the yet unaddressed segregation is "why those [school finance reform] policies may not have yielded their maximal return in impacts for children in our state." Indeed, a recent study found that New Jersey's schools are among the most segregated in the nation. If the combination of pre-K investments and school finance reform work synergistically, then Stein's musing serves as an endorsement of a greater synergy that includes not just those two dimensions but a third one: desegregation. This three-dimensional synergy is precisely the policy prescription we believe the nation needs to implement in order to overcome the legacy of segregation. To understand why, we must first acquaint ourselves with other, sometimes surprising synergies beyond the pre-K and school-funding duo we have discussed.[26]

————

DR. MARTIN LUTHER King Jr. once proclaimed that "of all the forms of inequality, injustice in health care is the most shocking and inhumane." It is that sentiment that animated the push to desegregate hospitals in the Mississippi Delta region in the 1960s. Hospital desegregation was a monumental policy shift that, alongside the rollout of school desegregation, impacted the overall long-term well-being of minority children of the post-*Brown* era. The desegregation of hospitals in the South started in 1963. Developments in all three branches of government—judicial, executive, and legislative—were influential. First, the US Court of Appeals for the Fourth Circuit ruled, in *Simkins v. Moses H. Cone Memorial Hospital* (1963), that the separate-but-equal clause in the Hospital Survey and Construct Act (or Hill-Burton Act) of 1946 was unconstitutional, rendering segregation unlawful in certain hospitals that had received federal funding in a handful of southern states under the court's purview. Second, Title VI of the Civil Rights Act of 1964 broadened the evisceration of the separate-but-equal doctrine beyond select hospitals and beyond Virginia, North Carolina, and other Fourth Circuit states, making it illegal for *any* private institution receiving government funds to withhold services on the basis of race. Third, with the introduction of Medicaid and Medicare in 1965, a hospital had to be racially desegregated in order to be eligible to receive Medicaid and Medicare funding.[27]

The staggered timing of hospital desegregation in the South led to timing differences both in improved access to hospital care for minorities and in the implementation of Medicare and Medicaid in parts of the South. "Staggered timing," "differences in implementation"—if these terms sound familiar, that is not an accident. The staggered timing of school desegregation and Head Start implementation mirrored the staggered timing of hospital desegregation, and just as in education, in health care these variations created opportunities to assess the impacts of different elements of the changes that were occurring across the nation.

We found that, by the end of 1966, 25 percent of the counties in the South—and 75 percent of the counties in the Mississippi Delta—were not yet in compliance with the order to desegregate hospitals. The economists Doug Almond, Ken Chay, and Michael Greenstone used the variation in the timing of hospital desegregation in Mississippi to document substantial declines in black infant deaths occurring one to twelve months after birth (post-neonatal mortality) from diarrhea and pneumonia in counties that had desegregated by February 1969 relative to counties where the hospitals remained segregated through the late 1960s. These are early-life health conditions that require immediate access to adequate hospital care to prevent mortality. In particular, they reported that black "post-neonatal death rates due to diarrheal dehydration (gastroenteritis) and pneumonia in Mississippi . . . were 10-times higher than the rates for whites" prior to hospital desegregation, but that these black mortality rates "plummeted by 65 percent by 1971," following hospital desegregation. The authors concluded that hospital desegregation enabled around 7,000 additional black infants to survive infancy from 1965 to 1975. Subsequent research by other scholars provides evidence that racial convergence in early-life health and hospital access from birth to age five led to a significant narrowing of the black-white test-score gap for cohorts born during the mid- to late 1960s.[28]

These results demonstrate a critical, often ignored link. Good health early in life can impact later educational attainment. When one considers the incredible pace of cognitive development in the early years, this finding is not altogether surprising. But it does point to a whole range of synergistic investments that we have not yet taken into account: those combining health and educational investments to strike at the legacy of segregation. This research inspired us to assess a new synergy: the combination of hospital desegregation and school desegregation. And as with our research into the synergy of pre-K and school funding reform, we asked ourselves the same question. Was the combination of the two investments greater than the sum of their individual parts?[29]

In short, yes. We looked at the timing of both school desegregation and hospital desegregation in the same model and linked those figures with nationally representative data. The analysis used measures of the age at which hospital desegregation occurred and the distance to the nearest hospital as an index of segregation and access during childhood (where the location of black hospitals were included as well as whether the nearest public hospital was open to blacks). We explored how improved access to school quality and health-care services interacted with blacks' subsequent life trajectories, adult socioeconomic status, and health outcomes.

The findings show that healthier children are better learners. We discovered significant synergistic impacts between hospital desegregation and school desegregation that led to significant reductions in racial health disparities in adulthood, which once again underscored the importance of considering the interrelationship between early childhood investments in health and public school spending. When these two types of investments occur together, the combined effect can be substantial.[30]

———

UNLIKE THE OTHER policies we've explored, *funding* is an enabling condition. That means it matters in part because it is a prerequisite for combining multiple potentially effective policies, such as class size reductions, increases in instructional time, and teacher salaries. But what happens when we have funding reforms without desegregation? Does funding work independently, or does it work best when it is combined synergistically with the right policies? A clue can be found in the Los Angeles Unified School District, or LAUSD.

Unlike in many other districts of the era, in the LA school district in the 1970s the courts and other branches of government attempted to work together to develop a desegregation plan that included student reassignment. Working together with the California District Court, the LAUSD passed a desegregation plan pairing student reassignment with funding increases in places that, despite reassignment efforts, would still have large percentages of minority students. The district was poised to take on segregation. Then, in 1979, California voters passed Proposition 1, which stated that California's courts could not require a district to reassign students absent evidence of de jure segregation—or segregation on the books. After a long line of cases, in 1982 the US Supreme Court held that such de jure segregation had not occurred in Los Angeles, and, just like that, Los Angeles was left in the peculiar position of being required to have a desegregation plan, but being prohibited from reassigning students based on race. In other words, the desegregation plan could do many things—such as increase funding to majority minority schools—it just couldn't desegregate. The past three decades in the LAUSD thus represent a natural experiment into what happens when you *do not* have the synergy we've been describing. In other words: what happens when you increase funding, but don't take on segregation?[31]

A 2011 report by the Office for Civil Rights (OCR) within the US Department of Education seemed to supply an answer. OCR independently conducted a review of the Los Angeles Unified School District to verify its compliance with various equity programs. The report assessed whether the district provided comparable resources to schools that were predominantly black and schools that were predominantly white. OCR found patterns of school resource disparities across the district along race and class lines. The report noted that the "ratio of books per pupil at District schools ranges from three books per student to 41 books per student." It also found a disparity in the books in the libraries: the "average publication date of the U.S. history books at the libraries at the African American schools OCR visited was 1986; the average publication date of the U.S. history books at the white schools visited was 1996." OCR reported that in the 2009–2010 school year, 42 percent of the teachers were absent for ten or more days for reasons unrelated to instructional activities at the predominantly black schools, whereas at the white schools, 27 percent of the teachers were absent for ten or more days for such reasons. The researchers found that in the 2008–2009 school year, 5.7 percent of African American and 6.6 percent of Latino students participated in programs for gifted and talented students district-wide, but 24.7 percent of white students and 29.9 percent of Asian students participated in them. They also looked at the referral rate for the gifted and talented program, which entails testing by district psychologists (not test scores). In the 2009–2010 school year, each of the five predominately white elementary schools referred more than forty-five students to the program. In contrast, four of the five predominantly African American schools referred less than seven students to the program. Regarding student discipline, OCR found extreme disparities in the rate of African American suspension and expulsion as compared to their white peers.[32]

What happened? One explanation is that the funding increases that flowed from the desegregation plan were far less effective when they were not coupled with actual desegregation efforts. In other words, perhaps the logic of *Brown*—that you cannot undo the legacy of segregation without investing in actual integration—is presciently, profoundly accurate.

We evaluated this question by comparing otherwise similar children from districts like Los Angeles, which had low levels of integration and high levels of funding increases, with children in places such as Louisiana, where court-ordered desegregation had led to both substantial school resource equalization and integration. Which factor would prove to be dominant in fueling the long-term beneficial effects of school desegregation? Increases in school resources, or exposure to more diverse classroom peers? Or would the two need to be working together to get the beneficial effects? From a research perspective, the substantial geographic variations in when and *how* desegregation was implemented across districts was revealing, as these differences led to differences in the degree of racial integration and resource equalization achieved through a district's desegregation court order. In some districts, there were large increases in black-white student exposure, but limited increases in school resources; in others, there were modest decreases in racial segregation, but larger increases in school spending on minority children. In Louisiana, court-ordered desegregation brought more state funding to integrated schools, while in Los Angeles, more segregated schools received more compensatory funding.[33]

As it turned out, improved school resources explained a significant amount of the beneficial effects of desegregation when contrasting the subsequent outcomes of black and white children from districts in which court-ordered desegregation led to larger (versus smaller) changes in school segregation and school resources, respectively. Among blacks, in districts in which desegregation court orders led to more significant increases in school spending, the more years children were exposed to desegregated schools, the greater the gains they made in terms of their educational attainments and adult socioeconomic status. In court-ordered desegregated districts in which school spending for black children did not appreciably change, however, although the children experienced greater classroom exposure to their white peers, they did not make a comparable improvement in their educational and socioeconomic trajectories.[34]

This finding means, first and foremost, that in some cases, synergy has the power to take two policies that, in isolation, seem flat and transform them into one package of policies with profound promise.

———

IT IS IMPORTANT to observe the nuances here. The lesson from our research into the synergy of integration and school funding is not that money does not matter. We have shown repeatedly that it does. Rather, the lesson is that school funding reforms can make a huge difference so long as the money is spent on the right things. If we zoom out from Los Angeles and look at the whole state of California, we can see this effect more clearly.

In 2011, the State of California rolled out a set of new, ambitious school finance reforms similar to what New Jersey had implemented over the course of many years in *Abbott*. The Local Control Funding Formula (LCFF) is California's first major school finance reform since 1971, and it is now one of the most progressive state funding formulas in the nation. One in eight students in the United States is educated in California's public school system, the largest state school system in the country. Prior to LCFF, the state used an outdated school funding formula that had grown cumbersome—featuring dozens of categorical programs—and highly inequitable. The prior funding system had done little to help shield school district revenues from the impacts of the Great Recession, during which district budgets dropped by 20 percent over two years, a fall from which they had not meaningfully recovered by 2012, just prior to passage of LCFF. Recognizing the urgency of a funding overhaul, with LCFF, Governor Jerry Brown proposed what will likely be his flagship legislative achievement.

Uncertainty about available funding from year to year often precludes a district's ability to enact bold, transformative curricular reform that can span a decade. Although many districts experience such unpredictability, urban and low-income districts bear the burden most often. School funding instability, much like household income instability, causes short-term, inferior investments that impede long-term, continual improvements. The eight-year, $18 billion LCFF plan is designed to bring fiscal stability and predictability to California's schools as the state recovers from the Great Recession and rebuilds its education infrastructure.

LCFF attempts to address school resource inequity by (1) reallocating district revenues based almost entirely on the proportion of disadvantaged students in each district (rather than on district property wealth), and (2) removing many of the restrictions on how the revenue can be spent. Disadvantaged students are defined as those who qualify for free or reduced-price lunches, have limited English proficiency, or are in foster care.

The architects of LCFF understood that addressing rapid growth in the number of high-need students would require that districts have both more money than previously and greater autonomy over how the funding is distributed to meet those needs. To address the deleterious effects of concentrated poverty, the funding formula allocates concentration grants to school districts where more than 55 percent of the students are classified as high need. The LCFF, which went into effect in the 2013–2014 school year, replaces the complex web of regulations and rules that California districts had to wade through in the past with a more transparent school funding system.

A reform is only as good as its results. A new study that I conducted with one of my recent PhD students, Sean Tanner, is among the first to provide evidence of LCFF's impacts on student outcomes. Using detailed annual district finance data for all public schools in California from 1995 to 2016, and analyzing the impacts of reform-induced increases in district per-pupil spending on high school graduation rates and student achievement in high school math and reading, we found evidence of LCFF's positive effects.[35]

In order to isolate the causal effects of increased school spending on student success, we compared changes in average student outcomes across cohorts from the same school both before and after LCFF-induced changes in district per-pupil revenue (over and beyond statewide, cohort-specific time trends). We found that LCFF-induced increases in district revenue led to significant reductions in average class sizes and significant increases in average teacher salaries and instructional expenditures. Thus, a significant portion of the increase in spending made it to the classroom.

Our results also show that LCFF-induced increases in school spending led to significant increases in high school graduation rates and academic achievement, particularly among poor and minority

FIGURE 5.1

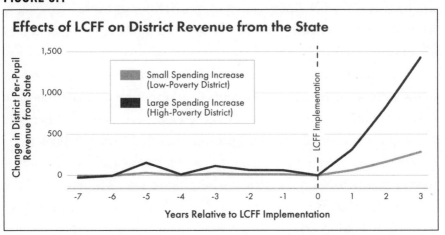

Effects of LCFF on District Revenue from the State

Small Spending Increase
(Low-Poverty District)

Large Spending Increase
(High-Poverty District)

Change in District Per-Pupil Revenue from State

LCFF Implementation

Years Relative to LCFF Implementation

students (Figures 5.1–5.3). A $1,000 increase in district per-pupil spending experienced in grades ten through twelve led to an increase of 5.9 percentage points in high school graduation rates, on average, among all children, with similar effects by race and poverty.

For low-income students, we found that a $1,000 increase in district per-pupil spending during ages thirteen through sixteen increased high school math achievement an amount equivalent to approximately seven months of learning. It was also equivalent to 37 percent of the average mathematics achievement gap between poor and non-poor students in the eleventh grade; 24 percent of the average mathematics achievement gap between black and white students in the eleventh grade; or 34 percent of the average mathematics achievement gap between Hispanic and white students in the eleventh grade (based on data from all California public schools from 2003 to 2016). The corresponding school-spending effect increased high school reading achievement (resulting from a $1,000 increase in district per-pupil revenue during ages thirteen to sixteen) by approximately three months of learning. The magnitude of these effects are large, particularly in light of the fact that LCFF is only in its fourth year. The results are broadly similar to those found in the Abbott reforms in New Jersey and other recent studies that use quasi-experimental methods. In sum, the evidence suggests

FIGURE 5.2

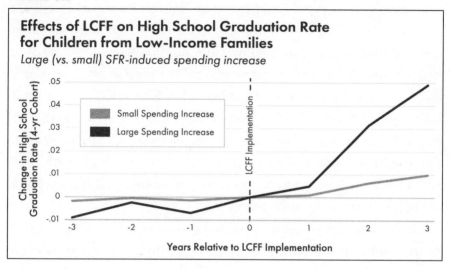

Effects of LCFF on High School Graduation Rate for Children from Low-Income Families
Large (vs. small) SFR-induced spending increase

FIGURE 5.3

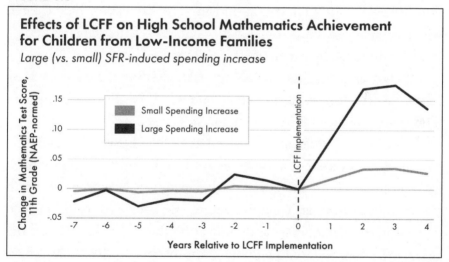

Effects of LCFF on High School Mathematics Achievement for Children from Low-Income Families
Large (vs. small) SFR-induced spending increase

that money targeted to students' needs can make a significant difference in student outcomes and can narrow achievement gaps. If that sounds obvious, good. The point is that so many policies that have been seen as useless or counterproductive are anything but.[36]

THUS FAR, WE have shown that spending works, as long as it is applied strategically, consistently, and over the course of a student's time in school. Given the power of the synergies we've detailed, one might think districts would run headlong into funding them. Unfortunately, nationwide trends are not encouraging. Matthew Chingos, an education scholar at the Brookings Institution, has found that "overall funding progressivity remains low despite two decades of reforms enacted by courts and state legislatures." In other words, we are investing in public education more than we used to, but not nearly as much as we should. That, Chingos wrote, "suggests a troubling lack of progress on equitable funding of public schools."[37]

In New Jersey, some of the stalled progress in educational investment is due to the effects of the Great Recession, particularly because so many of its residents worked on Wall Street. In 2010, Governor Chris Christie—a Republican with national ambitions—cut $820 million from the state's education budget. The Education Law Center, which sued once again, estimated that since 2009, the state has underfunded education by a total of $9.07 billion.[38]

"I know that the funding has helped," says Stein, the former New Jersey justice. "But it hasn't helped enough. It hasn't closed the gap. They have narrowed the gap, but it hasn't closed it."[39]

Racial gaps in education, as well as in health, are large and persistent. But they are not immutable. And so the fight continues. Back in New Jersey, both the governor's mansion in Drumthwacket and the state legislature at Trenton have swung back and forth between control by the Democrats and control by the Republicans, and the two parties have offered competing approaches to *Abbott*. In 2007, for example, Democratic governor Jon Corzine proposed doing away with *Abbott*, which he said had "no rational basis of explanation." Instead, he wanted to devote $400 million to implementing a new funding formula, giving aid to any district that was deemed to be in need, including non-Abbott districts.[40]

He faced opposition with his proposal, however. "The effect would be to dismantle the unprecedented success that we've been making in improving student achievement in our high-poverty urban schools," said the head of the Education Law Center, which had brought the original *Abbott* case nearly three decades before. Ultimately, his proposal did not pass, and the *Abbott* decision remains the primary funding principle in the state.[41]

Although some of *Abbott*'s success has been deconstructed by various policy changes, and perhaps weakened by the high levels of school segregation that still prevail, *Abbott V* is a good illustration of what our research highlights: the *how* of school reform matters as much as or more than the *what*. In other words, beyond identifying which policies work on their own—be it integration, Head Start, or school finance reform—one must thoroughly investigate the inner workings of *how* the policy was implemented, and determine *why* it did or did not work. The synergy of policies working together plays an enormous role in their success.

Before the introduction of state school-finance reform or federal preschool programming, *Brown v. Board of Education* was the cornerstone of a truly equitable public school system. In the preceding chapters, we have endeavored to show that the other two types of policies also provide the building blocks of lifelong success for children. A foundation of a high-quality preschool, bolstered spending through funding-reform formulas, and, throughout, the powerful brace that is the integrated classroom are all effective. Our research shows that these, in fact, are the necessary components of the kind of education system most of us want, even if many of us haven't known how to get there.

Unfortunately, there are some who have explicitly fought against integration, and who have tried to tear down the fragile edifice of *Brown*. Their decades-long efforts have made school integration fraught and all too rare in America today. To understand how to achieve integration, we must understand the forces that oppose it (and that have long opposed it) as well as the other obstacles to real and enduring change.

PART II
THE DREAM REVERSED

·· 6 ··

BUSING IN BOSTON:
"WE WON'T GO TO SCHOOL
WITH N—RS

O F ALL THE MYTHS ABOUT INTEGRATION, THE MOST NOXIOUS MAY
be that we tried it, for a long time and in good faith, a nation wholly
and intensely dedicated to the effort. We did everything we could to
integrate the American classroom, this myth says. In many places, most
places even, we succeeded. In the places we failed, it was not for lack of
effort or conviction. Whatever the case, the experiment was done. Integration was noble, and principled, but is no longer a goal for which we
should be fighting. It is an idea whose time has come and gone.

The chapters that follow outline the troubling contours of our collective retreat from integration. That effort tracked closely with integration itself, a kind of malevolent shadow. There was, of course, the
ugliness in Little Rock, which demanded the intervention of President
Eisenhower. And there were similar battles across the Deep South.
But many of these occurred *before* the federal government began to
enforce judicial desegregation orders in the 1960s.

The fight against integration by no means ended. Instead, in
many ways it adopted the same tactics as the civil rights movement:
mass protest, legal activism, and voter registration. Faced with the

prospect of integration even outside the Deep South, recalcitrant whites manipulated and marshaled public will in a way that allowed opponents of integration to appear not to be racists. They resorted to powerful code words—like *neighborhood schools*, *local control*, and *forced busing*, to summon profound, if rarely spoken, racial fears. Though these efforts belong to history, they remain as viscerally powerful warnings to those who would upend the old racial order that, in many ways, still governs the land.

This strategy worked, and it contains a devilish dilemma: even as researchers like us have shown that integration works, much of the public has been erroneously convinced of the very opposite. In explaining how that came to be, we hope that future efforts at integration—which remain as necessary today as they were in 1954—do not succumb to the same pitfalls.

———

In 1960, Jean McGuire began teaching in Boston—the birthplace of public school education. She taught her first class at the Louisa May Alcott School. The school had been built in 1842, and 118 years of continuous use had taken their toll. So had forces more pernicious than the sound of children streaming through its halls: institutional neglect, settling like mold in the schoolhouse walls. That was in part because of the demographic changes that had taken place in the surrounding neighborhood of South End. Its brownstone blocks, once home to a white middle class, more recently had become populated by blacks. The Back Bay train station was nearby, and the neighborhood now had the largest population of Pullman porters in the world. Martin Luther King Jr. had briefly lived there. Much earlier, so had Harriet Tubman.

By the time McGuire began teaching at Louisa May Alcott, the school was entirely African American (McGuire was African American herself). "I had forty-two students, thirty-six seats," she would remember much later. "We didn't have new crayons, we had boxes of old nubbly crayons. Pencils had to be collected at the end of the day." One textbook she found contained a song called "Ten Little Niggers."[1]

There was no end to the indignities encountered at Louisa May Alcott—and hardly any remedies. "The yellow paper was brown on the edges," McGuire remembered. "It had been stored and saved and hoarded so there would be enough. Primary lined paper was very hard to come by. . . . We didn't have a tape recorder. We didn't have a music teacher to come in. There were no music lessons. . . . There were no science labs. There was no gymnasium."[2]

Six years after *Brown v. Board of Education*, this was the common experience of African Americans across the Northeast and the West, regions where, presumably, there had been no segregation to contend with, at least not of the legal variety that required federal intervention. But there had been something perhaps just as lethal, a collective silence about the plight of African Americans outside the Jim Crow states. "The Northerners want to hear as little as possible about the Negroes," wrote Gunnar Myrdal, the perceptive Swedish economist and sociologist, in 1944's *An American Dilemma*. "The result is an astonishing ignorance about the Negro on the part of the white public in the North." It was much easier and more convenient to blame the South for its shortcomings than to confront one's own shortcomings— shortcomings that haunted the ghettos of Boston and New York, San Francisco and Los Angeles.

The simple and ugly truth was that segregation was nearly as bad in the North and West as it was in the Deep South. Although the northern states had not erected a legal code around the separation of the races, individual laws and practices—particularly regarding housing, but also employment and the distribution of and access to social services—had almost exactly the same effect. Matthew Delmont, in his definitive and damning book *Why Busing Failed*, cited a 1955 report about New York City finding that "71 percent of elementary schools enrolled either 90 percent or more black and Puerto Rican students or over 90 percent white students." And although some officials uttered superficial vows of educational integration, children, whatever their skin color, stood little chance of attending school with other students who didn't look like them.[3]

The 1955 report, "The Status of the Public School Education of the Negro and Puerto Rican Children in New York City," came only a year after *Brown*, a ruling whose focus on the separate-but-equal policies of the Deep South took attention away from the de facto segregation in Boston, New York, and other cities across the North. Nor was there any material improvement in the racial balance of northern schools in the years that followed. In 1974, for example, Roxbury High School in Boston was 98 percent African American, while the schools of South Boston, a famous Irish American enclave, were uniformly white.

Two decades after *Brown*, in fact, one of the most notorious incidents in the history of resistance to school desegregation took place in Boston. It began with a ruling by Judge W. Arthur Garrity on June 21, 1974, in *Morgan v. Hennigan*, for the US District Court for the District of Massachusetts. In deciding a suit brought by African American parents, Garrity decreed that "a systematic program of segregation affecting all of the city's students, teachers and school facilities and have intentionally brought about and maintained a dual school system. Therefore the entire school system of Boston is unconstitutionally segregated."[4]

Even more painful than the diagnosis was the cure Garrity ordered: school busing.

———

How CAN YOU desegregate schools that aren't segregated? That was the sly question posed by northern politicians in the wake of *Brown v. Board of Education*. That ruling had struck down the legal framework of segregation predicated on the *Plessy v. Ferguson* decision of 1898, in which the Supreme Court had asserted, "We cannot say that a law which authorizes or even requires the separation of the two races in public conveyances is unreasonable." (Interestingly, the concept of separate but equal is mentioned nowhere in the decision itself.)

The separate-but-equal doctrine of *Plessy*, however, had never been legal in the North. Therefore, the remedy on integration was unnecessary, many said. From a legal perspective, there was nothing to integrate.

Much like Myrdal, southern politicians understood this northern strategy. "In my opinion the two Senators from New York are, at heart, pretty good segregationists," said Mississippi's unabashedly racist senator James O. Eastland. "But the conditions in their State are different from the conditions in ours." The implication was that if only the cultural differences between Mississippi and New York could be overcome, they could defeat their common foe: integration. The Yankees were his allies, even if they didn't know it quite yet.[5]

Eastland made that statement in 1964, ten years after *Brown*. At the time of that landmark decision, the president had been Dwight D. Eisenhower, a Republican who was not especially eager to wage social crusades on behalf of the dispossessed. Now the president was Lyndon B. Johnson, who wanted to do exactly that. A little more than two months after Eastland made his approving comments about his colleagues from New York, Johnson offered a different vision of the nation, promising the creation of a Great Society that would uplift all and exclude none. Education was crucial to this vision. "Our society will not be great until every young mind is set free to scan the farthest reaches of thought and imagination. We are still far from that goal," Johnson said.[6]

Many did not share that goal, particularly if it included black and white children going to school together. Johnson, a profoundly savvy politician who understood the fractures within the Democratic Party, knew that he would be punished for going too far. So, for example, while the Civil Rights Act that he signed into law that summer was rightly hailed as the most progressive race-related legislation in the nation's history, it also contained a provision that would forestall many of the efforts to integrate schools outside the Jim Crow states of the Deep South. That provision came in Title IV, section 401b, and it declared that desegregation "shall not mean the assignment of students to public schools in order to overcome racial imbalance." In other words, although segregation would be illegal, integration would not be compulsory. This was an assurance to northern states, which Johnson could not lose politically, that he would not force them to address conditions in their own cities, which in many cases mirrored those of the Deep South even without the haunting presence of Jim Crow.

In drawing this distinction, Johnson allowed northerners to plead a helplessness that was nearly like innocence. Yes, there was segregation in cities like Boston and New York, but this was just the way things were, not the product of malicious intent as it was in the South. You might hope the imbalances would be corrected, but they would only correct themselves, as part of natural human progress. Or maybe they wouldn't. Either way, it wasn't a matter for the government to adjudicate.

About ten years after passage of the Civil Rights Act, in the 1974 *Milliken v. Bradley* ruling on de facto segregation, Supreme Court Justice Potter Stewart declared that segregation in northern cities was "caused by unknown and perhaps unknowable forces such as immigration, birth rates, economic changes or cumulative acts of private racial fears."[7]

We know today that Stewart was entirely wrong in his assessment, so much so that one could rightly wonder if he was genuine in espousing this confusing view of the matter. The forces that had led to segregation in the North were neither unknowable nor unknown. To a large extent, northern and western cities had become segregated in the 1940s and the decades that followed during the Great Migration, when an estimated six million African Americans had moved there from the South in search of better living conditions and employment. The response was a migration of its own, known today as white flight. Scare-mongering tactics by the real estate industry and housing officials frightened whites into leaving for the suburbs (blockbusting); meanwhile, in a practice called "redlining," minorities were crammed into increasingly desperate inner-city neighborhoods. The whites were given federal mortgage assistance, but no such assistance was afforded to African American families. They were left on their own in ghettos that were abandoned, often cut off from the rest of the city by multilane highways that functioned like fences.

Stewart was right about "racial fears," even if he was right about little else. Those fears were not especially private. In 1941, a Catholic priest in Detroit became the face of white protest against the construction of a public housing project named for the abolitionist Sojourner Truth in a white neighborhood called Krainz Park. "The construction of a low-cost housing project in the vicinity," wrote Father Constantine Dzink, "would mean utter ruin for many people who have mortgaged their homes to the FHA [Federal Housing Administration], and not only that, but it would jeopardize the safety of many of our white girls." In particular, the sexualized fear of African American men would continue to inform fears of integration for decades to come.[8]

The FHA allowed whites to move to the suburbs while leaving the cities to blacks. Those cities, lacking social services, continued to deteriorate, driving out remaining whites. Sociologist William Julius Wilson and historian Beryl Satter described what it was like for African American families in the 1960s in Chicago: "Children were deprived of a full day of schooling, and left to fend for themselves in the after school hours. These conditions helped fuel the rise of gangs, which in turn terrorized shop owners and residents alike.

"In the end, whites fled these neighborhoods, not only because of the influx of black families, but also because they were upset about overcrowding, decaying schools and crime. . . . Whites could leave— blacks had to stay."[9]

———

BOSTON WAS ARGUABLY the site of the most infamous desegregation fight outside the South, a distinction that city would surely rather not have. Before there was Boston, though, there was Chicago. And before Chicago, there was New York. In all these cases, white parents resisted the suggestion that they were the benefactors of a racist system that could only function through the systematic deprivation of the civil liberties of African Americans. They certainly weren't its conscious perpetrators, they claimed. However, at the same time, they used their significant political capital to resist any remedies that would jostle them out of their comforts, either in the suburbs or in fortified urban enclaves like those in outer Brooklyn—Sheepshead Bay, Bay Ridge— where minorities had not penetrated and where they understood themselves to be most definitely unwelcome.

Northern whites could always use the South as a convenient foil, even as the schools of the North became ever more segregated them- selves. Much like Justice Stewart, they could—and did—plead igno- rance. As the head of New York's schools averred in 1954, "We did not provide Harlem with segregation. We have natural segregation here—it's accidental." And since government could not be responsible for accidents, it could not be responsible for segregation.[10]

Of course, New Yorkers of color did not feel a similar resignation to the status quo. Crammed into increasingly deteriorating slums such as Bushwick, in Brooklyn, or Harlem, in Manhattan, and large parts of the South Bronx, African Americans felt viscerally and understood intellectually the thoroughness with which myriad social forces had conspired to deprive them of educational and other opportunities. And by the early 1960s, they felt sufficiently empowered to do some- thing about it.

The push to desegregate New York's schools was actually as old as *Brown v. Board of Education*. And one of its main proponents had figured prominently in that court decision: Kenneth Clark, the sociol- ogist whose landmark doll study had shown the deeply harmful effects of segregation on children of color. Clark plainly recognized what was happening in his home city. "We felt that the people of New York City were not aware of public school segregation as an issue which faced the city itself," he wrote in 1958.[11]

The "busing" remedy had first been used in a Public Education Association (PEA) report from 1955. However schools were segre- gated—whether by accident or by law—the report said, the easiest way to integrate them was by mixing children from disparate neighbor-hoods into the same schools. And the easiest way to do that was to put them on buses. But that would prove, in the years that followed, an immensely controversial idea, with the yellow school bus coming to embody unspeakable—and misguided—racial fears.[12]

The media eagerly inflated those fears, vastly exaggerating the number of children who would be bused while giving inordinate voice to the prejudices of recalcitrant whites. This, for example, was the *Wall Street Journal* dispatch in response to the PEA report: "Hundreds of New York students are already criss-crossing the city by bus and subway to schools far from home. . . . Not only are children from Negro sections of Harlem traveling to hitherto all-white schools; in some instances, white pupils are crossing regular school zones to enter all-Negro schools."[13]

This is exactly what white parents feared the most. Many of them, too, had climbed out of the destitution of the Lower East Side and Brownsville, the immigrant ghettos of the early twentieth century. They were finally in the middle class—and just as they'd reached that coveted status, they were being asked to share perhaps their most precious commodity, good schools, with black and brown peo-ple they neither knew nor understood. A letter to the New York City Board of Education perfectly captured this sentiment: "The Negro is emerging from ignorance, savagery, disease and total lack of any culture. Is it necessary to foist the Negro on the White Americans for fair play?"[14]

Despite the evidence that the schools of New York were seg-regated, there was little movement on the issue in the decade after *Brown*. But neither was there the kind of widespread controversy that would push the school system in one direction or the other. That was until February 3, 1964, when the Citywide Committee for Integrated Schools, with the Brooklyn preacher Milton Arthur Galamison at its helm, sought a means to activate people of conscience to their cause. The committee hoped to engage white activism in the way that sim-ilar protests had in Mississippi or Alabama and organized a massive boycott, keeping 460,000 students from attending New York's public schools. The show of force did indeed activate Big Apple whites— but not as hoped. Quite to the contrary, the protest catalyzed white resistance.[15]

The response was swift. Many of the city's newspapers immediately described the protest as needlessly disruptive. And in a sign that would prove ominous for the proponents of integration, the *New York Times* seized on the literal matter of buses to discount the far greater matter of equal access to a decent education. "You can bus children just so far," it editorialized in response to the February walkout. "You can hire bus drivers when you ought to be hiring teachers. You can put children into buses for an hour and a half or more each day—as the board plans to do for some—but what do they learn in the bus?" In that moment, opponents of integration seized on a tacit understanding among whites that would prove fruitful in the decades to come: they reduced the complex issues of integrated education to the image of buses whisking children to distant schools where danger lurked.[16]

Strategically savvy, they also appropriated effective approaches that had been championed by civil rights heroes. In response to the boycott by the Citywide Committee for Integrated Schools, fifteen thousand white mothers marched over the water from Manhattan to Brooklyn—all the way to the grim board of education headquarters on Livingston Street. They carried signs that said, "I will not put my children on a bus," and, "We will not be bused." Then, at the start of the next school year, they organized a boycott of their own, keeping over a quarter of a million of their children from attending school.[17]

New York's legislators, many of them sharing these parents' concerns, were persuaded to embrace the status quo. No mass busing of students would take place in New York City—not then or ever since. Today, the city's education system is the largest in the country. It is also, by almost any measure, the most segregated.

New York made the depth of white animosity toward school integration in northern cities clear. Chicago underscored the point. By 1965, blacks fighting for integration could see that segregationists in high places were nurturing the roots of separation and degradation. Community activists complained to federal officials about the number of black students attending segregated schools, estimating them at 90 percent of the black student population. "Neither segregation nor integration just 'happens,'" the activists perceptively wrote. "Each is deliberately stalled or prevented. The school board, acting under advice of its general superintendent, pursues a deliberate policy of segregation." Community organizers were right to call out superintendent Benjamin Willis, in particular, who did nothing despite full knowledge that the black schools were so overcrowded that many of them were using trailers, or "Willis Wagons," as classrooms.[18]

Well, it is not precisely correct to say that Willis did nothing. Co-opting the preferred tool of the NAACP, he and other segregationists invoked Chicago's courts in support of *their* cause. They sought, and won, an injunction forbidding black activists from boycotting schools to protest segregation and the degradation that came with it. Unwilling to be intimidated, and in an act of true civil disobedience, black activists proceeded with their boycott, which included over one hundred thousand students.[19]

At the same time, to circumvent the parochial Chicago courts, activists filed a complaint in *federal* court claiming that Chicago's public schools had violated the newly passed Civil Rights Act. The US Department of Health, Education, and Welfare—the predecessor of today's Department of Health and Human Services—agreed, and withheld $30 million in funds from Chicago's school system.[20]

The response in the Windy City was a fast and fierce hurricane of racially charged antipathy. The *Chicago Tribune* called the activists "extremists." Congressman Roman Pucinski, a Democrat, said the federal department's move was "a violation of the civil rights act itself," a clever, if dishonest, characterization. Chicago's powerful mayor, Richard Daley, intervened, going directly to President Johnson to advocate for a resolution palatable to his city's segregationists. The $30 million was released to Chicago schools, with only token concessions demanded in return.[21]

In Chicago, as in New York, things would stay exactly as they were. And despite efforts at reform—some modest, some ambitious—things there remain today as they were fifty years ago. Surveying the socio-historical terrain of the mid-twentieth century in these cities gives us clues into why segregation continues to win the day *today*. The playbook hasn't changed—it has only evolved. What we often forget, but must not lose sight of, is that segregation in many northern cities is not an anomaly of unknowable origins. It was sought after by powerful elites in courts and congresses; fought for by fearful parents through marches and boycotts; and advocated in daily newspapers through heated rhetoric. In short, it was anything but accidental. To truly understand how we might leverage the policy power of desegregation, we must first acknowledge the sources of its decline, many of which descended into the American consciousness from the City on a Hill.

———

THE TURBULENT 1960s and 1970s were full of iconic images. A well-dressed African American man is held from behind, his torso exposed. In front of him, a long-haired white man wields an American flag. He seems prepared to spear his black victim, but is actually preparing to hit him over the head. This photo was taken on April 5, 1976, in the midst of a white riot against the integration of Boston's public schools, commonly known as the "busing crisis," a reductive phrase that misrepresents what the fight was really about. The African American being attacked was Ted Landsmark, a lawyer with two Yale degrees, as well as a doctorate from Boston University. As he recently told National Public Radio, he had a meeting downtown and didn't notice the riot until he was in its midst. "The first person to attack me hit me from behind, which knocked off my glasses and ended up breaking my nose," Landsmark recalled. "The flag being swung at me came at me just moments after that and missed my face by inches. The entire incident took about seven seconds."[22]

The photo of Landsmark being attacked is one of many from 1974 and 1975 that lay bare a battlefield that served as a kind of domestic counterpart to the jungles of Vietnam that US troops had recently left behind: white mothers leaning out of windows, holding a "Stop Busing" sign; busloads of African American children being pelted with rocks, while being protected by police escorts as if they were a presidential motorcade; neo-Nazis wearing swastika armbands, consulting a map of Boston, where they were about to join furious a battle that was being waged on behalf of segregation. Boston's whites, of course, didn't put it that way. They were fighting for schools, for neighborhoods. But it is hard to imagine that there could have been a Boston busing crisis to speak of if, at the core of the matter, there hadn't been a bunch of black children.

Little known is the fact that Bean Town's battle over integration predates *Brown* by a century. Benjamin Roberts sued the city over discriminatory schooling in 1849 because his daughter, five-year-old Sarah, had to walk past *five* schools for white children in order to reach the "colored" one she was allowed to attend. It was an experience that mirrored, in many ways, that of Linda Brown in Topeka, Kansas, a hundred years later.

In his opinion in *Roberts v. City of Boston* in 1850 in the Massachusetts Supreme Judicial Court, Judge Lemuel Shaw showed no sympathy for Roberts's plea. "The increased distance, to which the plaintiff was obliged to go to school from her father's house, is not such, in our opinion, as to render the regulation in question unreasonable, still less illegal," Shaw wrote. Fifteen years before the abolition of slavery in the United States, Shaw demonstrated an Oscar-worthy feigning of ignorance and impotence, writing, "This prejudice, if it exists, is not created by law, and probably cannot be changed by law." Boston's potent prejudice would reveal itself repeatedly throughout the next century, propelling perhaps the nation's most astounding, and dispiriting, example of how de facto segregation can eventually win the day.[23]

During the portion of the Great Migration lasting from 1900 to 1940, it is estimated that the black population of Boston rose by 49 percent. But though the blacks moving north were surely hoping for employment, their luck was not so good. Three decades into the Great Migration, 77 percent of the city's African Americans worked in manual jobs that paid little. And Boston's schools were no more welcoming to these new migrants than the workplace. In 1964, the Advisory Committee on Racial Imbalance and Education in Massachusetts submitted a report noting that there yet existed fifty-five segregated schools in Massachusetts, and that forty-five of them were in Boston.[24]

An aspirational appeal, the report, titled "Because It Is Right—Educationally," featured a photo of an integrated classroom on the cover with studious black, white, and East Asian students sitting in close proximity to each other. In the foreword, Owen Kiernan, the state's education commissioner, wrote that the members of the committee "agreed unanimously . . . that responsible school officials have both a professional and moral duty to correct [racial] imbalance whenever and wherever it is found." But committee members also agreed that the duty was not limited to elected officials. Instead, the "problem of racial imbalance is the responsibility of all citizens."[25]

The introduction to the report included a question-and-answer section that seemed to anticipate the fears of ethnic whites—the Irish, Jewish, and Italian families living in the communities where desegregation efforts would take place:

> Q: Don't Negro Children Have Less Scholastic Aptitude than White Children?
>
> A: Given equally favorable circumstances, Negro children have shown that they can learn as quickly as white children.

The commission followed this report with one squarely focused on de facto segregation in Boston, writing that because students attended schools near their homes, Boston's challenges with housing discrimination had led to an untenable situation in its schools. "The heart of Boston's problem," the report argued, "is found in the 7 elementary districts which have an average of 95.96 percent Negro pupils. Forty-six percent of the Negro children in the public elementary schools—nearly one-half—are-enrolled in districts where 19 out of 20 pupils are Negroes."[26]

Faced with jarring evidence of segregation, in 1965 Massachusetts legislators passed the Racial Imbalance Act. It "called for local school systems to eliminate racial imbalance in any school where the enrollment was more than 50 percent nonwhite," warning that if a "district failed to comply, it would lose its state educational aid," according to a historian's summary of the act written in 1998.[27]

Boston did not trip over itself to comply. Reactions were so slow, in fact, that community members created, and self-funded, a busing organization. Operation Exodus shuttled hundreds of African American children from the impoverished Boston communities of Roxbury and Dorchester to open seats in white schools in other Boston neighborhoods. This initiative would eventually give new educational opportunities to nearly 1,000 black youths. But because Operation Exodus received no municipal, state, or federal funds, it shut down shop in 1969. In its place, the Metropolitan Council for Educational Opportunity (METCO)—a state-funded grant program run by the Massachusetts Department of Elementary and Secondary Education—bused students from Boston and Springfield to suburban public schools. It remains in operation to this day, but it continues to make only a marginal difference, serving just 3,300 of the Boston Metropolitan Area's more than 800,000 students.[28]

Despite these admittedly meager efforts, progress was not just slow in the first years after the Racial Imbalance Act—it was nonexistent. By 1969, there were sixty-two racially imbalanced schools in Boston, seventeen *more* than four years before. What explained Boston's regression into segregation? As in New York and Chicago, opponents of integration in Boston wielded every possible tool, and they had a weapon that would prove brutally effective: Louise Day Hicks.[29]

———

IN LATER YEARS, Hicks would be inextricably connected with South Boston, that legendary enclave of working-class Irish Americans. She, too, would come to embody some of the stereotypes associated with that place and its people. Hailed as a hero by her peers for defending the interests of blue-collar whites, by the time of her death in 2003 she was a reminder of one of the ugliest episodes of racial tension in American history. And while time rehabilitates some reputations, it is unlikely to have that effect on Hicks. She remains a crucial figure for understanding resistance to integration outside the Deep South and in the modern era.

Hicks came from South Boston, but not from the kind of poverty that was endemic to that neighborhood. Hicks's mother was a model, and her father, William J. Day, was a judge. Hicks's mother died when she was a teenager; her father, she would later say, was "the greatest influence in my life."[30]

Unlike many other women in South Boston, Hicks did not marry young and settle down for a life of childrearing and homemaking. Instead, she went to college and then to law school. At Boston University, she was one of 9 women in a class of 232. Her true interest was not law, however, but politics. And for a woman in the early 1960s, the easiest route into politics was through whatever elected body concerned itself with the education of children. So, in 1961, Hicks ran for the Boston School Committee. Winning on a reform ticket, she proved, at first, to be "quiet and uncontroversial." In 1963, she became the chairwoman.[31]

Racial issues were rising to the fore all across America, and that was as true in Boston as it was anywhere else. That summer, the NAACP confronted the Boston School District. Speaking in front of the committee, one of the activists, Ruth Batson, said, "I know that the word 'desegregation' is a word disliked by many public officials, but I am afraid that it is too late for pleading, begging, requesting, or even reasoning. We are here because the clamor from the community is too anxious to be ignored."[32]

That was, in some ways, the first public salvo in a battle that would last for over a decade. Some of that battle would be fought with words, some of it with rocks, much of it on national television. In some ways, it is still being fought today, a kind of shadow campaign over school segregation that informs the chapters of this book.

After its defiant statement, the NAACP and its supporters in the African American community threatened a boycott. Hicks put her name to a statement that acknowledged the ills of "ghetto living" and committed all sides to a "sympathetic, cooperative solution to these problems." Although she publicly praised the statement at first, she withdrew her name after several days.[33]

Indeed, though Hicks rebuffed the advances of Alabama's segregationist governor George Wallace, who invited her to join him on a presidential ticket, most of her energies went toward ensuring that no integration took place. That endeavor dovetailed with her bid, throughout the 1960s and early 1970s, for more political power—as a member of the US House of Representatives, as a member of the Boston City Council, and, twice, as an unsuccessful candidate for the mayoralty of that city. Although she did not always win these bids to expand her political reach, each one deepened her reach into the living rooms of America.[34]

Through it all, Hicks's desire to keep black children out of white schools was the main—maybe the sole—source of her appeal to her constituents, which was only bolstered by the 1965 Racial Imbalance Act and Judge Garrity's subsequent district court decision that Boston must use busing to end segregation. These developments gave Hicks the perfect foil to fight against. During her 1967 run for the mayor's office, she used the now famous slogan "You know where I stand." Everyone did know: she stood with the whites.[35]

Hicks played on fears of dark-skinned invaders, of undeserving outsiders taking what was not rightfully theirs. She knew exactly what she needed to say, and more importantly, what could be left unsaid. Much like Trump's team did in 2016, Hicks "focused on 'the special interests,' 'the rich people in the suburbs,' 'the establishment,' 'the outside power structure,' 'the forces who attempt to invade us,'" as the journalist J. Anthony Lukas has said. It was the politics of grievance, masterfully conveyed.[36]

But then came Garrity's ruling in 1974, and everything Louise Day Hicks was working toward was suddenly threatened. That would do wonders for her political career, while harming Boston's reputation for decades to come.

———

IT WAS REALLY Judge Garrity's ruling in *Morgan v. Hennigan*—the NAACP case brought in 1972—that precipitated what we call today the Boston busing crisis. And, of course, the crisis was not about the use of buses, or any other mode of transportation. It was about who went to school where, how much people owed to each other, and how much they deserved to keep to themselves.

When Garrity released his ruling in June 1974, it left an entire summer for the city to work out a solution to its segregation problem. And that such a solution was necessary was made clear in Garrity's ruling. He concluded that the men and women in charge of Boston's schools had "knowingly carried out a systematic program of segregation affecting all of the city's students, teachers and school faculties and . . . intentionally brought about and maintained a dual school system." "Therefore," he said, "the entire school system of Boston is unconstitutionally segregated."[37]

Now came something no less daunting: the integration plan itself. This project would be undertaken by Charles Glenn, a thirty-five-year-old white Harvard graduate with a social conscience—one particularly attuned to the plight of blacks. At the time of his selection by Garrity to come up with a busing plan, he was on the state's Bureau of Equal Education Opportunity.[38]

Glenn would later explain how the busing plan came to be, telling J. Anthony Lukas, "We simply took a large map and started moving across the city in a big arc from northwest to southeast, dividing it into districts so that each school would include the right proportion of black and white kids. When we got to the end of the arc, we were left with South Boston and Roxbury. We didn't have any choice but to mix those two neighborhoods."[39]

Garrity's remedy, ham-handed as it was, did not single out the Irish Americans of South Boston specifically, but it did make odd bedfellows of all-white South Boston and all-black Roxbury. Why force such a turbulent union? According to one Boston official, Lukas wrote, Glenn wanted to teach whites in South Boston a lesson—the official believed that Glenn was thinking: "We've had enough of you racists in South Boston; you're going to Roxbury; let's see how you like that."[40]

They didn't like it much, unsurprisingly.

Hicks and her supporters quickly mobilized, using the kinds of tactics they had learned from the civil rights movement—and which they had seen used effectively by the fifteen thousand mothers who had organized a boycott in New York City a decade before. After seeing a stuffed lion in the backseat of a car and thinking that its roaring made for a good symbol of South Boston's rage, Hicks started a group called ROAR. Only later did she and her supporters come up with the words for the acronym: Restore Our Alienated Rights.

Supporters, many of whom were working-class mothers with children in public schools, wore T-shirts with slogans like "Stop Forced Busing." At public meetings, they spoke passionately about their own experiences. There was Pixie Palladino, an Italian American counterpart to Hicks, and Fran Johnnene, who rendered her opposition to busing in personal terms: "Three different schools, three different areas of Boston, and me with no car, no choice, no exception, and no appeal!" This cadre of "militant mothers" would be crucial to Boston's efforts to oppose integration.[41]

But whereas the civil rights movement was predicated on nonviolence, by shows of dignity before which even the most flagrant shows of racism would cower, the mothers in Boston did not engender a social movement for the good of all. Instead, groups like ROAR encouraged violence and bigotry, all to preserve the rule of segregation.

When Garrity delayed the opening of school until mid-September (so that that the desegregation plan could be implemented), opponents seized the opportunity. Two African American teachers assigned to South Boston High School were accosted by protesters. One had his car vandalized, and the other was "threatened by a white youth who held a pellet rifle to his head."[42]

ROAR activists also hounded Democratic senator Ted Kennedy of Massachusetts. The Kennedys had been the pride of Irish Boston, but because Kennedy supported busing, he was now considered "a disgrace to the Irish," a traitor to his own people. "Let your daughter get bused there so she can get raped," one protester said. Another alluded to the assassinations of his brothers Robert and John, saying, "Why don't you let them shoot you like they shot your two brothers?"[43]

School started on September 12. The black children who were presumably to be the benefactors of integration were greeted by some three hundred protesters at South Boston High, who pelted their buses with rocks. White students assigned to schools in black neighborhoods simply didn't come to school: at Roxbury High, for example, only twenty whites came for the first day of class.

The stonings continued on the second day, causing injury to at least one African American student. Jean McGuire, who'd been dismayed by the conditions at the Louisa May Alcott school a decade before, recalled the scene: "I remember riding the buses to protect the kids going up to South Boston High School. And the bricks through the window. Signs hanging out those buildings, 'Nigger Go Home.' Pictures of monkeys. The words. The spit. People just felt it was all right to attack children."[44]

The violence continued inside the schools and on the streets of Boston. The Ku Klux Klan showed up, vowing to protect "white people here in the cradle of liberty against the deprivation of their civil rights."[45]

By late September, more white students were coming to school. On October 11, there was a major sign of progress: only a single bus carrying black students was met with a hail of stones. But even if the violence would ebb, it would not cease that year. And it continued in the year to come. The ugliness included fights, riots, and walkouts. Thomas H. O'Connor, a Southie native, later described that fall at South Boston High: "Almost without let-up, there were confrontations in the corridors, fistfights in the lunchrooms, clashes in the lavatories and shoving matches in the locker rooms. One day white students would walk out of classes; the next black students would boycott. White parents charged Headmaster William Reid with showing partiality toward black students; black parents insisted he was favoring whites."[46]

Judge Garrity, meanwhile, held the line, continuing against all odds with the implementation of the desegregation plan that had been nearly a decade in the making. Throughout that year, he and several appointed experts worked on Phase II of the busing plan. Under this new, more comprehensive plan, according to Lukas, "the city was divided into nine community school districts like slices of a pie, each wedge including black neighborhoods towards the pie's center and white communities towards the edge. Integration was achieved by busing whites toward the center of each slice and blacks toward the periphery." Parents were also given the option of enrolling their children in magnet schools, in a foreshadowing of a tactic that has been used by other districts wanting to integrate their schools in a somewhat more gentle fashion. During the new phase, 2,100 students would travel to school by bus.[47]

Opposition continued, but so did the busing. If the battle was merely over whether busing would continue, then Garrity won. But if the battle was against segregation, or for the future of Boston's children—black and white alike—then victory is far less clear.

———

DESPITE THE VIOLENCE that marked the 1974–1975 school year, Judge Garrity's desegregation order continued apace until it was lifted in 1987 by a federal appellate court. In *Morgan v. Nucci*, the three-judge panel for the US Court of Appeals for the First Circuit "ruled the city had 'performed in good faith in recent years' to end racial imbalance in the city's 123 public schools," reported United Press International. The judges noted that thirteen schools remained "racially identifiable," but they conceded that little could be done about this, as the mono-racial composition of those schools was "rooted not in discrimination but in more intractable demographic obstacles."[48]

Boston school officials were understandably pleased. John Nucci, head of the Boston School Committee, told UPI: "It says very clearly that because we've been committed to the principles of desegregation, because we do not ever want to run a segregated school system again, and because we have grown and matured as a city, we now can have some flexibility and perhaps can give parents significantly greater choice in where their children attend school."[49]

Boston had spent thirteen years under the integration order, but it did not achieve lasting integration in that time. Garrity's order would, in the end, prove a Pyrrhic victory. Because if the goal was to have white and black children learning together, that goal was not achieved. Faced with the prospect of integration, white parents simply fled. It should not be surprising that the Boston suburbs have some of the best public schools in the country, many of them functioning as feeders into the Ivy League. But Boston's schools continue to flounder. This arrangement is replicated in almost every other American city.

In 2012, only 13 percent of the children attending Boston's public schools were white. In 1967, the schools had been 72 percent white. "Now, there are no white kids to be integrated," one former supporter of busing lamented.[50]

Hicks and her allies, abetted by an insufficiently critical media, successfully managed to paint busing as a grotesque abuse of power. Busing became a code-word, and those who understood how to appeal to the fears of whites, how to swamp facts with emotions, knew how to use it effectively. Unexamined by many opponents of integration was the assumption that neighborhood schools were indeed a civil right, that one was somehow entitled to attend the closest school possible—and that the government has no say in where, and how, children are educated. The busing wasn't "forced" any more than parking rules are "forced." It was a delusion of whites in Boston—and elsewhere—that they had untrammeled freedom to educate their children in whatever school they saw fit. It was an even greater delusion that the busing issue was about anything other than race.

A report by the NAACP put the matter pithily: "It's Not the Distance, It's the Niggers."[51]

Boston was the first victory by anti-integration activists in the post-LBJ era. But it was a tenuous victory, and a hint of how deep the sentiments against integration ran. Opposition to integration would continue to manifest itself in ensuing decades, sabotaging the nascent experiment.

HOW CHARLOTTE (BRIEFLY) GOT IT RIGHT

I N 1974, OPPOSITION TO INTEGRATION TURNED FROM RHETORIC TO violence in Boston. But eight hundred miles southwest, in swampy North Carolina, West Charlotte High School's black and white students banded together with a clear message. They invited students from South Boston to show that yellow buses did not portend the nightmares that northern politicians warned of. At West Charlotte, the scions of some of the city's preeminent white families went to school with working-class blacks. They went willingly, without violence, and often with great affection. That's not to say that Charlotte was a paradise. Instead, it was refreshingly ordinary. That was the promise, and the point.[1]

Integration in Charlotte was so ordinary, in fact, that it became a status quo worthy of protection—and black and white families would indeed attempt to protect it over the course of the ensuing decades, but to no avail. Today, Charlotte's schools are as segregated as they were before 1971, when integration there began in earnest. To truly understand how integration can blossom, and how resegregation can uproot even vaunted progress, we must understand the history of this proudly modern city. Therein lies a lesson in political impatience and expedience. Schooling, unfortunately, does not function like the stock market, with

Dorothy Counts, fifteen, walks to school among a seething crowd of white students and parents on September 4, 1957. A day of firsts: first day of school; first to integrate Charlotte-Mecklenburg Public Schools. (Photo courtesy of *Charlotte Observer*)

gains and losses flashing across a screen. Instead, it progresses through subtle, powerful, orderly social progress. Despite its challenges, though, Charlotte's story is also one of determination that echoes the value of integration and provides clues into how to realize its promise.

———

ON A BRIGHT North Carolina morning in 1957, Dorothy Counts walks to Harding High. She is smartly dressed, even for a proper southern girl, with a ribbon stretching down to her knees above the hem of her plaid dress. Two paces behind, her father marches dutifully. But a grim expression grips his face. Between them, and surrounding them, dozens of jeering whites—mostly, but not all, children—heckle and hound their every step. Dorothy knows that what will follow will be trial and tribulation, and so does her father. At Harding High, there will be no welcome but this, of unmitigated hostility.[2]

Many years later, Dorothy would recall that students continued to harass her inside the school. She thought she might be making friends with one white girl, but hopes of a genuine connection were quickly dashed. "The very next day, as we passed in the hallway, my newfound friend ignored me," she said. "Our eyes met and she looked away. Guilt and discomfort were displayed all over her face." After four days, Dorothy's parents pulled her from Harding, sending her to finish school with relatives in Philadelphia. She eventually graduated, but she did not return to Charlotte for many years.[3]

Dorothy served as the vanguard for an early attempt at integration in the Charlotte-Mecklenburg schools, and the district did realize some integration through this early effort. But seven years after her fateful march and eventual retreat, "segregation was still the reality in Charlotte-Mecklenburg": "[By] 1964, the system had 88 segregated schools—57 white and 31 black," by the school district's own count.[4]

If Charlotte was to realize integration, it would need to do more than simply allow black families to walk through white neighborhoods and into white schools. But what?

———

IN A DOWNTOWN Charlotte office filled with civil-rights-era memorabilia, James E. Ferguson II recalls being in junior high school when *Brown* was decided. "I'm thinking, 'Oh wow, this means I'm gonna have a new educational experience,'" he says. "That initial excitement didn't last long, because nothing changed." He did not experience any form of integration until he went to law school at Columbia University. "That was when I first realized the tremendously powerful impact segregation had on me and everyone else who was subject to it." He felt socially ill at ease around his white peers.[5]

But Ferguson, determined to create a different future for his home state, returned to Charlotte to create North Carolina's first racially integrated law firm. There, he represented both blacks and whites, including the "Wilmington Ten," nine young men and a woman who had been convicted in 1971 of charges, including arson, resulting from school desegregation protests. Ferguson is credited with helping to get the convictions overturned when the US Court of Appeals for the Fourth Circuit ruled in 1980, in *Chavez v. State of North Carolina*, that they had been wrongfully convicted, with the judges citing an attempt by authorities to stifle their nonviolent opposition to segregation. While Ferguson protected North Carolinians from constitutional abuses in the criminal courts, his friend and colleague Julius Chambers would handle the civil side as a general, of sorts, in the war for integration.

Chambers had graduated from the University of North Carolina Law School and had interned under Thurgood Marshall at the NAACP's Legal Defense Fund. He had learned much under the man many called "Mr. Civil Rights," and he put what he had learned to good use when, in 1964, he was approached by a curious couple. Darius and Vera Swann were black Presbyterians who had served as missionaries in India. Time away from home has a way of shifting our perspective, and so it was with the Swanns. When they returned to Charlotte and "were told that their eldest child, aged six, must attend an all-black school," they knew it was wrong. So, with Chambers's aid, they sued.[6]

The resulting lawsuit, known as *Swann v. Charlotte-Mecklenburg County Board of Education* when it reached the US Supreme Court, was brought by Chambers while he was still at the NAACP Legal Defense Fund. Throughout the latter half of the 1960s, Chambers argued vigorously on behalf of the Swanns and other families seeking to integrate North Carolina, persevering even as opponents firebombed his house, his car, and his office. Then, in 1969, after a string of victories, he found himself arguing that the only way for Charlotte to rectify its history of segregation was to implement busing, or, more precisely, the strategic placement of children in schools managed in such a way as to achieve racial balance.[7]

In the earlier 1970 case of *Swann*, Chambers made this impassioned plea before James B. McMillan, a judge for the US District Court for the Western District of North Carolina. Judge McMillan, who had previously publicly opposed busing, seemed anything but an impartial arbiter. But his ruling would shock the world and prove he was perfectly suited to adjudicate the matter. "He decided to do something unusual," Ferguson remembers. "He decided to listen to the evidence."[8]

And the evidence was clear—the integration plan offered by the school board included a great deal of the status quo, with Chambers maintaining that "school choice" was not up to the task of unsettling generations of segregation. So McMillan invited a scholar at Rhode Island College, Dr. John A. Finger, to come up with a superior desegregation plan. The "Finger Plan," which involved busing a large number of students to achieve a greater degree of racial balance—would prove far more ambitious than anything the district might have dreamed up. And it would ultimately win over Judge McMillan. The plan was designed to, as much as practicable, "reach a [71 percent white, 29 percent black] ratio in [each of the] various schools so that there will be no basis for contending that one school is racially different from the others."[9]

In the order mandating that the district adopt key aspects of the Finger Plan, McMillan reminded critics that the need to desegregate "is a matter of law, not anarchy; of constitutional right, not popular sentiment." And he discussed the frustration, in Charlotte and in courtrooms around the country, with the slow pace of desegregation since *Brown*, writing that "recent appellate court decisions have hammered home the message that sixteen years of 'deliberate speed' are long enough to desegregate tax supported schools." Finally, he held that the ambitious plan was supported by a constitutional requirement to realize desegregation immediately, writing, "There remains no judicial discretion to postpone immediate implementation." And so he ordered that Charlotte not only provide transportation to "all children whose reassignment to any school is necessary to bring about the reduction of segregation," but also fully desegregate elementary schools, high schools, and school faculty, not eventually, but by later *that year*.[10]

BUSING BEGAN IN Charlotte on September 9, 1970, the first day of the new school year. Attendance that first day was about 80 percent, much higher than it would be on the equivalent first day of integration in Boston. There were, however, some protests, which were staged by the Concerned Parents Association. As the *New York Times* would report, the association "told nearly 6,000 white parents that it was their patriotic as well as their strategic duty to peacefully disrupt the busing plan by keeping their children home."[11]

More promising to the opponents of integration than a protest was the 1970 appeal of McMillan's ruling to the Supreme Court, which at the time had four justices who had been appointed by Republican president Richard Nixon. While the Warren Court of the late 1960s had been led by a justice whom many considered a liberal activist, the Burger Court—so named for Chief Justice Warren Burger—signaled a kind of conservative return that has continued to this day.

The ruling in *Brown v. Board of Education* had been unanimous, reflecting an increasing national discomfort with the separate-but-equal doctrine prevalent in the Jim Crow South. It had been informed by social science research suggesting the deep psychological harm of segregation on the developing mind. By the time *Swann* arrived at the Supreme Court, the nation had changed considerably in terms of race relations, and not exactly for the better.

The nonviolent protests of the early 1960s had given way to the images of armed Black Panthers confronting police officers on the streets of Oakland and even in the California statehouse in Sacramento. There were riots in Newark and Detroit, as well as assassinations of police officers in Manhattan. The neighborhood of Watts burned in Los Angeles in 1965. By 1968, 95 percent of American households had a television set, and the continuing conflicts on the streets played out nightly on the screens in America's living rooms. That spring, the nation watched as Chicago exploded in fiery civil unrest upon the news that Dr. Martin Luther King Jr. had been assassinated in Memphis.

For many white Americans, these images led to a dour and un-
pleasant conclusion: something had gone horribly wrong in the civil
rights movement. The people looting stores and setting fires could
not be the disciples of Martin Luther King, or even, for that matter,
the more confrontational Malcolm X. Now, there was a raw anger
nothing like the locked-arm unity of Selma. Many whites, watching
the tumult of the late 1960s, had concluded that their earlier fears
and prejudices were now being horrifically confirmed. If they had
not fled the cities for the suburbs in the 1950s, they certainly did
so now. Otherwise, they clustered in heavily ethnic enclaves—South
Boston, Staten Island, parts of the San Fernando Valley—that seemed
immune to "intrusion" by people of color.

Busing, especially in a district that represented a mix of both city
and suburb like Charlotte-Mecklenburg, suggested a pulling-back of
whites into the roiling city core they had sought to escape. On both
the left and the right, various opponents, from a young Joe Biden to a
grizzled Richard Nixon, railed against "forced busing."

For Nixon, opposition to busing was a means of feeding a ravenous
Republican base. He was tuned perfectly to the grievances of whites
who believed themselves to be victims of liberal elites. The year before
the *Swann* decision, when he gave a speech on school desegregation,
he cautioned against "massive" busing, reminding his constituents, "I
have consistently expressed my opposition to any compulsory busing
of pupils beyond normal geographic school zones for the purpose of
achieving racial balance."[12]

Nixon extended that opposition beyond the bully pulpit, stacking
the Supreme Court with social conservatives. Opponents of *Swann*
took solace knowing that Nixon's picks were ready to snuff out any
budding attempts at integration. They were further delighted by the
knowledge that Julius Chambers, who was then only thirty-four years
old, would argue the case for the plaintiff. They assumed that the combination of an inexperienced attorney and a conservative bench would
spell early doom for McMillan's decision and Charlotte's efforts to

integrate. But, much to their chagrin, Chambers would prove to be more than equipped for the task, and the justices Nixon had appointed would shift leftward once installed. The Nine ruled *unanimously* that Charlotte's plan—including its student reassignments—was a constitutionally permissible tactic to rectify segregation.[13]

The opinion, written by Burger, was short and to the point. "Today's objective is to eliminate from the public schools all vestiges of state-imposed segregation," it opened, foreshadowing that Chambers had won a sweeping victory that would redound to the children of Charlotte. The justices, speaking with a unified voice, asserted that "the remedial technique of requiring bus transportation as a tool of school desegregation was within [Judge McMillan's] power." And that meant it was within the power of any district court judge in a similar circumstance.[14]

The busing in Charlotte would therefore continue—and busing around the country would begin. For now, at least, integration was the victor.

———

WEST CHARLOTTE HIGH School is, in many ways, the symbol of integration's heyday in that city. It is an especially powerful—and unique—symbol of how blacks and whites can work together to make integration work. In many places, whites felt as if integration had been foisted upon them by the courts; blacks sometimes felt the same way. Charlotte, and West Charlotte High in particular, was that rare example of blacks and whites joining in a common cause.

West Charlotte High had been founded in 1938, and it soon had become a point of pride for the city's African American community, even if it had no "lunchroom, auditorium or gymnasium," as the historian Pamela Grundy noted in her book about the school. Despite the dearth of resources that was the hallmark of separate-but-equal schooling, West Charlotte was a place where African American students could excel under the tutelage of African American teachers. Whatever they may have lacked, they didn't lack for role models. "We were really taught," one graduate recalled later in an interview with Grundy. "They taught us to have so much dignity and self-assurance. And not to be afraid."[15]

The desegregation effort brought about by *Swann* called for Charlotte's schools to reconstitute their student bodies starting in the fall of 1970 so that they would reflect the overall racial dynamic of the county. About 43,000 out of 80,000 students in Charlotte-Mecklenburg would therefore have to partake in the dreaded (if widely misunderstood) ritual of "forced" busing.[16]

West Charlotte, which had been entirely black, now accepted its first white students. "Many of the whites who came were absolutely scared out of their minds," one former student recalled. Because the teaching corps also had to be integrated, there were also suddenly white teachers at the high school. They were seen, whether fairly or not, as intruders.[17]

In fact, some African Americans resisted integration as fiercely as their white counterparts did, an undercurrent that complicates the broader narrative about who supported efforts at racial balancing (and who didn't). On the cusp of Judge McMillan's plan becoming a reality, teachers from one all-black school in the city wrote, "We have watched the efforts of integration, always meaning that blacks were to assimilate and, in fact, be absorbed by white institutions, white programs, white cultures. To this we say we are tired and resent your insult that you still presume our inferiority, that you still will presume that we are incapable of performing equally as well as whites."[18]

Given the difficulties of the 1970–1971 school year, integration could have easily proven a disaster in Charlotte. Disaster, in fact, was expected. Yet, while there were occasional fights, the school somehow held together. The student editors of the 1971 high school yearbook reflected somberly on the year that had been with little of what might be called a carefree teenaged spirit: "It is the dawn of a new era, and we, the sobered survivors of the turbulent sixties, are determined that the mistakes of that decade shall not reoccur."[19]

What truly saved West Charlotte—and, in fact, the entire integration experience in the Queen City—was something that rarely makes its appearance in American civic life today: unity. In effect, both blacks and whites realized that much of the rest of the nation was watching what was happening in North Carolina, and that their city's reputation would rise or fall based on the integration experiment. Some business owners and civic leaders across the Deep South—in cities like Birmingham and Montgomery—already grasped many years before that images of black protesters being beaten in the streets and drenched by water hoses would only further sully the already troubled image of the region. But that insight had largely remained below the surface, or at least had been drowned out by the much louder shouts of the segregationists. Years later, and many miles to the north, it was the voices of the integrationists that were heard.

In 1973, black and white parents in Charlotte formed an advisory group to make sure that integration would go more smoothly there than it had in other American cities. Crucially, the whites on the committee included some of the city's wealthiest and most prominent civic leaders. Their involvement effectively signaled to "ordinary" whites that it was acceptable to partake in integration.

Recall that the working-class whites of South Boston would later feel like Judge Garrity had foisted integration on them, while leaving better-off whites out of the fraught and painful process. Although this wasn't quite true, the belief was deeply held by many Irish Americans in the city. By preaching integration to them without partaking in it themselves, Boston's civic leaders only made the situation worse. Charlotte was the opposite, with elites leading the way, defanging any charges that they were exempting their own children from integration.

West Charlotte became the epicenter of this new, joint effort, a kind of showpiece of what integration could be. "The plan assigned several of the city's most prestigious white enclaves to the school," according to Grundy. And perhaps because of the inclusion of well-to-do whites in the integration plan, Grundy noted, "even those residents most staunchly opposed to busing agreed the plan was fair." A similar effort in Boston would have had the scions of Back Bay blue bloods heading off to Roxbury High, to show that they understood the importance of integration. Of course, no such effort ever took place.[20]

Integration has never been easy, but Charlotte's example shows that it doesn't have to be tragic. James "Smudgie" Mitchell, who later became a city councilman in Charlotte, attended West Charlotte in those days. Thinking back on his time at the school, he now realizes what an important role the students themselves played in the success of the integration plan. "I don't know if they wanted us to succeed though," he recently said. "I think that's where we proved them wrong. I really thought they thought it was going to be racial tension every day. 'Here we go again. Six o'clock news. A riot at West Charlotte again.' Never happened."[21]

But the majority of the citizens of Charlotte understood how rare it was to make a smooth transition to integrated schools, and they remained fiercely protective of their experiment at schooling black and white children together. In 1984, President Ronald Reagan was blindsided by the Queen City's embrace of integration. During a speech on his reelection tour, he maligned his liberal detractors, who, he argued, "favor busing that takes innocent children out of the neighborhood school and makes them pawns in a social experiment that nobody wants." But the response from the otherwise jubilant crowd was, as one observer would describe it later, "dead silence." Republicans elsewhere may have shared Reagan's hostility to busing, but such detractors were not in this crowd.[22]

The Charlotte Observer later ran an editorial, "You Were Wrong, Mr. President," that reminded Reagan that even if there was resistance to integration in his adopted home of California, or across the Northeast, Charlotte was another matter. "Charlotte-Mecklenburg's proudest achievement of the past 20 years is not the city's impressive new skyline or its strong, growing economy," the editorial said. "Its proudest achievement is its fully integrated schools." Fully aware that Charlotte's integration had started with a surprising decision in *Swann*, the editor implored Reagan not to put justices on the Supreme Court who would "force this community to dismantle its integrated school system." Such a move, the writer said, would force "a tragedy" on "future generations of our children."[23]

Buttressed by biracial support, Charlotte's integration efforts would continue, and they would remake West Charlotte High. The white students brought resources with them, bolstering the argument that integration equalizes schools like no other force. "Within a year, West Charlotte boasted a new, paved parking lot for student cars, two new tennis courts, and a thoroughly refurbished interior," according to Grundy. Black and white students gained a deeper understanding of each other. And their desire to share that understanding was what led them to invite South Boston students to see their schools in person in 1974.[24]

West Charlotte High would remain a national model for the promise of integration for the next twenty-five years. In 1991, the *Wall Street Journal* profiled the school on its front page. "Against the Odds: As Others Scale Back on School Integration, Charlotte Presses On," the headline read. It continued with a subtitle: "Parents Have Helped Create a Model Busing Program." The school, and the city, had endured much to realize a quarter century of continuous progress. But new threats loomed just out of view.[25]

———

TWO WEEKS AFTER the 2017 mayoral election in Charlotte, a high school junior named Kaycee Hailey published an op-ed in the *Charlotte Observer*, the same newspaper that had excoriated Reagan for his dig at school busing thirty-three years before. Hailey described the current situation, saying that Charlotte-Mecklenburg is now "a segregated district." "I go to a segregated school," she wrote. And the school she attended was none other than West Charlotte High, once the pride of the city and a paragon of school integration. The school was no longer either pride or paragon. Hailey wrote: "I've seen teachers storm out of classrooms and quit halfway through a class. I am often advised to take more rigorous classes, such as AP courses, but few are available at my school."[26]

About 85 percent of Hailey's peers at the school are black, like her. The same share of students are poor. The school once described by the *Wall Street Journal* as "a warm picture of integrated young America" is no more, and with it, the summer of Charlotte's fame has also faded into the past. James Ferguson, who cofounded Charlotte's first integrated law firm in the era of *Swann*, watched the shift take place. His assessment: "There is no core of people who are actively pushing for school desegregation. We're almost back to where we started from."[27]

How could Charlotte recede from its idyllic version of integration, protected by cross-racial unity, to become yet another resegregated school district? It was derailed, in essence, by the triumph of self-interest over the collective good.

———

NEW YORK BECAME the financial center of the country in the early nineteenth century. San Francisco made a meteoric rise to prominence during the tech boom. As both examples show, major American cities often evolve in rapid, unexpected ways. Charlotte certainly began a rapid transition in the late 1970s. Bob Morgan, the current president of the city's chamber of commerce, recalls that shift: "In 1978, IBM moved 1,000 families from upstate New York [to Charlotte]," he said. "That was the first big influx. You couldn't buy pasta. You couldn't buy a bagel in Charlotte. The IBMers really began to change the community." With these shifts came other signs of growth: the rapid expansion of Charlotte Douglas International Airport as a major southeastern hub and the growth of Duke Energy into a national powerhouse.[28]

In 1987, there were 473,760 people in Mecklenburg County, which includes Charlotte and its suburbs. By 1997, there were 617,328. Most of this influx flowed to the suburbs rather than to Charlotte's inner core. Although they were connected by municipal government and the school district, the city and the suburbs represented different sets of values. Many of the suburbs were new, arising out of previously empty land. By 1976, only 12.5 percent of all the land in Mecklenburg County had been developed. By 2006, 57.6 percent of the land had been developed, an astonishing increase.[29]

Many of the newcomers to Charlotte were from the Northeast and the West, and often they did not want to participate in busing or integration. "Charlotte has been a model for shifting children from one end of the county to the other and not a model for educational excellence by any means," one white parent complained in 1988.[30]

One of the discontented suburbanite transplants was William Capacchione. Twice, Capacchione tried to get his daughter into Olde Providence, a "sparkling" magnet school "set in Charlotte's fast-growing Southeast quadrant." In a single year, the parents of the children attending Olde Providence had "raised $26,000 for supplies and student activities," according to a *New York Times* article, and it had brand-new Apple computers and other technology. For some in Charlotte, magnet schools had become a popular solution to rising dissatisfaction with integrated schools. Capacchione, who had come from elsewhere, for example, didn't remember the struggles over integration that had taken place twenty years before.[31]

When Olde Providence decided not to admit his daughter, who was white, because her name was not drawn in a lottery, Capacchione did what Darius Swann had done before him—he sued. Six other families joined him in the suit, *Capacchione v. Charlotte-Mecklenburg Schools*, which went to the US District Court for the Western District of North Carolina. As if fate had conspired against Charlotte's efforts to integrate, Capacchione's case was heard by Judge Robert Potter. Potter had been appointed by President Reagan and had maligned Charlotte-Mecklenburg's integration efforts during his visit there in 1984. He had also worked as an anti-integration activist in 1970 and had worked for Jesse Helms, the famous segregationist US senator from North Carolina. Later, as a federal judge, his tough sentences earned him the nickname of "Maximum Bob."

But danger signs from the judiciary appeared long before *Capac-chione* arrived in Potter's courtroom. In the mid-1980s, courts began ruling that school districts formerly under orders to integrate had reached "unitary" status, meaning their schools were sufficiently desegregated that they no longer needed to follow desegregation plans. For a time, it seemed unclear whether such rulings were constitutionally permissible. Many of these districts had schools that were certainly still racially segregated, and that were even resegregating. But the courts often held that such segregation was inevitable given the choices of the families in those districts, and that the districts had done all they could to realize the hopes of *Brown* and the mandates of cases like *Swann*. Then, in 1991, the Supreme Court clarified, in *Board of Education of Oklahoma City v. Dowell*, that even if a school district was segregated, and even if it was becoming more segregated, if a district court found that it had complied with past desegregation plans "for a reasonable time," and "was unlikely" to "return to its former ways," it would render any further court supervision of desegregation efforts unnecessary. In other words, so long as a school district had *tried*, it did not matter whether it had succeeded; nor did it matter what would be likely to happen if it ceased its efforts.[32]

Although Potter was one of Reagan's earliest nominations, he was not the last. Reagan appointed close to three hundred right-leaning district court judges who, like Potter, were willing to find that school districts had *tried*, to confer upon them the coveted "unitary status" they sought, and to relinquish them from the promise of integration. Charlotte had certainly tried, and it had even realized a true, if fragile, success. But the families at West Charlotte High and throughout the city knew that integration took effort—both heroic and sustained—to realize its incredible promise.

In *Capacchione*, James Ferguson, whose firm had long been a stalwart sentry in the effort to protect integration, jumped to the defense of Charlotte's pride, representing plaintiffs from the *Swann* case who had banded together with the school district to protect their joint integration project. It is important to understand just how strange the arrangement of parties was. On one side, claiming that integration efforts must continue for the benefit of all, were long-established Charlotte parents and former students and the school district itself—who had seen integration blossom from its fragile infancy. On the other, a newcomer to Charlotte's suburbs was seeking relief for suburban families who wanted nothing to do with integration.

The *Swann* plaintiffs and school district argued in *Capacchione* that unitary status was inappropriate because "there has been more [racial] imbalance in recent years than at any time since the desegregation orders have been in place." In addition, "almost all newly constructed schools have been built in predominately white areas." The few that had opened in predominately black areas were magnet schools, like the one Capacchione coveted for his daughter. Their argument was simple. They could not end integration efforts when they had not yet achieved integration, especially when new threats, like a shift in educational resources to Charlotte's white suburbs, stood ready to unsettle a generation of progress.[33]

Judge Potter was unmoved. He remained satisfied that Charlotte had *tried*, and said it need not try any longer. He held that because Charlotte had "complied with the thirty-year-old desegregation order in good faith," any "racial imbalances existing in schools today are no longer vestiges of the dual system." Instead, Charlotte had "achieved unitary status," which "dissolve[d] the [*Swann*] desegregation order."[34]

Potter could have stopped there, and most judges would have. But integration offended Potter at a deep and visceral level. He had opposed the policy for much of his life. So he continued, writing, "The Court also finds that [race-based] student assignment practices [to magnet schools] went beyond constitutionally permissible bounds." Finally, he said, "The continued use of [these] race-based policies are hereinafter prohibited." Even if the school district wanted to sustain and further the success it had realized through its student reassignment program, Potter made clear that it would do so at its own peril. The court, he said, was watching—no longer to stamp out the vestiges of segregation, but to speedily squelch any efforts, even those by the school district itself, to revitalize integration.[35]

Defenders of integration did what they have always done when faced with defeat—they persevered, this time in the form of an appeal to the US Court of Appeals for the Fourth Circuit, in the case *Belk v. Charlotte Mecklenburg Board of Education*. There, however, they encountered seven judges who had been nominated by Reagan, Nixon, and George H. W. Bush. In an opinion by Judge William Traxler, they affirmed Potter's decision that Charlotte's school district, against its own protestation, had achieved unitary status, and that the school district should, in its assignment policies moving forward, be guided by "the principles of non-discrimination"—meaning they must ignore race.[36]

With that, Charlotte's efforts to achieve integration were effectively ended.

——

AT THE TURN of the millennium, when West Charlotte High School students heard Judge Potter's decision, they were shocked. Had the nation learned nothing from their incredible efforts? One student, Justin Perry, immediately did the only thing that made sense. He left school, went downtown to the district courthouse, and protested. Perry, and many of his peers, understood that Potter had used unfounded racial fears to destroy one of the few spaces where those fears were allayed, for blacks and whites alike.

"In our space, we actually talked about these differences," Perry remembers. The controversy around busing, he explains, is not about buses. "It's about what the end of the ride leads to." And while a ride to an integrated system might lead to deeper harmony, the end of integration harms all Americans at a psychological level. And Perry should know. After graduating from high school, he went on to the University of North Carolina at Chapel Hill, one of the finest public universities in the nation, to earn a graduate degree in social work and counseling. Today, he works with young people in Charlotte-Mecklenburg. Some of them come from the wealthy white suburbs, the very ones where newcomers in the 1990s sought to live so their children would not have to attend integrated schools. Instead, these students now attend what Perry calls "real estate orchestrated schools." But these schools, he says, are places where the pressures of achievement can lead to stress, anxiety, and other psychological ills.[37]

"You can't have a high-quality education without diversity," says Perry. The rollback of integration efforts, he believes, signals a deeper social breakdown, an atomization of American society. "We sold our soul," he says, "and now we're gonna have to deal with it." Research backs up his assertion, suggesting that children who go to integrated schools are more likely than those attending segregated ones to learn resilience and empathy, along with other skills likely to help them in an increasingly complex world.[38]

Other graduates of Charlotte's schools during its era of integration feel similarly. Sam Fulwood III, who is now a Senior Fellow at the Center for American Progress, recalls his schooldays with the kind of deep appreciation that can only be gained with age. "Nostalgia floods my memories of Charlotte," he wrote on his website, recalling how his time at Garinger High when it was integrated "prepared me for life in the multicultural world that I have known all my adult life." He explained, "I recall my school years as rough and tumble but a period of growing pains that offered me an opportunity for later success in career and life. I want that for every student who now attends my hometown's schools."[39]

Today, that dream seems further away than ever. As Perry, Fulwood, and countless others feared, the end of busing led to rapid re-segregation in Charlotte. The *Charlotte Observer* recently reported that "more than half of Charlotte-Mecklenburg Schools' black and Hispanic students now attend schools . . . where at least 90 percent of their classmates are nonwhite[,] and poverty levels are high." What would it take to undo this shift? The Education and Law Project of the North Carolina Justice Center, a research and advocacy organization, recently calculated the percentage of students who would need to be reassigned in each district in North Carolina to achieve integration. The larger the reassignment needed to achieve integration, the worse the segregation—and the district that topped the list was Charlotte-Mecklenburg. Today, in the district that was once the epitome of progress, over *half* of the district's students would need to be reassigned to achieve integration.[40]

And, as feared, with segregation came other problems. A pioneering, influential study of intergenerational mobility published in 2013 found that Charlotte ranked last among the fifty largest cities in the United States in terms of a child's prospects for escaping poverty. That is, children born poor are more likely to remain poor as adults in Charlotte than in any other major metropolitan area in the country. The deepest poverty in the state lies in neighborhood pockets of Charlotte, with high levels of school segregation and resource disparities contributing to the glacial rate of upward mobility there.[41]

Charlotte's economic challenges relate to its educational challenges in the kind of vicious cycle that can be seen in many resource-poor school districts throughout the state. Over the past two decades, the already sizable disparities in per-pupil spending between the highest- and lowest-wealth districts in North Carolina have increased. In particular, for the most recent year we have data (2015–2016), the ten highest-spending districts spent four times more per pupil than the ten lowest-spending districts. This is true despite the fact that most of the funding for North Carolina schools is disbursed at the state level. Residential housing patterns that lock a large proportion of black children into concentrated poverty and often under-resourced schools are partly to blame. Decreased state-level investment is also a culprit, as is the state legislature's failure to replace the existing state school finance system with a more progressive funding formula. The vast wealth differences in local property bases explain the lion's share of the funding gap, although the ten lowest-wealth districts are taxing themselves at nearly twice the rate of the highest-wealth districts. The district spending disparities contribute to disparities in teacher salaries, class size, and curricular offerings.[42]

IF CHARLOTTE'S HISTORY reveals anything, it is that the Queen City's citizens do not take defeat lying down. And the school district is, in some important respects, well positioned for renewed effort at integration. However, in this new era, the obstacles to integration seem ever to multiply, and although many of them come from within the Tar Heel State, others flow from outside. Understanding what Charlotte can and must overcome provides a valuable lesson for any district hoping to breathe new life into integration.

PUTTING THE "STRICT" IN "DISTRICT BOUNDARIES"

Despite its many setbacks, Charlotte dodged one major bullet that affected integration efforts in dozens of other districts in the 1970s— and that yet encumbers such efforts. One example comes from Detroit, where a black father of three, Ray Litt, wanted his children to attend integrated schools. White flight had left Detroit so thoroughly segregated that any successful integration would require cooperation from neighboring, essentially all-white school districts in the suburbs. The question was whether the courts could order integration *between* districts, rather than just *within* them. In *Milliken v. Bradley*, originally filed on behalf of Litt's children by the NAACP, a divided US Supreme Court ruled 5–4, in 1974, that integration efforts could not cross district lines unless *both* districts were found to have discrimination policies on the books. Not surprisingly, Detroit's suburban school districts, like many districts around the country, lacked any formal segregation policies. Having been essentially segregated from their inception, they had never needed formal policies to achieve their goal. This did not matter to the five justices who joined the majority opinion, in which Chief Justice Warren Burger chastised those who sought to casually ignore district lines. In the 1970s, unlike Detroit, Charlotte-Mecklenburg was 70 percent white and 30 percent black, and thus integration could be achieved within the district. *Milliken* was not a barrier. Today, however, within-district integration would be substantially harder to achieve, as only 30 percent of Charlotte-Mecklenburg students are now white.[43]

THE REVISIONIST HISTORY OF *BROWN*

Changing demographics present only one of the challenges facing Charlotte's efforts to revive integration. In Judge Potter's 1999 decision conferring "unitary" status on Charlotte, he claimed that Charlotte's use of a student reassignment policy that considered race was a violation of the Fourteenth Amendment to the US Constitution. While the US Court of Appeals for the Fourth Circuit affirmed Potter's finding that Charlotte was "unitary," it fell just short of supporting his constitutional analysis on the issue of racial assignments.[44]

But, in 2007, a Supreme Court that had been stocked with conservatives by President George W. Bush proved far more amenable to Potter's argument. The lead-up to the case, *Parents Involved in Community Schools v. Seattle School District No. 1*, might sound familiar. In 2000, Kathleen Brose, a white mother, applied to have her daughter Elisabeth attend the "oversubscribed" and well-resourced Ballard High. Seattle Public Schools assigned Elisabeth to Franklin High, an integrated school that, while held in high regard, lacked the luster of Ballard. So Brose sued to end Seattle's public school enrollment policy, which used student race as a "tie-breaker" in school placement decisions. Just like in *Capacchione*, opposing Brose were not only parents who saw the benefits of Seattle's integrating policy, but the school district itself.[45]

Supporters of Seattle's integration policy had found a sympathetic ear in the US Court of Appeals for the Ninth Circuit, which ruled in 2005 that the race-based tie-breaker was constitutionally permissible. Brose, undaunted, promised an appeal to the Supreme Court. "It's too important a decision for the city of Seattle. These children need access to their neighborhood schools, and they're not going to get it if the district uses a racial tiebreaker," Brose said, inadvertently revealing, in her choice of words, that—as many had suspected—*neighborhood school* was the opposite of a school that was racially integrated. *Neighborhood* meant *white*.[46]

Despite Brose's apparent racial motives, a divided Supreme Court issued a devastating opinion, siding 5–4 with Brose. In the majority opinion, Chief Justice John Roberts, erecting an essentially insurmountable barrier to any district hoping to consider race in student assignments, held that the racial tie-breaker violated the US Constitution. In a portion of the opinion that proved too divisive even for Justice Anthony Kennedy, who often sided with the conservatives on the Court, Roberts invoked *Brown v. Board of Education*, which he argued meant to end the practice of admitting or denying school admission based on race. "Before *Brown*," Roberts wrote, "school-children were told where they could and could not go to school based on the color of their skin. The school districts in these cases have not carried the heavy burden of demonstrating that we should allow this once again—even for very different reasons." Then came the decision's most famous line: "The way to stop discrimination on the basis of race is to stop discriminating on the basis of race."[47]

It is not hyperbole to say that *Parents Involved* is the greatest legal barrier to integration in the modern era. The decision rendered all race-based admissions policies the same, equating racism (segregation) with attempts to end racism (integration). In a dissenting opinion, Justice John Paul Stevens seized on this very point. "The Chief Justice," he wrote, "fails to note that it was only black school children who were [kept out of white schools]; indeed, the history books do not tell stories of white children struggling to attend black schools. In this and other ways, The Chief Justice rewrites the history of one of this Court's most important decisions." Stevens's point was simple. Roberts was rewriting *Brown*, which was never intended to prohibit remedial racial classifications. Nevertheless, Roberts's revision now protects segregation everywhere.

CHARTING A PATHWAY TO SEGREGATION

"There's a word for what happens when majority-white suburbs pull their children from a majority-minority school district and place them into exclusionary, majority-white schools: segregation." So began an incendiary article regarding North Carolina House Bill 514, which was signed into law in June 2018. The bill allowed four wealthy, predominantly white suburbs in Mecklenburg County to create charter districts for their own residents, effectively permitting their secession from the Charlotte-Mecklenburg public school system. The permissible admissions policy for these schools will give preference and priority to students who live in the immediate neighborhoods of the schools, who are, of course, largely white. This law will only exacerbate the racial and socioeconomic segregation in the area's schools, which, as noted before, are already only 30 percent white.[48]

In a cruel irony, because these charter schools receive government funding, taxpayers throughout the district—including those parents who might prefer integration—are being forced to subsidize these split-offs. Whereas in the era of integration during the 1970s, "white families seeking to withdraw from public school to avoid integration were forced to bear the financial burden of their prejudices," as the co-directors of the nonprofit Julius L. Chambers Center for Civil Rights put it, with House Bill 514, such costs are to be borne by parents throughout the district and the state.[49]

ALL POLITICS IS LOCAL

The tug of war over integration continues in North Carolina. But who is tugging in which direction? A 2017 study by the economists Hugh Macartney and John Singleton documented how changes in the political composition of the state's elected local school boards had affected school segregation. They found that board members who were Democrats had taken significantly more actions to reduce school segregation than those who were Republican. The effects were driven by differences in the propensity of the board members to redraw the boundaries of school zones in ways that promoted either integration or segregation, where Republican-majority members were found significantly more likely to do the latter.[50]

This is not to say that Democrats universally champion integration. As noted previously, even Joe Biden once railed against busing. Today, in New York City, the self-styled progressive visionary Bill de Blasio shies away from calling the schools segregated, acutely aware that he might need the votes of upper-middle-class whites in order to secure reelection to City Hall. "I don't get lost in terminology," he recently said when asked if New York's schools were segregated. They are, and horrifically so, and anyone who has spent time in destitute outer-borough enclaves like East New York knows that perfectly well.[51]

But Macartney and Singleton's research suggests that, at least in North Carolina, if proponents of integration seek to hitch their wagon to one of the two major parties, the choice is clear. It also suggests that the actions of local school boards, and the elections that determine them, can have a real impact, even today, on the battle for integration.

SEGREGATION'S HIDDEN FACETS: TEACHERS AND CLASSROOMS

In the pre-segregation era, West Charlotte High School's students exceeded expectations largely due to teachers who "really taught," and who inculcated "dignity and self-assurance" and showed black students "not to be afraid," one former student told the historian Pamela Grundy. In 1970, Judge McMillan ordered Charlotte to undertake integration in elementary and high schools, yes, but it was not only among students: it was also among *faculty*. And in the resegregation era, when the student Kaycee Hailey described the challenges at West Charlotte, she recounted "teachers [who] storm out of classrooms and quit halfway through a class." A factor that is underappreciated in the search for solutions to school segregation and resource disparities—the "elephant in the room"—is the one at the front of every classroom: teachers, along with teacher quality.[52]

Among female college graduates in 1960 nationwide, more than 30 percent of those who were white and more than 50 percent of those who were black were teachers; by 1990, only 20 percent of the female college graduates nationwide—black and white—were teachers. As outside employment opportunities improved for women and blacks in recent decades, fewer chose to teach, and those who did teach tended to be less skilled than previously, resulting in an overall decline in teacher quality. Although this is the general pattern across the country, it has been felt disproportionately in poor urban schools, like those in Charlotte.[53]

However, to Judge McMillan, teacher quality was not the only challenge facing districts like Charlotte-Mecklenburg: they were also dealing with the problems wrought by teacher segregation, meaning that the demographics of the teachers in many schools did not match the demographics of the students. Research confirms this concern, but not in quite the way one might expect. In today's public schools, across the country, while minority students constitute more than half of K-12 school enrollments, in the typical district roughly 84 percent of the teachers are white, and only 2 percent of the teachers are black men. Although the segregation of students has received most of the attention, the lack of teacher diversity is a growing problem, and not just for students of color. Teacher segregation can have important educational consequences for student achievement, because teacher expectations often operate through colored lenses. It also keeps minority students from having role models who look like them. It is difficult to become what you never see. When there is diversity both among the teachers and among the students, students of all races benefit.

Research has demonstrated the positive outcomes experienced by minority students when they are exposed to teachers of color in elementary school. Tom Dee and other economists have found that black students who were in Tennessee's class size reduction experiment, Project Star (Student Teacher Achievement Ratio), who started kindergarten in the late 1980s, benefited from both smaller class sizes and having a black teacher in any of their elementary school years. Compared to their peers with no black teachers, students who had a black teacher in these years were more likely to graduate from high school and more likely to take a college entrance exam. Similarly, a study of public school students in North Carolina showed that poor black students who started third grade between 2001 and 2005, and who had a black teacher anytime in the third through the fifth grades, were significantly more likely than their peers who had not had a black teacher in those years to graduate from high school and express interest in attending college.[54]

A national study from 2016, based on three years of data collected on tenth-grade public school students, revealed large differences in the expectations of black and white teachers when asked to predict the outcomes of the same black students. The white teachers were roughly 40 percent less likely than the black teachers to predict that a student would finish high school and about 30 percent less likely to predict that a student would complete a four-year college degree. The academic performance, and even the potential for academic success, of black students could well be negatively impacted by the lower expectations of some white teachers. Their more dismal projections could also affect whether black students are placed on the college-prep academic track. Such lower expectations could contribute to racial disparities in school disciplinary behavior as well—suspensions and expulsions—elements of a student's experience that may be connected to his or her chances of getting stuck in the school-to-prison pipeline. The study showed no difference, however, between black and white teachers' academic ratings of white students.[55]

These troubling patterns of systematic racial bias in teachers' expectations have been highlighted elsewhere as well. In another 2016 analysis, researchers used national data on more than ten thousand elementary school students and found that among students with high standardized test scores, black students were about 50 percent less likely to be placed in gifted programs in math and reading than comparable white students. The likelihood of placement in gifted programs is equally low for Hispanic students. Black students were three times more likely to be assigned to gifted programs, however, when they were being taught by a black teacher instead of a white one—the racial gap in the likelihood of being placed in a gifted program was altogether eliminated, in fact, when black students had a black teacher.[56]

Research has also shown that policy can dramatically change the gaps in teacher expectations and the placement of students in gifted and talented programs. In 2012, Florida's Broward County schools—a large, diverse district—began a shift from referral-based consideration for gifted placement in favor of universal screening of students and training to help teachers recognize giftedness in diverse schools. A 2015 study showed that, with the new protocol, twice as many qualified black and Hispanic students were recognized for placement in gifted and talented curricular programs in their public schools. And there were significant improvements as well in the subsequent academic performance of minority students newly placed into these gifted programs.[57]

Taken together, this research shows that to stamp out the vestiges of segregation, we must focus not only on students, but also on teachers, on their demographics, on their attitudes toward their students, and, most of all, on their preparation. With the diversity of school-age children in the United States increasing, schools seeking to realize the promise of integration should tailor their curricular offerings and provide unique supports for students' cultural, ethnic, and linguistic needs. Educators should provide both academically rigorous and culturally affirming learning environments. And districts and states should ensure that teacher preparation brings the aspirations of integration into reach.

RAYS OF HOPE OVER BLUE MOUNTAINS

Supreme Court decisions sap opportunities for integration; state statutes green-light subsidized segregation via charter schools; teacher segregation accelerates student segregation at the classroom level and speeds the flow of the school-to-prison pipeline. In the face of these challenges, one might think the residents of Charlotte would throw up their hands and give in to despair. Yet many of them have instead redoubled their efforts. And the city that was once the model for integration now provides key lessons in how it might be achieved in this more complex era.

———

ANTHONY FOXX IS a product of Charlotte's successful integration period. He embodies the vast possibilities that integration affords individuals and society at large. While attending Charlotte's desegregated public schools, he and his peers were part of the "new school" who would help define what desegregation truly meant. The influential voices of a remnant of "'old school' educators . . . who had been in the segregated system" helped inspire Foxx's tenacious character. He recalled one teacher who always pulled him aside with a charge: "It's not enough to be just as good as, you have to do more. . . . You gotta be serious and go after what you want." Foxx lived out those words to the fullest, becoming Charlotte's second black mayor, and then the nation's first black secretary of transportation, serving in the Obama administration.[58]

When Foxx considered running for mayor, he despaired to see Charlotte and the schools reverting back to pre-desegregation statistics and regimes. "I felt like there was a moment when the city was either going to confront itself again or the moment would pass," he said. He knew "someone who had been around [during the years of integration] needed to step out there and reassert what [he thought] was the city's greatest strength: its ability to pull together and create a much more clear idea of what an interconnected, inclusive community should look like." Foxx's words echoed the sentiments of many other personal stories in this book: "It's messy, it's hard, it's frustrating, it's maybe inefficient on some level, but it's the only solution we have in a democracy like ours," he said. "And our biggest challenge as a country is to get beyond appearances. And the only way you can do that is to be in the trenches with people—and the schoolhouse is one of the best places for that to happen."

Foxx knew how to do that. On his mayoral watch, he significantly improved the conditions of his old high-school neighborhood. "We put a business park in the West Corridor near Johnson C. Smith [University]," he said. "It's actually bringing jobs into that area, [which] has been historically depressed." Moreover, "we passed the most significant neighborhood improvement bonds—many of which went into the west and the east side." In one area, McCorry Heights, where the residents "had been promised sidewalks fifty years before, and never got them," the city finally put in the sidewalks. It also "put the after-school programs on a competitive basis, on the theory that we needed to improve quality and improve access," said Foxx. The city increased funding for affordable housing and improved the transit system, too.

Foxx considers himself "a fire starter" on issues of equality and partly attributes his boldness to his experiences in desegregated schools. Before he and his childhood peers had "a chance to absorb all these societal impressions people have of various races," he said, they realized "you're people." The "whites and blacks, and others, whom I went to school with in those years, are certainly more well-rounded and understand American culture in a more true light than most of us do": "Black kids like me, we saw whites as our counterparts. . . . Your parents may have had a huge disparity in what they were making, but in classes, we were all just there. It was as equal a position as I've been in in anytime of my life, even since."

———

Foxx is not the only fire-starter in Charlotte who is used to seeing blacks and whites working together as equals. A racially diverse coalition of leaders from business, education, housing, faith, and philanthropic communities, as well as local policymakers, have united to reverse the tide of segregation. Their effort is the result of the Charlotte-Mecklenburg Opportunity Task Force, a group of twenty community leaders who spent 2015 and 2016 working to devise a new plan to expand access to opportunity-rich neighborhoods for all children. They consulted with fifty national, regional, and local experts on the best ways to break down the barriers to economic mobility in the city. James Ford, an educational consultant who was named North Carolina Teacher of the Year for 2014–2015, and who cochairs the task force, explained how "at the inception of our work we viewed it as a multigenerational problem—and we developed solutions in like manner."[59]

The coalition's evidenced-based advocacy helped launch a number of initiatives in 2016: expanded access to quality child care and pre-K, with the pre-K program anticipated to reach more than 6,500 children by its sixth year; a $20.8 million project funded by the city's Housing Trust Fund to build five new affordable housing developments in Charlotte; a new community strategy on economic mobility with a $16.4 million investment from United Way of Central Carolinas; and funding commitments by leaders such as Brian Moynihan, the CEO of Bank of America, to allow thirty-six Charlotte nonprofits, including Communities in Schools and the Charlotte-Mecklenburg Housing Partnership, to increase economic mobility among the area's black residents.

Admittedly, there is much work yet to be done, as some in Charlotte do not want to revive the city's successful experiment with integration. But the city's grassroots coalition of leaders embodies the type of intersectional integration mission work that is essential for social change and shared prosperity. Yes, when it comes to school desegregation, the city has backslidden, as has much of the nation. But integration remains a dream we can recover if we are willing to fight hard enough for it.

··8··

THE BATTLE OF JEFFERSON COUNTY

Segregation now, segregation tomorrow, segregation forever.

—GEORGE WALLACE, GOVERNOR OF ALABAMA, 1963

TWO WHITE MEN IN SUITS FACED OFF IN FRONT OF THE SWINGING double door to a university gymnasium. A lectern divided them. Armed guards stood ready. Two black students waited in the wings for this nightmarish show of force to end. Their wish? To register for classes that they might be part of a new day for Alabama. But the man blocking the doors, Governor George Wallace, seemed more interested in returning his state to the days of cotton fields. The standoff would come to represent Alabama's deep, and seemingly intractable, resistance to integration.

Today, perhaps the most pernicious export in Cotton Country is not a product stemming from black degradation—it is a tool for it. When North Carolina passed House Bill 514 in June 2018, and allowed wealthy, predominantly white suburbs to secede from the Charlotte-Mecklenburg schools, it seemed they were wielding a new blade. But segregationists in Alabama have been using the tactic of secession for at least seven decades.

To understand one of integration's strongest and oldest foes, we must travel to two Jefferson Counties, the first being in Alabama.

There, we will also uncover the many harms not just of segregation, but of *resegregation*. And we will explore the promise held by new innovations in integration that may have the power to overcome threats new and old, enabling districts around the country to rekindle the familiar, faltering flame first ignited in *Brown*.

———

JUST BEYOND THE city limits of Birmingham lie some of the wealthiest suburbs in Alabama. The schools in these suburbs frequently make it onto national best-schools lists, even as Birmingham includes some of the worst. The 1971 case *Stout v. Jefferson County Board of Education* resulted in a court order that addressed these disparities by demanding the integration of Jefferson County. The man who argued that case was U. W. Clemon, who, as Alabama's first black judge, worked to protect that progress from constitutional encroachment for nearly three decades.[1]

Clemon retired in early 2009, but for the past two years he has been back in court rearguing *Stout*, the same case he won nearly half a century ago. The case returned after a middle-class Birmingham suburb called Gardendale sought to leave the Jefferson County school system and control its own schools.

Gardendale is not unique in its pursuit of "local control." Municipalities in states as liberal as New York and California have sought to form their own school districts by seceding from larger ones. Yet much like the antibusing movement that preceded it, the local control movement uses coded language and seemingly commonsense arguments to achieve fundamentally corrosive goals.

The districts seeking to assert local control via secession today all have their reasons, some of which sound reasonable enough. But since the days of Jim Crow, Clemon has watched waves of Jefferson County segregationists employ such tactics repeatedly, vigorously, and successfully. And he wants to be absolutely sure they don't win again.[2]

AL LINGO. GEORGE Wallace. Bull Connor. It is no accident that three of the most notorious segregationists in American history come from Alabama. Nor is it happenstance that Alabama was the site of the 16th Street Baptist Church bombing, which was designed in part to terminate, via terror, the integration efforts of the Armstrong family. Segregationists in Alabama have proven themselves fanatically devoted to their cause. But while the three mentioned above used demonstrations of force, other segregationists used subtler means to achieve their ends. In the wake of *Brown v. Board of Education*, they uncovered a tool that would not only slow integration, but reverse it, opening the floodgates of resegregation.

Just as integrationists leaned on a brilliant revitalization of the Fourteenth Amendment, Alabama's segregationists looked to a legal provision in the state code that had existed long before integration. Under a 1903 statute, cities in Alabama "with more than 5,000 residents . . . can secede from their county school districts by negotiating an agreement with the county district," and once "a new city school district is formed," taxes paid by its citizens, and property contained within its borders, "will automatically go to the new city school district." Separation, money, and property—what more could a segregationist ask for? With this statute at the ready, after *Brown*, Alabama witnessed a steady exodus of wealthy, white communities from school districts.[3]

The 1974 case *Milliken v. Bradley*, which forbade inter-district desegregation remedies absent a showing of segregation on the books in both districts, only sped up the transition. Since *Milliken*, to escape a desegregation decree, parents need only successfully petition for their communities to become part of newly created "districts." That these new districts are often far whiter and wealthier than the districts they escape is often irrelevant and ignored.[4]

To be fair, segregation may not be the only goal of secessionists. Rebecca Sibilia, the CEO of EdBuild, a nonprofit shining a light on regressive education funding structures, calls *Milliken* "the single most damaging Supreme Court decision" not just for integration, but for educational equity. She believes many communities seek to control their schools because they know districts that pay more property taxes have more school funding. If *Milliken* provides the legal cover for segregation, she says, "the way we fund schools creates the incentive." At the same time, she adds that "you can't fault a community for wanting to provide for their own."[5]

The dual, and related, desires of secessionists—to segregate and to hoard resources—can be seen most plainly in Jefferson County, Alabama. Today the county is carved into about a dozen school districts. Segregationists erected new school district borders against integration as early as 1959, and they have continued the practice in city school district after city school district, from Mountain Brook to Vestavia Hills to Homewood to Hoover to Trussville. Each district is substantially whiter, on average, than Jefferson County (which is about half white). Two districts are approximately 85 percent white, and one (Mountain Brook) is 98.7 percent white. These five districts share another distinction. Out of the 129 Alabama districts ranked in terms of reading, math, and science test scores, each of these post-*Brown* secession cases is ranked in the top ten. Four are in the top five. Finally, like districts in other wealthy communities, they generally spend more per pupil than the state average.[6]

But the staggering whiteness, wealth, and academic success of these split-off "city districts" is only half the story of Jefferson County. Five of the county's school districts are ranked among Alabama's 20 *worst* school districts. Each has a disproportionately low white population, and in 4 of these districts, *less than 4 percent* of the students are white. Among these, Birmingham, which serves over 30,000 students and is the second-biggest district in the county, is 1.1 percent white and ranks 112th out of the 129 districts.[7]

A 2016 EdBuild report found that the border around Birmingham (which separates it from Vestavia and Mountain Brook—the two highest-performing districts in the state) was the second most segregating border in the entire country. On one side, the poverty rate is below 7 percent, median property values are above $339,000, and median household income is above $81,000. On the other, nearly *half* of the citizens are in poverty, median property values are below $87,000, and median household income is a staggeringly low $31,217. To cross into Birmingham is to plunge into an educational ravine. And similar ravines are popping up across the country.[8]

Another EdBuild report noted that, since 2000, segregationists have formed 47 breakaway districts and are working to form 9 more. Twenty-nine other states besides Alabama now have "explicit secession policies" codified in law, and "only nine require a study of the funding impact of a proposed split," according to EdBuild, while "just six require consideration of the effects on racial and socioeconomic diversity and equality of opportunity for groups of students." And unlike during the Civil War, not all secession is in the South. In the San Francisco Bay Area, a wealthy suburb called Northgate has spent several years trying to separate from the Mt. Diablo Unified School District. Northgate's median income is $126,000, about $50,000 higher than Mt. Diablo's. If Northgate breaks away, it will be 65 percent white and only 8 percent Latino, a far cry from the district as a whole, which is 32 percent white and 42 percent Latino.[9]

The authors of the EdBuild report noted that these secessions are hugely deleterious to students. They warn that a "splintered school system of haves and have-nots today lays the groundwork for a fractured society in the future." "We are deluding ourselves," they continued, "if we believe that we can maintain a fair and inclusive culture without putting in the collective effort to support the education of our most vulnerable students—and if we don't unify around that goal, we will surely fail to realize a society in which all children may reach their full potential."[10]

Against this backdrop, yet another community seeks to secede from Jefferson County. At the center of the fight is a rare commodity in cash-strapped Alabama. The district, and the parents hoping to secede, are locked in a tug-of-war to determine who will control a $55 million school building.

———

ONCE THE SITE of a jug factory and a coal mine, Gardendale retains vestiges of a blue-collar past. Its median household income is $60,000, and though some live comfortably, not all are wealthy. But Gardendale is 88 percent white. And in the fall of 2013, the town decided it was going to split from the county school system, holding a vote on a new property tax that would serve as a referendum on secession.

Right before the tax vote, an advertisement appeared in the *North Jefferson News* that made the racial subtext plain. Above a picture of a white girl was a question: "Which path will Gardendale choose?" The ad listed "Places that chose NOT to form and support their own school system," including Center Point, Pleasant Grove, and Hueytown, all of which are majority black. It also listed districts that had already seceded from Jefferson County, which were some of the "best places to live in the country": Homewood, Hoover, Vestavia, and Trussville. These districts are indeed very good, but they are also very white.

Like the secession measures of other Jefferson County "city districts," the property tax measure passed, and the following spring, Gardendale formed its own board of education. For the position of superintendent, the city council hired Dr. Patrick M. Martin, a young administrator who had run a school district in Central Illinois.

The Gardendale school system prepared to open in the fall of 2014. Jefferson County, however, proved less willing to go through with the divorce. There was the $55 million high school that had just been built, and there was the *Stout* desegregation order, which the county argued would be hurt by Gardendale pulling away so many white students. Gardendale, for its part, tried to avoid arguments about race, which it must have known it could not win. It claimed instead a basic American right, which is the right to be left alone.

The separation seemed to be moving forward until the spring of 2014, when Jefferson County asked Gardendale for $33.1 million to compensate for the loss of its new high school. Gardendale appealed to the state superintendent of schools, who said in February 2015 that Gardendale owed only $8 million. The dispute entered the courts the following month, when Jefferson County filed a motion that went to US District Court Judge Madeline H. Haikala, who oversees the *Stout* integration order.

The county argued that every secession had left its district poorer and less diverse. "In Jefferson County, splinter districts have historically been predominantly Caucasian and comparatively affluent," wrote the lead Jefferson County attorney. "They are widely perceived as offering a superior public education experience and are magnets for families who can afford to pay the 'tuition' represented by comparatively high property values."

Although it was under an integration order, Gardendale High School was only about 27 percent black, while the county was 43 percent black. Still, Gardendale was one of the few schools in the county that afforded minority students the opportunity to transfer into a majority-white high school. The student body at Gardendale High included 26 of these "racial desegregation transfer" students, which amounted to 10 percent of its black population. Meanwhile, approximately 150 black students from across the county took classes in the school's vocational facilities.

Under the new system, the exclusion of North Smithfield from Gardendale's schools would have the greatest demographic impact. The small, unincorporated community of North Smithfield sent about 130 black students to Gardendale schools, and would now be excluded, unlike two overwhelmingly white unincorporated areas, Mt. Olive and Brookside. As the fight with Jefferson County intensified, the newly formed Gardendale Board of Education decided to allow North Smithfield students to attend Gardendale schools after all—but did so without consulting with North Smithfield residents. And although the board permitted North Smithfield students to attend Gardendale schools indefinitely, North Smithfield would have no seats on Gardendale's board of education.

It became evident to black parents that Gardendale did not make this decision because it wanted the diversity the North Smithfield students would bring—indeed, the Gardendale board sought nothing more than the bare minimum necessary to comply with the *Stout* order. Parents of the few North Smithfield students who were granted slots were understandably wary of becoming unwanted guests of Gardendale's schools, uncertain whether their granted token stay would last about as long as the lip service paid to them. North Smithfield residents would have the ability to influence decisions and ensure that their inclusion was permanent only if they received a place on the board.

———

OF COURSE, IT is always easier to apportion blame than to find a solution. But maybe the blame is misplaced, to some degree. Try to see the resegregation debate from the point of view of a Gardendale parent. If racial equality is so important, then why are those wealthy over-the-mountain suburbs exempt from it? Is integration only the job of working-class whites? Shouldn't the suburbs that have the most— Mountain Brook, Vestavia Hills—be the ones required to share before those who have less? Thinking this way, a white parent in Gardendale is likely to reach a conclusion very similar to one reached by a black parent: *The system is overwhelmingly, crushingly unfair*.

Beyond the color line, segregation influenced access to equitable facilities. Few Jefferson County schools were multimillion-dollar edifices like the new $55 million Gardendale High School. Some schools in the poorer neighborhoods had invested little in renovations, and looked much like they had when they had been built fifty years before. About one-third of the blacks attended one of the six new high school buildings in Jefferson County, and if Gardendale seceded, their access to those schools would drop significantly. At Fultondale High School, just three miles away from Gardendale, paint didn't even cover the letter "N," a stain from the Jim Crow days when the school was the all-black New Castle High. But buildings weren't the only things that needed to be brought into the twenty-first century. In the building of creative minds, evidence demonstrated that Gardendale was increasing the reading and math proficiencies of its elementary-school black students. Such gains would likely be lost in a secession, along with a host of resources.[11]

The hearing reached its dramatic climax when Judge Haikala asked Patrick Martin, the Gardendale superintendent, if he'd ever read the 1954 *Brown v. Board of Education* ruling. Clearly surprised, Martin admitted that he had not read the Supreme Court decision "in its entirety," though he correctly identified the school district in question as being in Topeka, Kansas.

"I can't remember if it was Thurgood Marshall or who that argued that case," Martin said.

Haikala asked about *Brown v. Board* to underscore that the case before her was not about a single high school, or even a single town. It was about a nation of free and equal persons, and whether that nation still committed itself to the ideals of freedom and equality.

In April 2017, Judge Haikala issued her ruling. While acknowledging her own concern that Gardendale's true motive was to refashion itself as a predominantly white city, she acceded to Gardendale's wishes by allowing for a separation that would begin at the elementary level and take place over three years. "The Court is giving the Gardendale Board of Education an opportunity to demonstrate good faith," Judge Haikala wrote.

Yet Clemon was undaunted. He had won the original *Stout* case, and in February 2018, his perseverance paid off once again. Seventy-two years after Clemon decided, at the age of thirteen, that he wanted to be a civil rights lawyer, he won yet another victory—this time, to protect the promise of the progress he had fought his entire career to achieve. In the Eleventh Circuit, Judge William Poyer reversed Judge Haikala's ruling, roundly rejecting her Solomonic approach.

"The district court found that the Gardendale Board acted with a discriminatory purpose to exclude black children from the proposed school system and, alternatively, that the secession of the Gardendale Board would impede the efforts of the Jefferson County Board to fulfill its desegregation obligations," he began. "Despite these findings," he continued, "the district court devised and permitted a partial secession that neither party requested." Judge Poyer, vexed by this inconsistency, "conclude[d] that the district court committed no clear error in its findings of a discriminatory purpose and of impeding the desegregation of the Jefferson County schools, but that it abused its discretion when it sua sponte allowed a partial secession."[12]

With Judge Poyer's strong words, the legal battle was won. Gardendale meant to segregate. Allowing Gardendale to secede would lead to segregation. But, given Jefferson County's obligation to *integrate*, Gardendale would be afforded no such opportunity. Yes, the legal battle was over. But the battle for the *soul* of Jefferson County remained. One question, raised repeatedly during the trial, yet lingered. Was the resegregation that Gardendale sought, and that five districts before had realized, truly harmful?

———

FORTUNATELY, WE DO not have to guess what the impacts of resegregation are. History has given us a way to find the answer. The vast majority of school desegregation was achieved through court orders. Peak integration was reached in the late 1980s, when almost 45 percent of black students were attending majority-white schools. By that point, roughly 1,100 school districts had been subject to court-ordered desegregation, but some of that desegregation also resulted from pressure applied by the US Department of Health, Education, and Welfare. Since the early 1990s, a host of districts have sought—and been granted—unitary status, which released them from federal oversight. More than one-half of all districts that were ever under

FIGURE 8.1

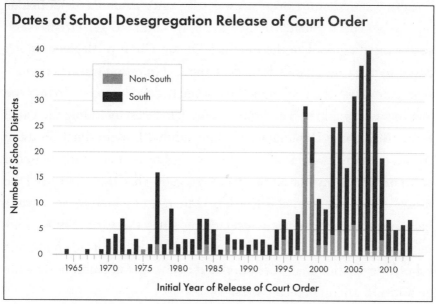

Dates of School Desegregation Release of Court Order

court-ordered desegregation have been released from court oversight, with more than 200 districts released from court orders between 1991 and 2013 (see Figure 8.1). Immediately following the release of court orders, students are often reassigned to neighborhood schools. Districts then experience sharp rises in school segregation by both race and poverty. In the districts that have been released from desegregation court orders since 1990, more than half of the black students now attend racially isolated schools (i.e., schools in which more than 90 percent of the students are members of minority groups), nearly double the percentage when busing began.[13]

Why does resegregation harm students of color? For one thing, it depletes the teaching corps of its most capable members. The racial and socioeconomic composition of schools significantly influences this factor, because concentrated-poverty, majority-minority schools are significantly less able than wealthier, whiter districts to successfully recruit and retain the highest-quality teachers. As the student composition of a school becomes more heavily minority and poor, the most qualified teachers tend to transfer to other schools.[14]

By the early 1990s, judges had become wary of maintaining politically charged court orders, especially since evidence demonstrating the beneficial impacts of integration was limited. That trend made
secession attempts like the one in Jefferson County, Alabama, much
easier to carry out than before. Still, the real question was whether resegregation was the malicious force some believed it to be. To find the
answer, we combined data from several databases, including the Panel
Study of Income Dynamics and the National Longitudinal Study of
Adolescent to Adult Health. But instead of using the timing of initial
court orders (as my first study on desegregation had done), we used the
timing of *releases* from court orders. The rate at which these releases
have been issued has been accelerating since the early 1990s. This
method allowed us to isolate the impacts of policy-induced changes in
school segregation that were unrelated to changes in childhood family
factors and other characteristics.

We found that, for minority children, increases in school segregation (following court-order releases) led to worse educational outcomes, but these were offset in large part by the beneficial effects of
increases in school spending. In the longer run, however, the exodus
of a district's high-quality teachers from schools with concentrated
poverty to more affluent ones (coupled with the high degree of teacher
turnover in economically disadvantaged minority schools) erodes
achievement gains for minority children.

Leading up to the release of court orders, the likelihood of African American children graduating from high school increased by
3 percentage points with each additional school-age year of exposure
to desegregation. This improvement came to an abrupt halt after
districts were released from court orders. For black students, a 15
percent increase in school segregation experienced in half of one's
school-age years resulted in 0.25 fewer years of completed education,
which was offset by the beneficial effects of a 5 percent increase in
school district spending (experienced, again, in half of one's school-
age years). Similarly, for blacks, a 15 percent increase in school segregation experienced in half of one's school-age years resulted in a

decline of 7 percentage points in the likelihood of attending college. This decrease, however, was offset in part by the fact that a 5 percent increase in school spending experienced in half of one's school-age years led to an increase of 5 percentage points in the likelihood of attending college.

Adult earnings are similarly affected by resegregation. For African Americans, a 15 percent increase in school segregation experienced in half of one's school-age years was associated with a 7 percent reduction in adult wages. This negative effect of increased school segregation experienced for half of one's school-age years was offset by the impact of a 5 percent increase in school spending, which led to a 5 percent increase in wages.

In addition, a 15 percent increase in school segregation experienced in half of one's school-age years resulted in an increase of 4 percentage points in the likelihood of being arrested, an increase of 2 percentage points in the likelihood of being convicted of a crime in adulthood, and an increase of 3.5 percentage points in the likelihood of being incarcerated.

What about white children? If integration broadens their horizons, a countervailing movement necessarily has the opposite effect. Whites who were not exposed to diverse schools during their K-12 years were more likely to have no racial diversity among their friends in adulthood, to live in neighborhoods in adulthood without racial diversity, to express significantly stronger preferences for same-race partners, and to be significantly less likely to ever have been in an interracial relationship. Whites who were not exposed to diversity in schools as children expressed significantly more conservative political views in adulthood. Taken together, the results show that, for whites, greater school-age exposure to more diverse school environments (particularly beginning in the elementary school years) leads to greater racial tolerance, more diverse friendship networks in adulthood, and more progressive political views (as self-reported). The social integration aspect of schools and exposure to peers of different races has long-term consequences. Over the past three decades, there has been significant growth in jobs requiring high levels of social interaction—particularly in terms of the ability to work on diverse teams. Those holding such jobs earn higher wages, on average, than those holding jobs where relating to people of different backgrounds matters less. Social skills in the workplace are becoming increasingly more valuable and necessary than in the past.[15]

This evidence also strongly supports a long line of social science research on the "contact hypothesis," which proposes that interpersonal peer contact can reduce prejudice, increase racial tolerance, and influence an individual's values. Dr. Martin Luther King Jr. poignantly described the hypothesis this way: "People fail to get along because they fear each other; they fear each other because they don't know each other; they don't know each other because they have not communicated with each other." Nowhere is the potential greater to foster racial harmony and be enriched by diversity than in our public schools, beginning in the earliest grades. But the longer the exposure, the better: when contact is only temporary, one may have just enough contact to see the differences, but not enough to appreciate the similarities. A clear message emerges from both our quantitative analyses and our qualitative interviews: exposure to diversity in grade school significantly impacts one's outlook on race. Socioeconomic status colors perspectives on race as well.[16]

Moving from desegregation to integration means moving from access to inclusion, and moving from exposure to understanding. The results of our studies underscore that integration is a not a zero-sum game. Segregation may appear to be good for the individual, but it is not good for society as a whole. In fact, it is a type of market failure.

But this focus on the negative outcomes of resegregation misses a key point. It is not simply that resegregation portends a loss of opportunity, mobility, and unity. It is that integration has the power to transform communities, and society, in ways we have only begun to realize.

We must therefore resist the temptation to settle at halting resegregation, as the Eleventh Circuit did. We must ask for more: we must revive the dream, and bring together the people whom redlining, white flight, secession statutes, conservative Supreme Court precedent, gentrification, and other social forces would keep apart. But how?

To answer that question, we must travel four hundred miles due north from Jefferson County to another, very different Jefferson County.

———

TWO DECADES AFTER *Brown*, more than 90 percent of the students in Louisville's city schools were black. Roughly the same proportion of students in the neighboring suburban schools of Jefferson County were white. One black student, Pamela Smith, recalled the unequal learning opportunities in her all-black school during those pre-integration years, saying, "We would read about science experiments, what was supposed to happen. But we didn't actually get to see it because we didn't have working Bunsen burners or chemicals to do experiments with. We had to get the same information without the same resources."[17]

As was the case for many other districts, only a court order would compel Jefferson County Public Schools (JCPS) to integrate with Louisville's urban district. Immediately after the gavel sounded in the fall of 1975, the southern metropolitan district retorted with the same vitriolic resistance that befell Boston, Birmingham, and Little Rock. Bricks were hurled at buses carrying courageous children. Rioters set fires amid protests against the influx of not only students, but also teachers. One unique aspect of the court's mandate was that both students *and* teachers of Louisville's predominantly black urban school district were required to merge with the surrounding suburban district of Jefferson County. The Louisville–Jefferson County consolidation stood in stark contrast to Alabama's Jefferson County secession efforts.[18]

Louisville's initial heated resistance to the court mandate would, in time, simmer down, giving way to a process of integration that took hold in the 1980s. A small chorus of supporters grew into a broad, diverse coalition for integration. Early proponents of integration held that "belief can come after the mandate," and that the dissenters would convert after seeing their children experience the benefits. In Louisville, these hopes appeared to be realized, and by the 1990s Louisville had one of the most integrated school systems in the nation. It also was sustained longer than in almost any other district in the nation.[19]

But 2007 proved a turning point. In that year, the Supreme Court ruled, in *Parents Involved in Community Schools v. Seattle School District No. 1*, that it was unconstitutional for race to be the sole factor in student assignment plans to achieve school diversity. Chief Justice John Roberts wrote, "The way to stop discriminating on the basis of race is to stop discriminating on the basis of race."[20]

Louisville–Jefferson County's superintendent, Dr. Sheldon Berman, arrived that same year, inheriting what he called "one of the best integrated systems" in the country. Berman wanted to preserve the promise of integration in Louisville in spite of the Supreme Court decision. He committed to integration, resisting mounting legal and political pressures to succumb to resegregation. Inspired by his family history, he recalled that his father, a Holocaust survivor, had been "welcomed into the home of a Polish farmer and protected from the Nazis for almost two years." He remarked: "When it comes to protecting each other, ensuring each other's safety and well-being, confronting injustice and surviving oppression, we all depend on one another—we are all in this together." For these reasons and more, Berman understood the importance of diversity and access to equitable resources.[21]

This bold, principled stance met with no small amount of dissension. In our conversation with him, a reflective Berman shared that, "In Louisville, there remain deep-seated beliefs about community, and about who should be a part of that community, that go back a long way." Berman recalled that the residents who opposed integration cited two main reasons: first, they "want[ed] their children to be in neighborhood schools," he said. "That's why they chose that home in [that] neighborhood—they do not want to consider their child going to school across town, as it is an inconvenience." And second, he added, some people simply "do not value desegregation. They see it as representing no gain for them, but rather represents compromises they have to endure for the benefit of others."

In private, candid conversations with parents, Berman most often heard sentiments like, "I don't want my kids with those kids from the inner city. They bring drugs and crime into our schools, [and my kids] will be exposed to bad things and learn bad habits." He added that many people espoused the viewpoint that, "I want my schools to be *my* schools—neighborhood schools. I don't like the government messing around doing 'social engineering.'" Berman recounted, "We heard a lot about social engineering, [which] in my estimation is a code word for a race policy." In a concerned tone, Berman said, "There is deep-seated racism—institutional racism—that is a part of the cycle we see in this opposition to integration."

Despite the constant political battles and litigation, "We had very strong support from several communities—west Louisville was very supportive, [and] in the Highlands the Jewish community was very supportive of desegregation," Berman recalled. Given the legal advent of *Parents Involved*, the district needed to partner with the community that still believed in integration, because "there was no longer a court order that would impose integration," he said. "If [integration] happened, it would happen as a result of a mass community's voluntary adoption of an integration plan." It would only happen because the people wanted it and pursued it together.

There was a sliver of hope written into the Supreme Court decision, wherein school districts could use other factors to achieve diversity in their schools. Berman set about designing a new approach to integration that focused on both socioeconomic diversity and racial/ethnic composition to ensure access to high-quality schools for all students. Rather than divorcing quality from the school climate and diversity of its schools, this approach treated them as inseparable, aiming for more equitable distributions of curricular offerings and student-family backgrounds. This approach countered narrow racialized ideas about what makes a school great. "We wanted to give students in the West End, which was predominately African American, the opportunity to be in the best schools in the district," said Berman. That thrilled the West End community, and many of them exclaimed to Berman, "You're finally opening up the premier schools of the district to be desegregated." Berman added, "We believed that the entire district will become high performing and that it will benefit everyone. In fact, whether academically or socially, we are one community, we support each other, and this is the best way to build a cohesive democratic community."

To accomplish the district's new student-assignment plan, Berman enlisted the help of national experts, including John Powell from the University of California, Berkeley, and Gary Orfield from the University of California, Los Angeles, as well as leaders from other districts. An advisory group was formed, and the district forged its new plan under intense fire from opposition groups, who continually tried to foil the district's attempts to retain school integration.

District leaders had learned from experience that their previous race-based approach to desegregation could result in schools that, while integrated well by race, were almost entirely composed of students from poor families. In the school where this had happened previously, students had struggled academically and exhibited behavior problems, and the school had been forced to reckon with teacher staffing issues.[22]

The new plan placed schools in geographic groups of diverse neighborhoods based on socioeconomic characteristics and racial/ethnic composition. District leaders implemented a transparent process in which parents were given the opportunity to list on an application their preferences for specific schools in their geographic grouping. Ultimately, to ensure families had greater options and control, the district accounted for both parental choice and diversity goals in the assignment of students to schools.[23]

The push for diversity succeeded because it was combined with choice. The district endeavored to shift away from a forced plan of equity and diversity to adopt a plan of choice that still embodied those values. Recognizing that segregated schools with high concentrations of poverty tend to offer fewer science, math, and college-prep classes, and less access to counselors, high-quality teachers, and state-of-the-art facilities, Berman and his team sought to address this problem head-on. They introduced more than twenty magnet schools, which became a major part of the shift toward choice and comprehensive school excellence. Berman wanted people to "see the advantage in the themes [of the magnet schools] for themselves." He felt that the first-rate curricular themes would cause those who were still reluctant to accept integration to "rise above" the kind of self-interest that typically resulted in people "separating themselves from populations they didn't want to interact with." The district created an International Baccalaureate elementary school, for example, and a leadership academy, among others. Berman identified Lincoln Elementary as an excellent example: "It's a school on the edge of downtown," he said. "It was virtually all black when we started, and we made it into an arts magnet" because of its location. "We invested $6 million in renovations, put together an outstanding program. . . . We brought in a new principal to lead the efforts and help recruit more high-quality teachers to the school. It was a successfully integrated school," he fondly recalled.

In order to provide economic incentives for neighborhoods to become more diverse, superintendent Berman and his team elected to offer three exemptions to their school integration plan. One was for families already living in integrated neighborhoods that met the racial diversity goals established in the original court order. Another was for black families who moved to predominantly white neighborhoods using public housing vouchers. The third was for families living in neighborhoods that eventually evolved into integrated areas. This component of the policy was devised in consultation with national education equity and housing policy experts.[24]

The city-suburban comprehensive desegregation plan was bolstered by the fact that residential segregation had declined by more than 20 percent since 1990, in contrast to many other urban cities that have seen increases in housing segregation. It is important to note that the reduction in residential segregation witnessed in Louisville over this time period may also be in part both a cause and a consequence of a sustained, enduring commitment to integration in the community.

Establishing a new direction and new policies for the schools represented only half of the effort required to make the district-wide overhaul successful. Berman and his staff strove to ensure that families understood the benefits of integration, were aware of the educational resources that would now be available, and knew how to avail themselves of the new opportunities for their children. The district needed to form a coalition that would build public support for voluntary integration efforts. An informational campaign that incorporated human capital, financial resources, and media relations would help to show the public that integration could be an asset.

Berman reminisced with pride about how they "put together a powerful argument, collected the experts, leaders in the field, people who could be very articulate"—not only about the vision but about how it could be realized through the multipronged set of programs the district developed. He added, "The district [had] a wealth of resources: a research department with twenty-two people, a media [and] public relations department. We had television stations, three people who dealt with crises on a regular basis, writers, photographers. . . . It was an extraordinary group."

Following the decision of *Parents Involved*, the district distributed a "No Retreat" brochure to all parents. It aimed to express the district's unwavering commitment to integration. "We also developed another set of brochures that outlined our two-pronged approach to upgrade the district," Berman said. The brochures defended integration as an advantage for everyone and advertised the district's "highly attractive magnet schools," Berman said. These schools would "represent a more diverse population that would bring people together around a common theme." Berman explained that "we had a communications campaign and distributed media materials to counteract the incorrect perception that integration compromises student achievement." These documents also informed parents that what was needed was for "students to be equipped to function in a multiracial world," Berman said, "and the best way for students to learn to do that [was] for schools to be integrated, both racially and socioeconomically." The district told parents that it would be pursuing "schools that support student learning, student interactions and understanding, that broaden their interactions and their horizons," Berman said with a timbre of hope.

According to Berman, "students were our strongest advocates of integrated schools." They powerfully conveyed how much they "appreciated [integration] and how it enabled them to have friends from different cultures, from different experiences. . . . They felt it was advantageous. They understood the importance better than the adults." Whites and blacks alike who had grown up in Louisville's integrated environment rallied around grassroots efforts, forming advocacy groups that vocally endorsed the benefits of integration. This grassroots community even attended congressional hearings on school integration to provide testimonials of the ways in which their experiences in integrated schools had enhanced their critical thinking skills and broadened their perspectives.

Yet even though the district took great strides to communicate the value of integration, not everyone was pleased. Berman saw, in hindsight, that "one of the mistakes we made was not to hire an external public relations consultant," who could ensure that the message on the benefits of integration got distributed to everyone in the most effective way. "We spoke to the professionals, the leaders of the community who were behind us to some degree," he said, "but we didn't get to the heart and soul of the dissenters. We needed to pay much closer attention to the people living on the outskirts of Louisville who cared about their kids and had no understanding of why they had to be bused to a different school rather than attend the one just two miles away." This included a much more conservative-leaning political group that was more concentrated in the county areas both east of and south of Louisville.

Politically, Louisville is a blue area within a red state; it is aligned more with the North than the South. In Berman's words, "We're really a midwestern city in a southern state, but if you go to the hills of eastern Kentucky, now that's a southern state. There was real political tension there that remains." From our discussions with Berman, along with our own analyses, it became evident that the planners had done a good job of anticipating the educational issues, and had implemented some effective policy solutions—which were later demonstrated in improved learning outcomes—but that the political differences had tripped them up.

In direct opposition to the effort to establish socioeconomic school integration, in both 2011 and 2012 the Kentucky Legislature attempted to pass state laws that would have ended school busing programs. Congress was not the only place where power was surreptitiously, or overtly, used to further a segregation agenda. In 2015, the real estate businessman and legislator Hal Heiner announced a run for mayor. Central to his platform was a rebuttal to the desegregation plan. Heiner did not succeed, but his ideas persisted, and a bill that was put forth to mandate neighborhood schools across the state became the platform for another gubernatorial candidate's run for office. As argued in a 2016 Century Foundation report on school integration, "Desegregation is about shifting and restructuring concentrations of power that too often correlate with wealth and white skin, not solely about bringing together children who look different from one another."[25]

Berman remembered, "We had a lawsuit filed against our desegregation plan every single year I was there. We were in court over and over and over again." Few districts in the country made the same strides toward diversity and equity, and even fewer retained any significant amount of success compared to Louisville. One of the ones that did was Wake County, North Carolina. Berman and the Wake County superintendent were allies. When Louisville was targeted by opposition groups in the region, Berman said, "Wake County stood as a pillar of defense. We could always say, 'Look, they're doing it.'"

However, according to Berman, "*The most significant event* [directly affecting Louisville's integration efforts] was the election of four or five board members in Wake County—which had a socioeconomic integration plan that was a model we used." The Wake County plan and those who had developed it "had a lot of strength," Berman said, "[and] a great reputation." But immediately following the election of the new Wake County school board members, the board dismantled the plan. The superintendent subsequently resigned in protest, and a new superintendent, Donna Hargens, was appointed. But what stood out to everybody in Louisville was that a really effective integrated school system had been eliminated by a conservative political force exerting extraordinary power under the auspices essentially of the Republican Party. This outcome subsequently empowered Hal Heiner, the president of the state senate, and others to launch more aggressive anti-integration efforts. They realized that through their own political force they could change what was happening in the Jefferson County–Louisville public schools. The developments that had occurred in Wake County with the dismantling of a successful integration plan "sent a ripple effect through [our] entire district," Berman said. Its aftermath changed the nature of the debate that went on there. "That was a trauma for us," he said in a dispirited tone.

Once Wake County's desegregation plan disintegrated, Louisville stood out as one of the last urban areas standing for integration, which put a target on its back and empowered the forces of the opposition. Louisville was endlessly embroiled in federal and state court during the years that followed *Parents Involved*.

With Louisville left to battle for diversity and equity alone, Berman sought allies at the federal level. He made a plea for help to then secretary of education Arne Duncan. Louisville needed just one visit, or even a verbal endorsement, to signal to those near and far that integration was the nation's choice for twenty-first-century education policy. Berman remembered, "We got a phone call that said we are really behind you and they were working on a statement. But it wasn't until six months after I left that they issued a guidance around this, 4.5 years *after Parents Involved*. They wanted to avoid it like the plague."

At a later date, Berman and his staff received an invitation to present their record to Secretary Duncan and his staff. "We made the case that the department needed to take a strong stance around this issue," Berman said, "that they needed to support the districts that were still attempting to retain a desegregated system." But, he continued, "it went over like a lead balloon. Had they articulated a supportive voice for the kinds of work we were doing, we would've had much greater support."

Suits filed against the school district around state laws centered their arguments on the right to neighborhood schools. These arguments lost in court, as Louisville had the support in federal local district court rulings in its favor, but there were collateral consequences. The litigation remained in the news constantly, and it kept the fight very present. Perhaps what was most harmful to future progress was the barrage of litigation that began to sway public opinion. Not having the explicit support of the US Department of Education in a public statement presented its own challenges. Berman said, "Frankly, I wanted Obama to come and speak in the community about how important our efforts were. They didn't have to take sides, but come and talk about the great work we're doing." But the president never visited, and the dissenters were gaining ground. An excerpt of Dr. Berman's letter to the president read as follows:

> We firmly believe our current plan has the capacity to serve as a model for other urban and metropolitan districts of various sizes. Indeed, given the burgeoning challenges that most districts face in addressing the intertwined legacy of racial injustice and multi-generational poverty, elements of this plan will likely be perceived as a potential bridge for crossing the river of underachievement and hopelessness that has claimed so many of our young people since *Brown*.
>
> I am requesting a meeting to explain our plan in more detail, to seek your administration's endorsement of our efforts, and to

discuss the possibility of financial support that would bolster our work and simultaneously enable us to assist other districts that want to expand or preserve diversity in their schools.

Some would say that the day for talking about high-quality, integrated schools has come and gone. We disagree. We believe integration is a *choice*—a choice we are honor-bound to keep struggling for, even as we acknowledge the sacrifices of those who came before us. Again in your words, "the time has come . . . to choose our better history." We look forward to the opportunity to meet with you and key members of your staff and to further explore the implications of our student assignment plan for the children of our nation's public schools. They are indeed the product of our work—and they deserve that better history.[26]

Arne Duncan would later express regret that he'd done little to address the resegregation of schools during his tenure serving as education secretary in the Obama administration, acknowledging, "I would give myself a low grade on that."[27]

While the educational challenges would have been formidable to address alone, what made work in Jefferson County Public Schools twice as difficult was the political turbulence that had to be overcome. Berman didn't get fired for the educational policy, but for the political landmines that surrounded them. He lamented, though, that losing his job had been a casualty of the integration and equity efforts he had led. Wistfully, he said, "Over time, had I been able to stay, I would've refined some of the magnets and built a much stronger integrated program around them." Ironically, it would be Donna Hargens, the superintendent in Wake County after its integration program had been cut, who was hired to replace Berman.

———

LOUISVILLE'S CHALLENGING YET successful socioeconomic integration programs offer a partial blueprint for how diversity in schools can be achieved. In Louisville, this included efforts to reduce class sizes; to improve the distribution of high-quality teachers, combined with professional development to ensure that all kids had access to good instruction; and to integrate system-wide curricular reforms beginning in the early elementary grades, so that early tracking would not undermine access. The district reassigned its best principals to the lower-performing schools in order to attract higher-quality teachers to the schools where they were most needed. Finally, prior to Berman's appointment as superintendent, there were no nurses in the schools, particularly in low-income areas where students didn't have access to health care, and the absentee rate was extraordinarily high. To combat these health challenges, the district brought a nurse into every school, who would provide services not only to the kids, but also to the families. An internal study conducted by the district for the elementary schools showed that just having a nurse in the school improved attendance and student performance.

In 2011, Berman's last year as superintendent, close to 90 percent of the parents reported that they believed diversity in a school was desirable, and 87 percent were satisfied with the quality of their children's schools. As a sign of enthusiasm for integration, 42 percent of the parents had not chosen the closest school for their children. Those statistics were a stark contrast to the prevailing views from the 1970s, when nearly 98 percent of suburban parents were against integration.[28]

If the Jefferson County in Alabama were to emulate the Jefferson County in Kentucky, the urban school district in Birmingham would be combined with the county system, dissolving long-standing islands of privilege such as Mountain Brook and Vestavia Hills. Such a move, while challenging, would be feasible, and it could offer a new path forward for counties around the country.

———

THIS STORY OF two Jeffersons shows that segregation has mutated into secession—school districts breaking away from a larger district to avoid integration. This trend appeals to smaller local concerns over grander, more public ones. It asks parents, more and more, to see schools in the context of what they can achieve for their own children: *Education for all* is losing out to *Princeton for mine*.

But it also shows that integration has matured. In the face of legal barriers and new threats, champions for a connected society have found innovative ways to create a brighter future. The dream yet lives, so long as it can evolve.

How can we build on this new spark and breathe even more life into integration? To answer that question, we travel one last time, this time to study under the dogged crusaders of Grind City.

MEMPHIS CITY SCHOOL BLUES

Well, I don't know what will happen now. We've got some
difficult days ahead.

—DR. MARTIN LUTHER KING JR., FINAL SPEECH, APRIL 3, 1968,
MASON TEMPLE, MEMPHIS

THE FAMILIAR HEAT FLOWS THROUGH THE CLASSROOM WINDOWS,
signaling the end of the 2015–2016 school year at Booker T.
Washington High School, BTW for short, in Memphis, Tennessee.
Peering into one of those crowded classrooms, one can see rows of
students struggling earnestly to learn chemistry, each aware that an
end-of-year proficiency assessment looms. The previous year, only
half of the students in that class passed the test. This year, though,
one cannot help but predict a bleaker result. For this classroom lacks
something critical: a chemistry teacher. This has been the case for
most of the year. The previous teacher had left the challenges of BTW
behind to follow a promotion. But unlike the chemistry teacher, the
end-of-year assessment will come for these students. And every single
one of them, all sixty-five, will fail. Days later, BTW will make headlines—as the poster child for a failing education system.[1]

How quickly things change. In 2011, President Obama delivered BTW's commencement address before a still enchanted media
and a largely jubilant crowd that included Bill Haslam, Tennessee's

governor, and many state and local officials. They had all come to Memphis, and to BTW, to see the magical school that had increased its graduation rate from 55 percent to 82 percent in just four years. Obama deemed the moment "especially hopeful because some people say that schools like BTW just aren't supposed to succeed in America." "So that's why I came here today," he explained. "Because if success can happen here at Booker T. Washington, it can happen anywhere in Memphis. And if it can happen in Memphis, it can happen anywhere in Tennessee. And if it can happen anywhere in Tennessee, it can happen all across America."[2]

Obama painted a hopeful vision of education as a curative force primed to heal a society plagued by income inequality and racial prejudice. But five years later, even if nobody had taught BTW's chemistry students the properties of gases, they could tell Obama's vision for their school, and for Memphis, had ended up being little more than hot air whisked away by a local electorate and elected officials eager to regress to a state of two separate societies.

In this book, we have focused much on the role of the courts in promoting, and unwinding, the promise of integration. But the story of BTW, of Memphis, of Shelby County, and ultimately of Tennessee shows that we must focus not only on courts, but also on politicians and voters. In a way, this theme is nothing new. In Charlotte-Mecklenburg and Jefferson County, legislation empowered, and courts sanctioned, secessions that segregated North Carolina and Alabama even more deeply than they had been segregated before. We have already seen that no branch of government toils in isolation. But what happened to the students of BTW, and thousands more throughout Shelby County, evidences a new era of segregation empowered by political gamesmanship. If we hope to shelter, let alone nurture, integration, we must understand not only the legal arguments that grow from judicial antipathy to *Brown v. Board of Education*, but the tactics that flow from a burgeoning political will to undo its promise.

It is hard to think of a city more tragically instructive than Memphis: About promises made and promise squandered. About the disconnect between ideals and realities. About the ease with which we discard the former for the status quo. Above all, Memphis is a reminder of the lesson first taught by Kenneth Clark's doll study: segregation is a ruinous force, and it will gladly wreak havoc on individuals' psyches and on the fabric of our very society if we allow it to do so.

———

"I AIN'T SEEN cotton like that probably since I was a little girl," Dwania Kyles says. It was the autumn of 2017, and she was driving through Mississippi. For many years, she has lived in New York City, in Harlem, and she had not come back home to the South often. But now she was back, and the sight of the cotton fields confounded and beckoned her.[3]

"The way the sun was shining, and the way it looked silver, and it was cotton, and cotton, rows of cotton," Kyles remembers. Finally, she gestured to her companion to pull over. "I wanted to go pick some cotton. I wanted to go out in the fields."

Today, Kyles is an elegant woman in her early sixties with a life far removed from the cotton fields of the Deep South. But her roots are there, her story intimately tied to the effort, no more than half a century old, to integrate the schools of Memphis. She was a catalyst for its effort. She is also its product. Finally, she is a symbol of a promise of equal education that has been forgotten, at least in this western corner of Tennessee.

"I know where to start," Kyles says. When she speaks about the past, it is with great emotion. For this is not just a question of court orders and demographics. It is a question of longing—and belonging.

She starts with her parents. Her father, Samuel "Billy" Kyles, was a preacher. Her mother, Aurelia, was a dancer. They met in Chicago, but in 1959, Rev. Kyles got a job in Memphis, and the growing family moved down South. Up to that point, the home of the blues had not been a place of great educational promise for blacks. It had been explicitly segregated since its founding in 1848. As if to make the point as clear as possible, the header of one section of Memphis's original charter read, "Board to provide separate schools for white and colored pupils." In the 1960–1961 school year, a full six years after *Brown v. Board* had struck down the separate-but-equal doctrine, not a single one of the 44,812 black schoolchildren in Memphis had attended school with any of Memphis's 53,596 whites.[4]

By the early 1960s, however, African Americans were sufficiently emboldened to demand the integrated classrooms they had been promised. In 1960, the NAACP filed *Northcross v. Board of Education of Memphis City Schools*. Tennessee's system of "voluntary transfers" allowed blacks to *apply* to be in schools with whites, and also allowed districts like Memphis to deny those transfers out of hand. Not surprisingly, it yielded literally no integration, which, to the NAACP, seemed to counter the decree of *Brown* that de jure segregators like Memphis had an obligation to right their historical wrongs. After an initial defeat at the district court level, the NAACP appealed to the US Court of Appeals for the Sixth Circuit, whose judges did not come from Memphis and were willing to force intransigent southern cities to follow the law. For the first time in its history, the Memphis School District feared that it would have to end its long policy of segregation, and the NAACP knew it. So while the NAACP and the parents waited for a decision holding that the "voluntary transfer system" was inadequate, they decided to exploit the moment by showing that integration was nothing to be afraid of. Dozens of black parents applied to have their children accepted into white schools. These families were hand-picked not only for their willingness to avoid negative publicity, but also for another thing: having young children.

"We thought we would do something different," Rev. Billy Kyles, who was head of the NAACP's education committee, recalls, "and that is start with first grade. In all the other places, they started with high school. Our contention was that, no, those white high schoolers are already tainted. First graders? No, let's go with first grade." The image of the Little Rock Nine, who had been hounded on their way to Central High School, must have been especially haunting, doubly so because Little Rock was nearby. Having the work of integration done by younger children would, they hoped, prevent a similar paroxysm of violence in Memphis.[5]

Yet many parents were fearful of sending their little ones into a potential cauldron of hatred and even violence. That was how Billy Kyles's daughter, Dwania, ended up being part of the integration effort designed to pave the way for a grander shift: "We were a family on the front line," she remembers today. From the dozens that applied to attend white schools, only thirteen black children were admitted—including Dwania. Their meager forces were to be split up between three white schools.

The predictable resistance was quelled by an unlikely force. The police chief in Memphis at the time was Claude Armour. Billy Kyles vividly remembers how Armour described, and resolved, his inner conflict on the precipice of having thirteen black children attending white schools. "I'm a segregationist, I believe in segregation," he recalls Armour saying. "But I am the law and any policeman who can't go out there and protect these little nigra children, turn in your badge and your gun.'"[6]

Years later, Armour explained his thinking at the time to *Time* magazine, saying "I had to face the decision whether we were to have fear, strife and bloodshed or whether we were to enforce the law. I decided we would enforce the law and have peace, and that's what we have done." That was in contrast to other police chiefs across the South, most notably Bull Connor of Birmingham, who used any pretext, and sometimes none at all, to assail civil rights activists and throw them in jail, thereby hoping to discourage further efforts.[7]

Thanks in part to Armour's directive, that first day of school in September 1961 went smoothly. "The eight Negro girls and five boys were received as 'new pupils' by their white classmates in the first grade," the *Commercial Appeal* reported the following day. "They

"The Memphis 13": These students were the first to integrate the Memphis City Public Schools in 1961. Students' current names (not their names in 1961), and the schools they attended: Front row (left to right): Joyce Bell White (Rozelle); Harry Williams (Bruce); Deborah Ann Holt (Springdale); Clarence Williams (Rozelle); Dwania Kyles (Bruce); Alvin Freeman (Gordon). Back row (left to right): Leandrew Wiggins (Rozelle); Jacqueline Moore Christion (Springdale); Sheila Malone Conway (Gordon); Sharon Malone (Gordon); E. C. Freeman (Rozelle); Menelik Fombi (formerly Michael Willis) (Bruce). Not pictured: Pamela Mayes Evans (Gordon). (Photo courtesy of Daniel Kiel)

were welcomed upon their arrival as such by their homeroom teachers and were introduced to the class. During the day they joined the other children in drawing and other first-grade chores. At recess, they played Farmer-in-the Dell, Drop-the-Handkerchief and skipped rope on the school grounds, and at noontime they lunched with the other pupils."

But just because it was peaceful doesn't mean it was easy. Dwania Kyles explains how she was ostracized by both her white and black peers for attending an integrated school. "What was hard was, you go to school with kids that don't really like you because their parents say you're not supposed to like them," she says. "And then you go home to

First day of Memphis integration, September 1961. Left to right: Michael Willis (son of A. W. Willis), Harry Williams, and Dwania Kyles (daughter of Rev. Billy Kyles). (Photo credit: Withers Collection Museum and Gallery)

your neighborhood and the kids are like, 'Oh you think you're better than us 'cause you go to the white school.' So you get no relief.''

Dwania's experience on the vanguard of integration evidences an aspect of segregation well known by many blacks, but often misunderstood or missed by those who have not lived it. At six years old, Dwania had not yet developed what W. E. B. Du Bois termed the "dual consciousness"—the ability to exist in two racially and culturally separate societies, each with its own expectations and challenges. Arguably, no six-year-old should have to, as Du Bois put it, have "two souls, two thoughts, two unreconciled strivings; two warring ideals in one dark body, whose dogged strength alone keeps it from being torn asunder." And yet, that is precisely what segregation demands of blacks.[8]

Dwania's sacrifice was meant to help Memphis come one step closer to becoming a cohesive society where no person, let alone a child, need endure the challenges of cultivating a "double consciousness." It moved Armour to protect the "little nigra children," allowing for a peaceful transition to integration. It allowed photographers to capture images of adorable black children peering smilingly out of the back seats of cars headed for white schools—images suggesting brighter times ahead. And it led President John F. Kennedy to laud Memphis for an integration effort that, he said, "reflected credit on the United States throughout the world." Thanks to the sacrifice of thirteen little black children, Memphis was, at least for a moment, the pride of the nation.[9]

———

THE THIRTEEN BLACK first graders who attended just three white schools opened the hearts of many in Memphis to the prospect of integration. But thirteen youngsters alone certainly could not integrate all of Memphis's schools. And so, the year after Dwania stepped into an all-white school, the US Court of Appeals for the Sixth Circuit held that "the admission of thirteen Negro pupils . . . is not desegregation, nor is it the institution of a plan for a non-racial organization of the Memphis school system." In short, Memphis needed to do more to reverse the segregation written into its legislative DNA. But what, exactly? The Memphis School Board would do everything in its power to stall any answer and to ensure the court would ultimately set the bar laughably low. The final decision, which took effect in 1965, maintained an antiquated definition of an "integrated" school as one attended by at least one student of a different race. And yet, even by that deplorable standard, by 1966 there were only twenty "integrated" schools, which were attended by less than 3 percent of Memphis's black students.[10]

But this was only one of Memphis's jarring social problems. At the same time, workers throughout the city—black and white alike—were joining forces to advocate for economic justice. They were part of a broader multicultural effort led by Dr. Martin Luther King Jr. He was in the midst of his Poor People's Campaign, wondering why the nation was wasting billions of dollars bombing Vietnam when there were blocks upon blocks in cities around the country that looked as if they had been ravaged by an enemy force. Dwania Kyles was a preteen when Dr. King came to Memphis in the spring of 1968 to lend support to sanitation workers on strike.

On April 3, 1968, Dwania was at the church in Memphis where King would give what would turn out to be his final address. He alluded, near the end of the speech, to threats that had been leveled against him as he'd come to Memphis.

"Well, I don't know what will happen now," he said with tragic prescience. "We've got some difficult days ahead. But it really doesn't matter with me now, because I've been to the mountaintop. And I don't mind.

"Like anybody, I would like to live a long life. Longevity has its place. But I'm not concerned about that now. I just want to do God's will. And He's allowed me to go up to the mountain. And I've looked over. And I've seen the Promised Land. I may not get there with you. But I want you to know tonight, that we, as a people, will get to the Promised Land!"[11]

The following night, Dr. King was supposed to have dinner with Rev. Kyles, Dwania, and the whole Kyles family at their home. Rev. Kyles went to meet King and his delegation at the Lorraine Motel, a low-slung midcentury affair on the west side of town, near the Mississippi River. He and King spent an hour in room 306, engaged in what Rev. Kyles would later call "preacher talk." Shortly before 6:00 p.m., they went out to the balcony, intending to walk down to Kyles's borrowed Cadillac.

The party was lingering on the balcony of the Lorraine when a shot rang out. Dr. King dropped to the ground. Rev. Kyles later remembered the scene: "I thought I was having a nightmare, but the nightmare was that I was awake. And then we looked, and there was blood. So much blood."[12]

Dwania remembers the excitement of being at King's speech the previous night, the anticipation of awaiting his arrival at her home, the horror of learning that he'd been killed by an assassin. "Yeah, you got some scars behind some stuff like that," she says. Memphis would be similarly scarred, forever identified with the murder of the leader of the civil rights movement.

———

DR. KING'S DEATH would cast a shadow of racial enmity across Memphis that would confound all manner of civil rights efforts, from economic justice to integration. Gone were efforts that bridged racial divisions. The battle lines were drawn. In 1969, the NAACP staged a series of school walkout protests known as Black Mondays to highlight the lack of African Americans on the school board. The tactic had shifted from changing hearts and minds to wresting a modicum of power from Memphis's all-white, and increasingly combative, centers of political power and influence.

But even these efforts were stymied. "Ever since King's death eighteen months ago, his successors have tried to use the tactics of nonviolent mass actions he perfected to wring concessions from City Hall," *Newsweek* reported, lamenting that a recent effort at nonviolent protest had been frustrated when "teen-age black hooliganism and white resistance combined to confound their effort." *Newsweek* spoke with "a young Negro union official" who said that "Memphis has not changed since King's death. There seems to be a real attempt to undo some of the gains we've made."[13]

Efforts would come undone even more rapidly in the 1970s, after the Sixth Circuit demanded that Memphis begin busing students to achieve more rapid integration. Following the decision, a high-ranking Memphis school official predicted that "it would only be a matter of time until most of the areas of the city would be all black as the people move to adjoining communities and states to get out of what they would consider undesirable school situations." Indeed, Memphis became an increasingly poor and black city. Progressively, whites felt disconnected from their black neighbors in the wake of Dr. King's assassination, as did most Americans in the face of a busing decree. Busing was thus doomed to failure, "not because the court lost its will to demand it, but far more because the system ran out of whites to bus and predominantly white schools to which to bus black students."[14]

The shift was swift and thorough. In 1966, just over 50 percent of Memphis's schoolchildren were white. In the fall of 1973, as Memphis geared up for busing, whites represented 42 percent of the district's schoolchildren. During that first school year, more than twenty thousand white students would move to cities and suburbs in areas of Shelby County outside the city limits, or pay their way to attend private schools. In nine months, Memphis would lose nearly a third of its white students, and as a result, it would be left with a population that was only 32 percent white. In the years that followed, the share of Memphis students who were white would continue to plummet, all the way down to a low of 7 percent.[15]

Left behind in these turbulent Memphis schools were the black students who had given so much to integrate them. Unsurprisingly, Dwania Kyles does not remember her schooling in Memphis fondly. In fact, she wanted little to do with the city of her youth once she had the chance to leave it behind. "Once I graduated high school and went off to college, I really didn't come back to Memphis because I was ready to go away—and not understanding why until I got older, that I needed to heal," she says. "You know I had to be well into my late thirties or in my forties before I wanted to come back and participate in things that were going on with anything here in Memphis for the most part."

But the experience of being maligned as a black child attending white schools stayed with her. Kenneth and Mamie Clark had noted, in their doll study, that "color in a racist society was a very disturbing and traumatic component of an individual's sense of his own self-esteem and worth." Clearly, Kyles had carried the trauma of discrimination from Memphis to New York. "I had gone to New York to pursue a career in theater," she remembers, "but I did not like the auditioning process. And I was in my thirties before I figured out why. It made me feel like I was integrating a school all over again: to have mostly white people on the other side of the table telling me how I was supposed to act, telling me how I was supposed to be black."

Memphis's fight for integration was largely unsuccessful. Dwania's sacrifice, and that of twelve other black children in 1961 and hundreds more over the next five years, led to great loss and little gain: by 1966, only 3 percent of the city's blacks were attending integrated schools. The hard-fought busing plan of the 1970s was rendered impotent through a process of swift and massive white flight. And yet the champions of integration persisted.

They knew that the only barrier keeping many whites in Memphis, and around the state, from abandoning the integration project entirely was that they had to move, or go to private schools, in order to achieve their dishonorable discharges. And while many whites, like the twenty thousand who left Memphis in 1973, proved willing to make that trade, some of the others evidenced a willingness to brave integration rather than uproot themselves from their school communities.

But as we have seen, whites around the country would soon receive juridical permission to escape integrating school districts via secession—running away without going anywhere. As if able to see the future, Tennessee advocates for integration pushed for, and passed, a statute in 1982 that outlawed such secession. And for a time, the law, and the dim hope of integration, was protected against rescission by a Tennessee statehouse that was more purple than many gave it credit for. But all that would soon change.[16]

———

WHEN BARACK OBAMA came into office, he promised that "Yes We Can" would heal deep racial divisions. So it is not surprising that, in 2011, he traveled to Booker T. Washington High School (BTW), a school that, despite Memphis's white flight, had grown its graduation rate from 55 percent to 82 percent in just four years. It was as if he were pointing to BTW's new AP classes and improved school climate to say to Tennessee whites, "Come back! We can succeed together!"[17]

But before President Obama came to Memphis, powerful political forces aligned against him. Back in 2009, resistance to Obama had become known as the Tea Party, a term for a loosely affiliated coalition of conservative, libertarian, and, in a few cases, far-right groups. Some had concerns about his economic policies, others about his plans to reform the health-care system. What they shared, however, was a profound disdain for the man himself, and for everything his presidency represented: internationalism, multiculturalism, liberalism, and a willingness to take steps to overcome racial enmity.

Presidents are always expected to fare poorly in the midterm elections that take place two years into the first term. What Obama faced in 2010, however, was closer to a wave election. Democrats maintained control of the Senate, but Republicans won the House of Representatives. Less noticed, however, were their victories in statehouses around the country. These victories were powered by grassroots activists who were in turn funded by billionaires with a down-the-field vision of a conservative revolution. And while the schools of Memphis did not figure into their aims, those schools would nevertheless suffer from the rise of the Tea Party.

Several days after the election, the *Washington Post* deemed it a "GOP takeover in the states," noting that Republicans had picked up 675 seats in different legislatures nationwide. Now, the *Post* noted, Republicans fully controlled the legislatures and governorships in twenty-one states. Democrats were taken aback by the scope of their losses, while Republicans were ecstatic, aware that they had handed Obama a major defeat. Now, though, they would have to govern. "With hefty majorities in their state legislatures, Republican governors will now have the opportunity to show what they can do if they are in charge," the *Post* said. They were about to do just that.[18]

One of the states where Republicans had scored significant legislative victories in 2010 was Tennessee. Bill Haslam, a Republican, was voted in as governor, replacing Democrat Phil Bredesen, who had served two terms in Nashville (the Democratic candidate, Mike McWherter, finished with 33 percent of the vote to Haslam's

65 percent). Even more importantly, Republicans gained control of both chambers of the legislature, giving them immense power in Nashville. It was a power that was to be unchecked.

"Republicans gained control of the Tennessee Legislature and the governor's office for the first time since Reconstruction, and attained a majority in the state's Congressional delegation for the first time since 2002," reported the *New York Times*. Many whites who had wished to escape Memphis's integration plan in the 1970s had escaped to other areas of Shelby County. A generation later, all of the representatives that Shelby County sent to Nashville were white Republicans. The "flipping" of the Tennessee state government from blue to red would have a direct impact on Memphis schools, underscoring the powerful—if all-too-little discussed—relationship between voting and educational policy.[19]

———

THERE HAD BEEN tension between the school districts of Memphis and neighboring areas of Shelby County for years. This was not simply because many suburban residents of the county had intentionally fled Memphis to avoid integration. No, it was because the two had long been financially intertwined, and no amount of white flight could change the fact that the taxes of the urban residents of Memphis and the suburban Shelby County residents went into a pot enjoyed by students in both districts. Given the white flight of the 1970s, it may not be surprising that in the early 2010s, the median household income in other areas of Shelby County was more than double the median household income in Memphis. Thus, Shelby County residents paid more, per capita, to the school fund. That made the county's suburbanites feel like they were subsidizing the failing schools of Memphis without getting anything in return.[20]

Before the dust could even settle on the Republican drubbing in the Tennessee midterms, the Shelby County School Board, which was entirely white, began preparing to ask the state to confer upon it "special school district status," which would give the board "the authority to raise funds that would stay in just the suburban schools and potentially do away with the shared countywide property tax entirely." This would not quite be a divorce, since the districts were already separate. It was more like Shelby County's more suburban towns declaring that they no longer wanted to pay alimony to Memphis.[21]

There was only one problem. Three decades prior, advocates of integration had seen this coming, passing a law that outlawed the creation of these "special school districts." But this was 2010, not 1982. For the first time in decades, Republicans were on the verge of gaining unchecked power to roll back laws they didn't like without fearing either a legislative filibuster or a gubernatorial veto.[22]

Politicians and school officials in Memphis understood the looming threat of a full Shelby County split from the Memphis schools. They thus began considering one of the few moves available to them, a move at once counterintuitive and brazen: to ask Memphis voters to dissolve the school district entirely and *merge* with Shelby County. That way, Shelby County would have no way to escape its financial obligations to Memphis, since their schools would be one and the same.

Like the thirteen young black children who had integrated four Memphis schools in 1961, advocates moved swiftly and fearlessly. In December 2010, a month before the right-leaning legislature could begin its work, the Memphis School Board voted 5–4 to give voters a chance to dissolve the district. Like any 5–4 decision, this one evidenced real opposition to the audacious move, most notably by Memphis superintendent Kriner Cash, who called it "junior high street-fight nonsense." To Cash, the five who voted to dissolve were being too reactionary about the whispers they had heard that Shelby County would move to separate. "Now all of a sudden somebody heard somebody say something and you're ready to get revolutionary, radical," he said. He felt that relinquishing control of Memphis's schools to Shelby County would have unintended consequences, and told the five who voted to dissolve, "You've been running these schools for . . . the last 50 years. These are your schools. They are in the best hands now." He sounded much like those blacks who, at various points, have opposed integration fearing that black children will only be respected and nurtured if they are in black schools, with black principals and black teachers who care about black children.[23]

Some took exception to Cash's defense of the status quo, in which Memphis and the rest of Shelby County operated separate, parallel districts. One of these was board member Tomeka Hart, who told Cash, "My values don't allow me to put these babies in a system that is separate and inherently unequal," a poignant allusion to *Brown v. Board* and the doctrine it struck down.[24]

Both Cash and Hart were speaking deep truths. We have seen that black students are more likely to be selected for talented and gifted programs, and generally acknowledged for their abilities, when they have black teachers. Yet we have also seen that segregated systems predictably stifle their progress. Perhaps the two would have aligned had there been a third option—integration on equal terms with willing whites. But that solution had seemed impossible ever since a piercing gunshot had rung out on the steps of the Lorraine Motel in 1968.

Still, the final decision was not for the nine school board members to make, but for the citizens of Memphis. The issue remained contentious and created odd bedfellows among opponents of the merger, who included suburban Shelby County residents, Republican state lawmakers, a Memphis teachers' union, and several of the city's black ministers. Their motivations could not have been more different, but their interests were nonetheless aligned. They preferred the present separation to whatever might be on the horizon after a merger. On the other side, everyday Memphis parents sought something—a dream once promised and long deferred—for their children. The system was segregated, and it would only grow more so if something was not done. Sure, Booker T. Washington and other schools were seeing real progress under Cash, but no AP program could undo the stigma of being in a society divided. Months later, the citizens of Memphis voted by a 2-to-1 margin to merge their schools with those of Shelby County.[25]

Shelby County was not so enthusiastic about reigniting the promise of *Brown* and immediately sued, arguing that Memphis could not dissolve and force itself on the county school system. But in August 2011, a federal district court ruled in favor of Memphis and the dissolution, holding that the Memphis school district had been "abolished for all purposes except the winding down of its operations and the transfer of administration to the Shelby County Board of Education." The combined district would start operation in the fall of 2013.[26]

Now the true test was about to begin. In 2011, could the two districts—one white, suburban, and wealthy, the other black, inner-city, and poor—amicably unite? Memphis and Shelby County were much like the students at Booker T. Washington who had struggled to pass the end-of-year chemistry test with no chemistry teacher. They would surely be tested, but nobody had showed them the way to succeed. To the contrary, the decades since King's assassination had brought no racial healing to Memphis, where ancient suspicions remained as raw as they had ever been. In the days after the merger, a white school official in the newly united district recalled that "in the 1970s, it was a physical, personal fear. Today the fear is about the academic decline of the Shelby schools. As far as racial trust goes, I don't think we've improved much since the 1970s." Memphis and Shelby County would have to overcome the racial enmity that had grown unabated for a generation, all while engineering "the largest school district consolidation in American history."[27]

Perhaps many in Memphis were up to the task. But in Shelby County, tens of thousands of parents had already escaped Memphis once. And they would surely never be pulled back in. They answered Memphis's brash dissolution with a brash move of their own. If the law said their legacy of segregation forbade them from creating a special district, they would just change the law. Months before the merger would have started, the legislature passed, and Governor Haslam signed, a bill lifting the 1982 ban on the creation of special school districts. Shelby County's residents were given new wings, and a new era of white flight began.

That July, just six weeks before the start of the new, merged school year, voters in six Shelby County suburbs voted to secede. They did so with astonishing alacrity and alarming margins: in Arlington, 94 percent voted to secede; Bartlett, 91 percent; Collierville, 94 percent; Germantown, 93 percent; Lakeland, 87 percent; Millington, 74 percent. Equally astounding were the demographics in these neighborhoods: Arlington, 75 percent white; Bartlett, 63 percent; Collierville, 67 percent; Germantown, 73 percent; Lakeland, 79 percent; Millington, 47 percent. Shelby County's school district, now stripped of these six areas, looked quite different from the merged district that had been expected following the federal district court decision. Before the merger, the Shelby County area to be merged with Memphis had been 51 percent white. After the merger, and these secessions, it was 8 percent white. The message was clear: Just as tens of thousands of whites had fled Memphis public schools to avoid its black children in the 1970s, tens of thousands of Shelby County whites would now secede from their own school district for the same reason. This time, though, they took with them their favorite members of the combined school board, their fancy school buildings, their teachers, and, most importantly, to many, their tax revenues.[28]

Their stated intentions were, of course, anything but race based. The mayor of Millington sought to persuade viewers of WMC-TV that "anytime that you go out and talk to developers, and people that are looking to bring businesses to your community, the first thing they want to know is, 'Do you have an educated workforce that can come and fill those positions?' And now we can say, 'Yeah, we have a good quality school system.'" That's despite there being, as Penn State resegregation expert Erica Frankenberg says, no positive correlation ever demonstrated between local control and educational outcomes. To many Americans, especially those in the suburbs, if it's local, it must be good, and no amount of evidence can convince them otherwise.[29]

And what of those remaining in the inner-city schools? They are left to their own devices. Certainly, the schoolchildren of Memphis were left to struggle, now that those six Shelby County suburbs were leaving and taking their tax dollars with them. EdBuild reported that the "new districts have an average student poverty rate of 11 percent, lower than that of Beverly Hills. By comparison, a third of students in the shrunken Shelby County district lives below the poverty line—a rate higher even than that of Compton, California. In just one year, Shelby County's budget was slashed by 20 percent. Seven Memphis-area schools have closed since the 2014–15 school year alone, and the district laid off about 500 teachers in both 2015 and 2016."[30]

Supporters of the de-merger don't seem to mind this yawning inequality. If anything, it is reason for celebration. A local columnist wrote that it was "about time for suburbs to chant 'Told you so' to doubters of municipal school districts." "There is evidence the municipal districts are surviving just fine, thank you very much," he wrote. The proof? Collierville's new $100 million high school and $12 million in renovations to the Riverdale Elementary School in Germantown. But the main issue had never been whether six wealthy districts could succeed after secession. It was whether Shelby County could meet its obligation to educate all of its children—urban and otherwise—if it allowed its white children to flee.[31]

While Collierville and Germantown enjoyed sweeping success, in Memphis there were chemistry students without a chemistry teacher. The Memphis students were left out of the column. But in another sense, whites in these Shelby County districts had succeeded in doing what they wanted most, which was to keep their own schools separate from the city and its black students. Mission accomplished. If the sheer assertion of public will represents success, even if that will is used to selfish ends, then the congratulatory tone of the column fits. The buzzwords of the conservative movement, after all, are liberty and freedom. In this case, freedom meant *freedom from* being tethered to the troubled schools of Memphis, *freedom from* taxes that drained from the suburbs to the city. To the now-ascendant conservative base, this assertion is profoundly American; an appeal to the collective good, meanwhile, smacks of Soviet socialism.

The six-town Shelby County secession provided a neat template for other wealthy cities wishing to secede from less affluent districts. In 2016, Signal Mountain, a Tennessee suburb "where just 1 percent of students live in poverty," according to EdBuild, took steps to secede from Hamilton County, "which has a 21 percent student poverty rate." EdBuild noted that a local committee had estimated "that the new district would have an additional $1.8 million should it secede and take its tax base with it." Three other Shelby County districts also joined the quest for separation.[32]

Before the midterms of 2018, the Tennessee state legislature remained firmly in GOP control, with the Republicans controlling 74 percent of the seats in the House of Representatives and 85 percent of the seats in the Senate. With its overwhelming dominance in the statehouse, Tennessee's GOP seemed poised to foster this second wave of segregation for some time to come.

Was it all for naught? Did those who fought heroically to integrate Memphis sacrifice in vain? To answer that question, we must ask another one. What became of those who, like Dwania Kyles, integrated Memphis's schools? What sorts of lives did they live? And, perhaps even more interestingly, what sorts of lives did they pass on to their children and grandchildren?

———

THIS GENERATIONAL STORY can be found in the statistics of a study we recently conducted that provided new evidence on the impacts of parental education across generations. As in our other studies discussed in this book, we used the timing of court orders and childhood exposure to school desegregation to assess the impact of school desegregation on children and their families into the third generation. We found desegregation was such a powerful force that its beneficial impacts persist to influence the outcomes of the next generation. Its benefits show up as increased math and reading test scores, reduced likelihood of grade repetition, increased likelihood of high school

FIGURE 9.1

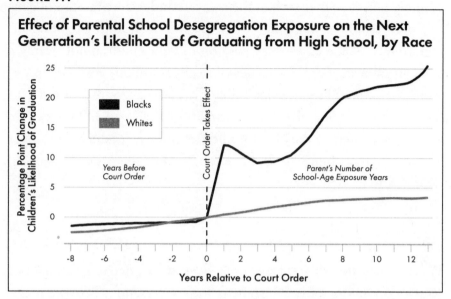

Effect of Parental School Desegregation Exposure on the Next Generation's Likelihood of Graduating from High School, by Race

graduation and college attendance, improvements in college quality and selectivity, and increased racial diversity of the student body at their selected colleges (Figure 9.1). The findings demonstrate that part of the intergenerational transmission of inequality can be attributed to school-quality-related influences. The results highlight that parental education is indeed a determinant of generational mobility.[33]

Dwania Kyles and the twelve other little children who integrated Memphis schools went through much turmoil in the process. Their efforts were ultimately stamped out, foreclosing opportunities for future generations to reap the benefits of their labor. Still, while Dwania may not remember her schooldays fondly, our study shows that she, and other black students who braved integration, did not fight in vain. Instead, integration opened doors and expanded opportunities, not simply for those on the vanguard, but for generations of their descendants.

But while integrators and their descendants often saw their lot improve, across freeways and train tracks and district lines throughout the country less fortunate, similarly situated blacks remained locked in segregated schools like those in Memphis. It would be wrong to assume, however, that each of them caved under the pressure of constrained resources. Many have joined, and now lead, the fight for integration. In some cases, they pass on to their children not simply a keen awareness of the challenges of segregation, but also a deep unwillingness to endure it, even if the only pathway to integration is to be one of just a few blacks in a primarily white space. This can be seen most acutely in the life of Willie Herenton, a graduate of Booker T. Washington High who became the head of the Memphis school district and then mayor.

———

WARM LIGHTING COMPLEMENTS a sleek wood decor at Houston's Restaurant in Memphis. The hum of the conversations between members of Memphis's well-to-do flows amid the opulence. Among the jubilant voices one might pick out is that of Willie Herenton. Now seventy-seven years old, he is in good spirits these days, which makes perfect sense: he is no longer in politics. He has become something of a beloved regular at Houston's, judging by the greetings he receives as he walks through the crowded space.

He did not receive quite so warm a reception when he was the mayor of Memphis, a position he held from 1991 until 2009, a service of five terms in City Hall. It was a contentious time, bookended by high crime in the 1990s and the Great Recession a decade ago. Herenton didn't help matters with his outspoken, unapologetic style, often escalating a fight instead of ignoring it.

Before becoming the mayor of Memphis, Herenton served as the superintendent of its schools, a post he held from 1979 until resigning to run for mayor in 1990. By the time he took over the schools, white flight had rendered the school system almost entirely black. But he convinced some 3,500 white students to reenter the Memphis schools in the early 1980s by offering specialized academic programs that would appeal to more affluent families.[34]

"The success of these enriched curriculum programs," the *New York Times* wrote in 1985, "can be traced in part to an innovative marketing plan that began when Mr. Herenton convinced some of the city's top corporations, including the Federal Express Corporation and Holiday Inns, Inc., to help him find ways to restore confidence in the public schools."[35]

Many years later, after leaving City Hall, Herenton started a network of charter schools that would give black Memphis parents trapped in the public school system a way out. The network is named after the early civil rights leader W. E. B. Du Bois.

Herenton was born in Memphis in 1940 and attended segregated schools. "I always considered Memphis to be the last bastion of a racially southern city," he says. He got his undergraduate degree from Le Moyne, a historically black college in Memphis, and then earned a doctorate in education from Southern Illinois University. He was thirty-nine when he became the city's first black school superintendent, and fifty-one when he became its first black mayor.[36]

"I was able to send my sons to Morehouse," he says proudly of the prestigious historically black college in Atlanta, which counts Dr. Martin Luther King Jr. among its alumni (and is my alma mater, too). He recalls how, many years ago, his son Rodney, who was an investment banker, wanted to go to business school.

"Dad, I want to go to Harvard. I want to get an MBA," he told his father.

Herenton remembers the exchange the way only a proud father can.

"Okay, well, why don't you apply to a number of schools?"

"No," Rodney answered. "I'm going to get into Harvard."

And he did. Now, one of his sons—whose grandfather attended segregated schools—attends Stanford, arguably the most coveted college in the nation.

"I was a part of the effort that integrated schools," Herenton says, proud of his sons and his own part in paving the way for them. "So, I always say that they're smarter than I am, but they're not tougher."

Herenton remembers how, when he was in graduate school in Illinois, he had been mocked by his peers over reports that whites in Memphis had buried a bus that was to carry black schoolchildren to the suburbs (this actually took place in Frayser, a suburb, in 1972).

"Man, is that your hometown?" Herenton remembers people asking him. "Memphis was so resistant that they literally buried a bus. I'm in graduate school writing my dissertation, and I'm embarrassed at my hometown."

Something else is at work, too, which is a flight of wealthier African Americans mirroring the earlier flight of middle-class whites. Herenton's own children didn't go to the failing schools in Memphis, and his grandchildren certainly didn't either. Very simply, you do not get to Morehouse or Stanford if you attend the public schools of Memphis, where only 24 percent of the high school graduates complete a college education.

"It's black *and* white flight," Herenton says. "I have found that African Americans who achieve success have the same barometers of success and expectations as whites—they have the same prejudice. Nobody wants to go to school with poor folks, they don't want to live in the same neighborhoods. Successful blacks take on the same behavior as successful whites."

Statistics back up this assertion. In 2015, the Brookings Institution found that between 2000 and 2010, many American cities experienced a decline in their African American populations. "Clearly, the black urban presence, which has been the mainstay of many large cities, is diminishing," wrote the study's author, William H. Frey. Families that had come to cities like Chicago and Detroit—which suffered the biggest population losses—during the Second Migration now decided they could find better opportunities elsewhere.

"Much of that population is suburbanizing," Frey wrote. "Leading black movement to the suburbs are the young, those with higher education, and married couples with children." The exact same thing could have been written about the white families that fled to the suburbs in the 1950s, as Frey himself noted.[37]

And as far as Herenton is concerned, black families have adopted some of the same attitudes held by their white counterparts. "When I tried to put housing, when I was mayor, in certain neighborhoods, you would've thought I was in a Ku Klux Klan neighborhood, and it was predominately African American middle class. They didn't want mixed-income housing either. They didn't want [their] kids to go to school [with poor kids]," he says.

Thurgood Marshall, who had successfully argued *Brown v. Board*, was criticized for sending his own son to Sidwell Friends School, the prestigious Washington, DC, private school. That was where, many years later, President Obama sent his own daughters. He was asked in 2010 if he would send his children to Washington's chronically failing public schools: "I'll be blunt with you: The answer is no, right now," he told his interviewer, instead electing to pay more than $60,000 a year for both Sasha and Malia to attend one of the most prestigious secondary institutions in the entire country.[38]

That leaves the residents of the inner city effectively trapped, shunned by their white and black peers alike.

"Until there's a broad brush," Herenton says, "that encompasses the horrible socioeconomic family disintegration, all the other societal/economic ills that influence education—until we begin to look at how you break generational poverty and all of the antisocial conditions that go along with it, we will not be successful.

"It takes all of these factors."

————

DESEGREGATION IS A law, but its realization is achieved through a spirit of belief in the potential of all children. Desegregation—whether via busing or district mergers—is a necessary, though inadequate, step. Memphis's experience shows that without a true appreciation for the value of black children, the promise of integration remains, at best, a fleeting hope that is too quickly dashed by white and middle-income flight, segregated classes within segregated schools, lower expectations for students of color, and disparate disciplinary measures.

Instead of this deep appreciation, we see evidence of bias. For example, studies have found that black third graders are about half as likely as their white peers to be placed into a "gifted" program—even when they have comparable test scores—and the Hispanic-white difference in the likelihood of selection into gifted programs is nearly as large. What's more, a national study showed that for black children, this differential selection in placement can be eliminated simply by giving black students at least some black teachers. This and related evidence suggests that we tend to underestimate the capacity of minority children to learn and perform at the highest levels, and that these beliefs may be internalized by the students themselves, which causes low expectations to become self-fulfilling prophecies. What we see evidenced today in the assumptions and judgments that teachers make about black boys, in particular, is that ultimately, without parent advocacy and agency, institutions will foster and sustain disparate outcomes.[39]

In common speech, there's a simpler label that may lie at the root of the problem: institutional racism, which may arise not only from conscious thoughts on the part of those who form an education system's policies and practices but also from unconscious bias.[40]

It is important to remember that we have more and better public data and research on what works in education than we had in the past (as we have demonstrated throughout this book). In earlier decades, we counted the percentage of students, black versus white, and if we got the school's racial composition balanced, we thought we were done. We did what the courts said. We now understand the importance of more nuanced data—data that offers a different and clearer picture of what leads to success, how disparate outcomes persist, which combinations of variables matter (for example, education, early childhood, jobs, safety, wages, and family support structures), and which levers to push.

———

THERE HAS BEEN a major school choice movement over the past two decades emphasizing individual concerns over the public mission of education, with an apparent willingness to sacrifice the latter. The contemporary language used by some proponents of school choice (and privatization of public education) is eerily similar to the older arguments of those who vehemently opposed integrated schools in the 1950s through the 1970s. We hear the same ideas reincarnated in the contemporary voices of the proponents of privatization (vouchers) without regard to the goals of equity, inclusion, and excellence, which, contrary to myth, can go hand in hand. This perspective is especially important given the current era of unprecedented racial and ethnic diversity among America's children, which are not leveraged as assets in our schools but too often viewed as deficits and barriers.

Consider, for example, the limited effectiveness of "No Child Left Behind," an unfunded mandate that fell short of providing requisite resources to narrow those gaps. Although it shone a light on the magnitude of the achievement gaps, via an emphasis on standardized test scores, it did nothing to truly improve education for the children who were being left behind. It was akin to testing to obtain a diagnosis without prescribing a cure—in this case, a cure for what ails America's schools, or at least a regimen that will begin to bring some improvement. Diagnosing the illness without prescribing any medicine ignores the reality that wherever we see achievement gaps we can trace them back to educational opportunity gaps that transpired earlier.

The world that existed during the era of integration and civil rights was not the same as the one we have inherited. The black-white dichotomy is an old paradigm. We have shifted from black and white communities to ones that are multiethnic in a globally competitive, international, twenty-first-century knowledge economy. Global community requires multicultural competencies. No matter where our children live and work in the future, their neighborhoods will be multicultural, part of the global community. Our failure will be in not adequately preparing them for that new reality.

It is not that we are looking in the wrong places; rather, we have made the faulty assumption that there is only one place to look. Whether it is desegregation, school finance reform, pre-K, or charter schools, all offer an answer, but none is a complete answer to addressing inequality. For that, we must turn to integrated solutions.

CONCLUSION:
COMING UP TOGETHER

None of us got where we are solely by pulling ourselves up by our bootstraps. We got here because somebody—a parent, a teacher, an Ivy League crony or a few nuns—bent down and helped us pick up our boots.

—THURGOOD MARSHALL

H OW MANY GENERATIONS DOES IT TAKE TO REVERSE THE ILLS OF segregation and inequities in education? The evidence in this book says just one—one generation. Not only do these school reforms have the power to break the intergenerational cycle of poverty, but the benefits extend into the third generation. Yes, three generations—and those in the third generation are the grandchildren of *Brown*. In fact, I (Rucker) am a grandchild of *Brown*. I am the third-generation benefactor of the policies discussed in these chapters, and my family history is a concrete portrait of this book's overture.

As I am an African American child of the latter phase of the integration era, my family tree is in virtually every chapter. Two generations before me, my grandfather took his GI Bill to the University of West Virginia to get a degree in education. Segregation denied him admission but offered to pay for him to be "shipped" to another university. Though he wasn't in a crowded galley on the Atlantic, the same social ill that had put slaves on ships now deported him to Columbia University, where he earned his master's degree. My father was born during those years in New York City. My grandfather then packed up his family and moved back to West Virginia, where he taught high school science in the public schools before being shipped off again—but this time, it was *integration* that drove the change, when he was fired from his teaching job, as black teachers were the first to be fired as white students began attending majority-black schools. Following the Great Migration's path, he moved to Minneapolis for job opportunities but was denied a teaching position. He would go on to have a distinguished career working for social justice at the National Urban League, the oldest and largest civil rights community-based organization of its kind in the nation. His son—my father—would be among the early cohorts of desegregation in Minneapolis public schools, a system my mother would later lead as superintendent. My siblings and I attended public schools from kindergarten through twelfth grade in the Minneapolis metro area. As a third-generation educator, I was never shipped or deported; instead, because of the legacy of my forefathers, I was privileged to be chosen and welcomed by the Russell Sage Foundation to New York City to begin writing this book. My daughter, the fourth generation of promise, was born in New York like her grandfather; and my son attended a high-quality preschool there, which helped lay a strong foundation for his dreams.

————

MUCH OF THIS book has dealt with our failures and shortcomings as a nation: The noble experiments we attempted but did not have the patience to stay with. The grand undertakings that we told ourselves were too difficult to even attempt, and that were thus better left to the dreams of ivory towers and think tanks. The excuses we made for inaction in the face of glaring inequality and desperate need. The baroque excuses with which we adorned the ugliness of plain old prejudice and hatred.

These are not easy things for the mind to rest on. Nor should it be the endpoint of this project, or of the greater project of school reform. It has not been our ultimate purpose here to tease out the complexities of some national sin, to reveal the rot at the heart of the American project. That may be satisfying to some, but it would be productive to none. Condemnation, on its own, cures no ills. Often, it only leads to counter-condemnation and recrimination. In the end, nothing gets done.

To the contrary, we believe that the American project is not so much imperfect as it is not yet fully realized. Our progress toward equality has been halting, and at times we have moved backward. This is indeed dismaying. But it need not be our collective fate.

Hope is justified. Time and again, Americans of all races, colors, and creeds have shown themselves to be willing to fight for equality in the schoolhouse, at the lunch counter, and on the public bus. They are proof positive that while the movement toward justice and equality is slow, it is also inexorable. We hope that this can serve as a guidebook to one important aspect of that journey. Like all guidebooks, it offers aspirations and recommendations—but also warnings based on painful experience.

We would therefore like to end the book with an image of progress. Although much of what has come before has been focused on the protracted, frustrated struggle to integrate the nation's public schools, we have also sought to highlight those moments—however fleeting or fraught, however thoroughly bookmarked by injustice—when prejudice was overcome, understanding achieved, and a better future imagined for all the children who will ever pass through the doors of a school, backpacks hanging from their shoulders.

It has been our primary contention in this volume that while prejudices held the practice of segregation in place, prejudice alone does not account for the more recent failure of integrated schooling. Prejudice has played a role, to be sure, but so have other factors. Foremost among these is our collective impatience, an unwillingness to see measures through, a willingness to abandon anything and everything that does not show immediate results—the destructive ethos of instant gratification transferred to the sphere of educational policy. Another problem has been siloed thinking, an inability to see problems in education from the high vantage point they deserve. No matter how well intentioned, reformers who toil in isolation from each other often toil at cross-purposes.

We believe these problems can be overcome. They will require an extraordinary coordination of resources and effort, but every solution proffered in these pages is fully within the realm of possibility. Simply put, a nation that can place a human being on the moon can figure out how to teach algebra to middle-schoolers in Baltimore. It has figured out how to do just that, in fact, but it has applied its zeal for public education selectively, and incompletely. Great effort has been expended. But it has not always been expended wisely or consistently.

Given the increasing racial and ethnic diversity of the US population, particularly among children, it is imperative that future work consider impacts on other racial and ethnic groups, particularly Hispanic and Asian American children.[1]

Solving school segregation will require renewed attention to several entrenched problems at once.

HOUSING POLICY

As we've seen, housing segregation did not happen by accident; nor did it only happen in those parts of the country where racism was openly celebrated. Instead, housing segregation was a strategic means to ensure segregation in every other part of American civic life. It was rooted in the devastatingly prescient insight that if people did not live together, and raise their children together, they would have little incentive to cross the color line in any other aspect of life, whether in the schoolhouse or the workplace.

Housing segregation, then, was a national phenomenon, one with troublingly deep roots. "Racial segregation in housing was not merely a project of southerners in the former slaveholding Confederacy," wrote Richard Rothstein in his authoritative 2017 study of housing segregation, *The Color of Law*. "It was a nationwide project of the federal government in the twentieth century, designed and implemented by its most liberal leaders."[2]

Segregated housing was, in particular, the pretext for segregated schooling. Conversely, school integration cannot be possible without integrated housing, which undoes the invisible borders that kept whites and blacks apart for much of the twentieth century. School busing failed in the 1970s because it brought children across the border without confronting the existence of that border in a way that was honest, explicit, and, in the end, conciliatory. Any solution that attempts to address schooling without addressing housing is bound to fail.

Trying to undo housing segregation may seem like a futile task bound to culminate in frustration and failure. But cities have succeeded in fighting against decades of strategic, entrenched discrimination. *Governing* magazine, for example, highlighted the Washington Park neighborhood of Cincinnati, where a stretch of "vacant buildings around a derelict park that was littered with needles and bullet casings" has been turned into "a diverse neighborhood where affordable housing was expanded along with market-rate condos."[3]

This is a small example, to be sure, but there are many others like it around the nation, with municipal governments, private developers, and community members working together to foster neighborhoods that are racially and economically diverse. Denver, for example, does not merely put low-income residents into housing projects, which concentrate poverty and exacerbate inequality. Instead of being sequestered in a remote project with other poor people, residents who qualify for the city's affordable housing program are assigned to units in different neighborhoods across the city.

"It's clear that low-income Latino and African-American kids do better on a variety of outcomes when they have folks of a higher occupational status surrounding them," said Wayne State University urban affairs professor George Galster, who studied the Denver experiment and deemed it a success.[4]

In December 2018, Minneapolis became the first major city to enact the bold policy reform to eliminate single-family zoning to address the history of racist housing segregationist practices and alleviate the affordable-housing crisis. This enables mixed-income housing neighborhood development and is part of the way forward. Will other cities follow their lead? Unfortunately, as of this writing, the Trump administration has delayed the implementation of Affirmatively Furthering Fair Housing, an Obama-era measure that would have required communities to state how they would combat housing segregation. That will make the fight against housing segregation more difficult, but it should not deter those who understand the importance of the mission.

HIGH-QUALITY PRESCHOOL

In the more than fifty years since its founding, Head Start has faced relentless criticism from those who judge it to be ineffective and inefficient, a waste of government funds for a feel-good program that achieves little. A Great Society program intended to help children whose parents could not otherwise afford preschool, it has always been maligned by the opponents of government "intrusion." The opponents of Head Start have been bolstered by studies that seem to show the program does not live up to its own mission. Such studies have been frequent. They are also deeply flawed.

As our research shows, the studies in question relied on narrow data sets that offered troubling but incomplete representations of the program. A more thorough look at Head Start—one that follows participants over a significant period of time—shows that Head Start is an effective program conferring lasting gains to participants, especially those who also received a high-quality K-12 education.

Yet, as *U.S. News & World Report* pointed out in a 2017 article, "the program has never had sufficient funding to serve all eligible children," an especially lamentable fact given that some fifteen million children are estimated to live in poverty in the United States.[5]

Nevertheless, as with housing, some cities have shown the way. Foremost among these is New York City, whose progressive mayor

Bill de Blasio made free universal prekindergarten a signature issue in his 2013 mayoral campaign. With a $300 million grant from the state legislature in Albany, de Blasio was able to start the program in the 2014–2015 school year. Today, some seventy thousand four- and five-year-old children attend the city's free pre-K program, and de Blasio is seeking to expand it to include three-year-olds as well.

What's more, the program is working, even as other parts of New York's public education system remain in a woeful condition. "The city's preschool program scores higher than the national average on assessments of the learning environment," wrote University of California, Berkeley, education policy scholar David Kirp in the *New York Times* in 2016, citing research data. "Parents give it a thumbs up, with 92 percent rating their child's experience as good or excellent. Not only has their youngsters' learning greatly improved, parents report, they are also better behaved."[6]

Overall, Kirp deemed New York City's pre-K program "impressive." Other cities have sought to replicate New York's success. More cities should do the same.[7]

CHILD HEALTH-CARE ACCESS

We now understand, much better than before, that learning is not solely the process of absorbing what a teacher has said in the classroom. Cognition is an ineffably complex process, one that is informed by physiology—the physical condition of the body. In other words, the mind needs the body to carry out its work.

Hunger, poor nutrition, lack of sleep, stress: these have all been shown to adversely affect a child's ability to learn. Children growing up in poverty are especially vulnerable in this regard, which is why providing them with health care is so important. Not only is doing so humane, it is sensible, ensuring that the thousands of dollars we invest in schooling—$10,615, on average, per child—aren't squandered because we haven't made other necessary investments. An airplane with wings but no engine simply won't fly.

One sensible solution, which has been around since 1997, has been the Children's Health Insurance Program, known as CHIP. In 2009, Phillip B. Levine and Diane Whitmore Schanzenbach published a study titled "The Impact of Children's Public Health Insurance Expansions on Educational Outcomes," in which they sought to quantify the above connection in the fourth and eighth grades by following children who were eligible for federally subsidized health insurance. Their findings were "strongly suggestive that improving children's health will improve their classroom performance."[8]

The founders of Head Start knew all of this, of course, even if they didn't have the data to back up their convictions. When announcing the creation of Head Start in 1965, President Johnson noted that children attending the program would "get medical and dental attention that they badly need," including free, nutritious food and health and dental checkups. Recently—and on a smaller scale—Geoffrey Canada's Harlem Children's Zone has supplemented its educational component with a Healthy Harlem initiative.

Much more is needed, however, to ensure that education is not sabotaged by poor physical conditions.

SCHOOL FUNDING REFORM

Money matters—a lot. This is an inconvenient fact, since the way we apportion money to public schools in the United States is fundamentally unfair. It also runs counter to the common complaint that we throw so much money at public schools to such paltry effect.

The answer to that complaint is that the money is not being spent wisely—and moreover, that the money is being spent only to correct—and to correct only partly—vast inequalities built into the system of school finance, which is rife with imbalances so old that we have come to take them for granted.

Schools are funded by property taxes, but even though these taxes are often quite high in poor, urban districts as a percentage of assessed value, they rarely add up to enough money to adequately fund the schools in those districts. This happens because property values in the poor districts are so low in the first place. Suburban districts, meanwhile, can use high property values to lavishly fund their schools, sometimes with somewhat lower taxes as a percentage of assessed value. At the same time, the cost of purchasing a home in, for example, Westchester County, north of New York, or in the San Francisco Bay Area, is so high as to serve as a barrier to entry. Prestigious public school districts thus also become exclusive ones.

Since the 1971 ruling in *Serrano v. Priest* in California, courts have sought to redress this inequality by forcing states to fund schools in low-income communities to levels that property taxes alone could not reach. While those efforts have been halting, and far from complete, they have shown the power of school funding reform to bring about improved educational outcomes.

As we found in a 2015 study, a 10 percent increase in per-pupil spending each year for all twelve years of public schooling leads to 0.3 more completed years of education, 7.3 percent higher wages, and a reduction of 3.7 percentage points in the annual incidence of poverty in adulthood. And these effects are much more pronounced for children from low-income families than for children from middle- and high-income families. Spending increases were also associated with sizable improvements in measured school quality, including reductions in student-to-teacher ratios, increases in teacher salaries, and longer school years.[9]

Continuing to advocate for school funding reform is therefore a crucial aspect of any successful effort at integration. And while lawyers and politicians may well prove necessary to that effort, the advocacy must also be undertaken by ordinary citizens themselves. Public education, in the end, will show no genuine improvement without public input.

———

DESPITE THE WORK that remains, we should not lose sight of the work that has already been done.

Plenty of communities around the United States have made incremental—but nevertheless significant—efforts to integrate their schools. Some of these are well known, like Louisville, Kentucky, where a long-standing integration plan remains a model for the nation. Recently, that model has been adopted by Hartford, Connecticut, which has had success in luring suburban parents to its system with the promise of high-performing magnet schools.

And then there are the schools of Clinton, Mississippi, which Jackie Mader of *The Hechinger Report* called "an academic powerhouse." The school-ranking site Niche agrees, giving the Clinton Public School District an A– and ranking it the seventh best in the state. This in a state with some of the ugliest history of racism in the nation. Also a state with some of the nation's worst schools.[10]

On the face of it, Clinton is not an exceptional place. Located to the south and west of the state capital, Jackson, it is a town of about 25,000 that is named one of Mississippi's "Most Livable Cities." The average family income there is about $53,000, which is about $6,000 lower than the national average. The town is 60 percent white, 34 percent African American, and 4 percent Asian.[11]

So how did this little town end up with what Jackie Mader called "extremely successful" schools, while also noting that they were "some of the most racially and economically diverse schools" in Mississippi?[12]

The answer begins in 1970, when a court order forced the schools of Hinds County to desegregate. Clinton, which is in Hinds County, split away and formed its own district, the Clinton Separate School District, the same year. That summer, as Mader noted, Dr. Virgil Belue arrived to serve as Clinton's first superintendent. What he saw was inauspicious: "He had no central office, no budget, and no bank account," Mader wrote. "The district's first school board meeting on August 3, 1970, had 19 agenda items, including determining the district's sick leave policy and finding furniture for the elementary school."[13]

"Well, heck, I can't fail at this place," Belue remembered thinking.[14]

Belue's innovation was to replace the neighborhood school, that long-standing bane of integration, with the community school. In his new conception of Clinton's schools, all the students in a particular grade would attend the same school, regardless of where they lived. So, for example, *all* first graders in Clinton went to school together, as did all second graders, and so on, right through high school.

Belue explained the wisdom of this plan: "You avoid having schools with wealthy parents supplementing support for one school on one side of town, and none of that going on on the other side of town." A seemingly simple solution erased the inequalities of neighborhood schools while also preventing the animosities that come from "forced" busing. Belue's grouping brought kids together without tearing the community apart. As one Clinton teacher who attended its schools in the 1970s would remember much later, "there are no rivalries within the district and no real concept of socioeconomic status. There is no poor school or wealthy school . . . we are all together from the very beginning."[15]

Clinton's schools were about 15 percent African American and 85 percent white when Belue took over nearly half a century ago. Today, they are majority black (54 percent), while retaining a significant white population (38 percent). The children continue to attend integrated schools, just as they did when Belue first came to Clinton. And they are thriving, with a high school graduate rate of 85 percent, and scores on state tests that are, for the most part, well above the Mississippi average. More than that, the children are learning *from* each other, using diversity as a source of collective strength and proving that it is more than just a pleasant byword.[16]

One parent put the matter perfectly: "By all of our kids being together, they're all held to the same standards. Every child in Clinton has the same opportunity, and it's important to teach our children that as well: that everyone should stand on the same foot, everyone should have equal opportunity."[17]

Critics may say that Clinton is a small town, where such an experiment is possible. They may note that the achievement gap between black and white students has not fully closed. They will point to the fact that many whites have moved out, or sent their children to private school, which seems to defeat the purpose of integration.

All of this is true, or at least partly so. But imperfection does not invalidate the noble experiment that is school integration. Too often, we balk at doing difficult work by finding excuses, seeking refuge in statistics and counterarguments. These may sometimes be valid. And yet the work remains. A sense of justice calls us. A yearning for equality demands we see past the imperfect present to an improved future.

As we've seen, we have tools that are, in some cases, decades old, but that nevertheless have the capacity to drastically correct some of the gravest inequalities in American society. Those measures include high-quality early childhood education, integrated schooling, and school finance reform. In concert, these measures could alleviate the devastating inequalities that have flummoxed policymakers for decades.

Only it won't be easy. Integration will take work. Equality will take work. But when it is achieved, that work will redound for generations.

Let us finish, then, with words from a generation that knew much struggle. In 2004, fifty years after she served as the most famous plaintiff in *Brown v. Board of Education*, the woman who was once little Linda Brown spoke at the University of Michigan. "I look a little different now," she said to laughter, recalling the famous picture of her on her way to school—a black school, because the white school would not have her.[18]

"I can still remember taking that bitter walk, and the terrible cold that would cause my tears to freeze upon my face," Brown remembered. Ironically, African American parents like Brown's merely wanted what the opponents of integration have asked for: neighborhood schools. "Black people were able to live all over town," she said, "but could not expect to send their children to schools closest to their home."

Brown then described the long legal battle for integration, of which she and her father became symbols. "My family became lost in the turmoil of the ensuing years—years that scarcely touched us. We lived in the calm of the hurricane's eye gazing out at the storm around us and wondering how it would all end," she said.

"I don't think my father ever got discouraged," she recalled, even if it was far from clear how the lawsuit would end. As it was, the suit would end with victory. There would be other victories, as well as defeats, and many more battles to be waged by future generations.

A collective consciousness about the urgency of the equity agenda is rarely ignited by the presentation of statistics alone, no matter how well assembled. With numbers *and* personal narratives, our goal has been to sound the alarm for today's generations, young and old, and to awaken understanding of the nature of segregation and its cascading long-term consequences when left unaddressed. Awareness is an important step in mobilizing collective action, developing sustainable solutions, and taking policy action steps to fulfill the promise of equal opportunity. Our inability to do everything should not undermine our efforts to do *something* in our relevant spheres of influence. It is not enough simply to write about the trends, talk about them, or analyze them; we must be trendsetters. We must cross the artificial walls that history has created and finish the work that *Brown* began—our collective destiny as a nation depends on it.

ACKNOWLEDGMENTS

I AM GRATEFUL FOR THE FUNDING SUPPORT FOR THIS PROJECT received from the Russell Sage Foundation (RSF), led by Sheldon Danziger, as well as the Carnegie Corporation, the National Institutes of Health, and the Alphonse Fletcher Fellowship (administered by Harvard University's W. E. B. Du Bois Institute). I also wish to thank the University of Michigan faculty members who direct the Panel Study of Income Dynamics (PSID) and the staff at the University of North Carolina (UNC) Carolina Population Center who direct the National Longitudinal Study of Adolescent to Adult Health (Add Health), especially for the access they provided to restricted-use geo-coded data. I deeply appreciate the generosity of those we had the opportunity to interview who shared their stories and unique experiences with us.

This work benefited from collaborations with colleagues Kirabo Jackson at Northwestern University and my former PhD student Sean Tanner. Invaluable, industrious research assistance from Sean Darling-Hammond sharpened my thinking and breathed new life into the book's legal storytelling (expect great scholarship from him in the future).

I would also like to thank Dan Gerstle for his detailed and thoughtful editorial support on successive drafts, the graphics designer Aaron Reeves, and all those at Basic Books and RSF who embraced my vision for this project. Finally, this work would not be possible without the enormous support and encouragement throughout from my wife, Candace; my mother, Carol; and my late father, Matthew Johnson Jr.

—*Rucker C. Johnson*

NOTES

INTRODUCTION: THE DREAM DEFERRED

1. "Black and Latino students make up 37% of students in high schools, 27% of students enrolled in at least one Advanced Placement (AP) course, and 18% of students receiving a qualifying score of 3 or above on an AP exam." "Civil Rights Data Collection, Data Snapshot: College and Career Readiness," US Department of Education, Office of Civil Rights, March 2014, https://www2.ed.gov/about/offices/list/ocr/docs/crdc-college-and-career-readiness-snapshot.pdf.

2. Organization for Economic Co-operation and Development (OECD), Programme for International Student Assessment (PISA), PISA 2015 Results (comparing student academic performance across countries), https://www.oecd-ilibrary.org/education/pisa_19963777; Jill Barshay, "U.S. Now Ranks Near the Bottom Among 35 Industrialized Nations in Math," *Hechinger Report*, December 9, 2017, http://hechingerreport.org/u-s-now-ranks-near-bottom-among-35-industrialized-nations-math; Sean F. Reardon, "School Segregation and Racial Achievement Gaps," *Russell Sage Foundation Journal of the Social Sciences* 2, no. 5 (2016): 34–57; Roland Fryer and Steven Levitt, "The Black-White Test Score Gap Through Third Grade," *American Law and Economics Review* 8, no. 2 (2006): 249–281; Linda Darling-Hammond, *The Flat World and Education: How America's Commitment to Equity Will Determine Our Future* (New York: Teachers College Press, 2010).

3. See Lindsey M. Burke, "Head Start Fails Poor Children," Heritage Foundation, January 28, 2013, https://www.heritage.org/education/commentary/head-start-fails-poor-children; President Ronald Reagan, State of the Union Address, January 25, 1988. Pointing to a misleading graph appearing to show that student outcomes haven't improved over the past thirty years alongside substantial

increases in per-pupil spending, US Secretary of Education Betsy DeVos concluded, "The Nation's Report Card shows that test scores continue to stagnate. This is not something we're going to spend our way out of and not something we're going to regulate our way out of." "Rise 2018: Panel 4, A Conversation with Secretaries and Closing Plenary," YouTube, posted by Reagan Foundation, streamed live April 12, 2018, https://m.youtube.com/watch?v=fUwZiMXK9k4. Hilary Hoynes, Diane Whitmore Schanzenbach, and Douglas Almond, "Long-Run Impacts of Childhood Access to the Safety Net," *American Economic Review* 106, no. 4 (2016): 903–934.

4. Such evidence will be discussed in detail in later chapters of this book, especially Chapter 8. Miles Hewstone and Rupert J. Brown, *Contact and Conflict in Intergroup Encounters* (Oxford: Basil Blackwell, 1986); Rupert Brown and Miles Hewstone, "An Integrative Theory of Intergroup Contact," *Advances in Experimental Social Psychology* 37 (2005): 255–343; Thomas F. Pettigrew, "Intergroup Contact Theory," *Annual Review of Psychology* 49 (1998): 65–85; Thomas F. Pettigrew and Linda R. Tropp, "A Meta-Analytic Test of Intergroup Contact Theory," *Journal of Personality and Social Psychology* 90, no. 5 (2006): 751–783; Johanne Boisjoly, Greg J. Duncan, Michael Kremer, Dan M. Levy, and Jacque Eccles, "Empathy or Antipathy? The Impact of Diversity," *American Economic Review* 96, no. 5 (2006): 1890–1905.

5. Jane Perlez, "New York Schools Consider the Use of Metal Detectors," *New York Times*, May 4, 1988, https://www.nytimes.com/1988/05/04/nyregion /new-york-schools-consider-the-use-of-metal-detectors.html; Joseph Berger, "Dropout Rate in New York Shows Decline," *New York Times*, June 13, 1991, https://www.nytimes.com/1991/06/13/nyregion/dropout-rate-in-new-york -shows-decline.html.

6. Quoted in Terrence McCoy, "Freddie Gray's Life a Study on the Effects of Lead Paint on Poor Blacks," *Washington Post*, April 30, 2015, https://www .washingtonpost.com/local/freddie-grays-life-a-study-in-the-sad-effects-of-lead -paint-on-poor-blacks/2015/04/29/0be898e6-eea8-11e4-8abc-d6aa3bad79dd _story.html?noredirect=on&utm_term=.a65e461a959f.

7. "The Integration Report," Civil Rights Project, University of California, Los Angeles, 2011; US Department of Education, Office of Civil Rights Data.

8. Carolyn Phenicie, "New Research Shows Achievement Gap Grows as Schools Become More Segregated," *The 74*, September 24, 2015, https://www .the74million.org/article/achievement-gap-grows-as-schools-become-more -segregated; Institute for Education Sciences, National Center for Education Statistics, "School Composition and the Black-White Achievement Gap," 2015, https:// nces.ed.gov/nationsreportcard/subject/studies/pdf/school_composition_and _the_bw_achievement_gap_2015.pdf.

9. Louis Serino, "What International Test Scores Reveal About American Education," Brookings Institution, April 17, 2017, https://www.brookings

.edu/blog/brown-center-chalkboard/2017/04/07/what-international-test-scores-reveal-about-american-education.

10. Gary Orfield, John Kuscera, and Genevieve Siegel-Hawley, "E. Pluribus...Separation: Deepening Double Segregation for More Students," Civil Rights Project at the University of California, Los Angeles, September 2012, https://www.civilrightsproject.ucla.edu/research/k-12-education/integration-and-diversity/mlk-national/e-pluribus...separation-deepening-double-segregation-for-more-students/orfield_epluribus_revised_omplete_2012.pdf.

11. US Department of Education, National Commission on Excellence in Education, *A Nation at Risk: The Imperative for Educational Reform. A Report to the Nation and the Secretary of Education*, April 1983, https://www.edreform.com/wp-content/uploads/2013/02/A_Nation_At_Risk_1983.pdf.

CHAPTER 1: BEFORE *BROWN*—AND BEYOND

1. Dwight Armstrong, interview by Rucker Johnson and Alexander Nazaryan, October 19, 2017.

2. *The Barber of Birmingham: Foot Soldier of the Civil Rights Movement*, directed by Robin Fryday and Gail Dolgin (New York: Chicken and Egg Pictures, 2011).

3. Quoted in James Patterson, *Grand Expectations* (New York: Oxford University Press, 1996), 23.

4. Shuttlesworth v. Birmingham Board of Education, 162 F. Supp. 372 (N.D. Ala. 1958).

5. Jack Peltason, *Fifty-Eight Lonely Men: Southern Federal Judges and School Desegregation* (Urbana: University of Illinois Press, 1978); Shuttlesworth v. Birmingham Board of Education, 162 F. Supp. 372 (N.D. Ala. 1958); Armstrong v. Board of Education of City of Birmingham, Ala., 220 F. Supp. 217, 219 (N.D. Ala. 1963).

6. Armstrong v. Board of Education of City of Birmingham, Ala., 220 F. Supp. 217, 219 (N.D. Ala. 1963).

7. Browder v. Gayle, 142 F. Supp. 707 (1956); Armstrong v. Board of Education of City of Birmingham, Ala., 220 F. Supp. 217, 219 (N.D. Ala. 1963).

8. Jack M. Balkin, "What Brown Teaches Us About Constitutional Theory," *Virginia Law Review* 90, no. 6 (2004): 1537–1577.

9. "Crises, February 1919: Lynching Record for the Year 1918," Old Magazine Articles, www.oldmagazinearticles.com/how_many_lynchings_in_1918#.W1PKx9JKhPY.

10. Quoted in Hortense Powdermaker, *After Freedom: A Cultural Study in the Deep South* (New York: Russell and Russell, 1968), 302.

11. James T. Patterson, *Brown v. Board of Education: A Civil Rights Milestone and Its Troubled Legacy* (New York: Oxford University Press, 2001); Horace Mann

Bond, *The Education of the Negro in the American Social Order* (New York: Prentice Hall, 1934); Robert A. Margo, *Race and Schooling in the South, 1880–1950: An Economic History*, NBER Monograph Series on Long-Term Factors in Economic Development (Chicago: University of Chicago Press, 1990), vii, 164; David Card and Alan Krueger, "Does School Quality Matter? Returns to Education and the Characteristics of Public Schools in the United States," *Journal of Political Economy* 100 (1992): 1–40; David Card and Alan Krueger, "School Resources and Student Outcomes: An Overview of the Literature and New Evidence from North and South Carolina," *Journal of Economic Perspectives* 10 (1996): 31–50.

12. Charles Hamilton Houston, quoted in *The Road to Brown*, film directed by William Elwood (1990), http://newsreel.org/video/THE-ROAD-TO-BROWN.

13. W. E. B. (William Edward Burghardt) Du Bois, *The Souls of Black Folk: Essays and Sketches* (Chicago: A. G. McClurg, 1903).

14. Quoted in James L. Conyers Jr., ed., *Charles H. Houston: An Interdisciplinary Study of Civil Rights Leadership* (Lanham, MD: Lexington Books, 2012), 181.

15. Patterson, *Brown v. Board of Education*.

16. Missouri ex rel. Gaines v. Canada, 305 U.S. 337, 349 (1938).

17. William Edward Macklin, "The Inevitable Mr. Gaines," *Missouri Student*, December 14, 1938, quoted in James Endersby and William T. Horner, *Lloyd Gaines and the Fight to End Segregation* (Columbia: University of Missouri Press, 2016).

18. Chad Garrison, "The Mystery of Lloyd Gaines," *River Front Times*, April 4, 2007.

19. Andrea Hsu, "'Sweatt V. Painter': Nearly Forgotten, But Landmark Texas Integration Case," National Public Radio, October 12, 2012, https://www.npr.org/sections/thetwo-way/2012/10/10/162650487/sweatt-vs-texas-nearly-forgotten-but-landmark-integration-case.

20. Ibid.

21. Sweatt v. Painter, 339 U.S. 629, 633 (1950).

22. Gary Lavergne, *Before Brown: Heman Marion Sweatt, Thurgood Marshall, and the Long Road to Justice* (Austin: University of Texas Press, 2010); Gary Lavergne, "Heman Marion Sweatt: The Unsung Civil Rights Hero," American Constitution Society, accessed April 23, 2018, https://www.acslaw.org/acsblog/node/17431; Jack Greenberg, *Crusaders in the Courts: How a Dedicated Band of Lawyers Fought for the Civil Rights Revolution* (New York: Basic Books, 2004).

23. "Linda Brown Thompson at the Brown v. Board of Education Anniversary," C-SPAN, January 12, 2004, accessed April 23, 2018, https://www.c-span.org/video/?c4675164/linda-brown-thompson-brown-v-board-education-anniversary.

24. James Patterson, *Brown v. Board of Education*.

25. Brown v. Board of Education of Topeka, 98 F. Supp. 797 (D. Kan. 1951). Findings of fact available at Douglas Linder, "Brown et al. v Board of Education

of Topeka, Shawnee County, Kansas et al.," *Famous Trials*, accessed July 21, 2018, www.famous-trials.com/brownvtopeka/658.

26. Mendez et al. v. Westminster [*sic*] School District of Orange County et al., 64 F. Supp. 544, 549 (S.D. Cal. 1946), aff'd, 161 F. 2d 774 (9th Cir. 1947); California Assembly Bill 1375, "An Act to Repeal Section 8003 and 8004 of the Education Code, Relating to the Establishment of Separate Schools for Certain Races," introduced January 29, 1947, signed into law June 14, 1947. For a history of California segregation laws, see Charles Wollenberg, "Mendez v. Westminster: Race, Nationality and Segregation in California Schools," *California Historical Quarterly* 53, no. 4 (Winter 1974): 317–332.

27. Michael O'Donnell, "Commander v. Chief: The Lessons of Eisenhower's Civil-Rights Struggle with His Chief Justice Earl Warren," *Atlantic*, April 2018, https://www.theatlantic.com/magazine/archive/2018/04/commander-v-chief/554045.

28. "Politician Rousselot," Getty Images, August 1964, accessed July 22, 2018, https://www.gettyimages.com/license/52260477.

29. James Patterson, *Brown v. Board of Education*; Jeffrey T. Leeds, "A Life on the Court," *New York Times Magazine*, October 5, 1968.

30. Brown v. Board of Education of Topeka, 347 U.S. 483, 493 (1954).

31. Ibid., 494, n. 11. Italics mine.

32. Michael Heise, "Equal Educational Opportunity by the Numbers: The Warren Court's Empirical Legacy," *Washington and Lee Law Review* 59 (2002): 1309, 1311, https://scholarship.law.cornell.edu/facpub/753.

33. Martha Minow, *In Brown's Wake: Legacies of America's Educational Landmark* (New York: Oxford University Press, 2012).

34. Gunnar Myrdal, *An American Dilemma: The Negro Problem and Modern Democracy* (New York: Harper and Brothers, 1944), lxix.

35. Kenneth Clark and Mamie Clark, "Racial Identification and Preference in Negro Children," in *Readings in Social Psychology*, Theodore Newcomb and Eugene Hartley, eds. (New York: Holt, Rinehart, and Winston, 1957), 602–611, available online at https://i2.cdn.turner.com/cnn/2010/images/05/13/doll.study.1947.pdf.

36. Ibid., 170, 177, in online version.

37. Ibid.; "Brown at 60: The Doll Test," *NAACP Legal Defense Fund*, n.d., accessed July 22, 2018, www.naacpldf.org/brown-at-60-the-doll-test.

38. "Equal Education for All," *Washington Post*, May 19, 1954; David Reynolds, *America, Empire of Liberty: A New History of the United States* (New York: Basic Books, 2011).

39. Quoted in Abby Phillip, "How the Washington Post Covered Brown v. Board of Education in 1954," *Washington Post*, May 16, 2014, https://www.washingtonpost.com/news/post-nation/wp/2014/05/16/how-the-washington-post-covered-brown-v-board-of-education-in-1954/?utm_term=.11cb1978ed23.

40. Patterson, *Brown v. Board of Education*; Brown v. Board of Education of Topeka, 349 U.S. 294, 301 (1955).

41. Charles Ogletree, *All Deliberate Speed: Reflections on the First Half-Century of Brown v. Board of Education* (New York: W. W. Norton and Company, 2005); J. Harvie Wilkinson, *From Brown to Bakke: The Supreme Court and School Integration: 1954–1978* (New York: Oxford University Press, 1981), 102.

42. Quoted in Melba Beals, *Warriors Don't Cry: The Searing Memoir of the Battle to Integrate Little Rock's Central High* (New York: Simon Pulse, 2007).

43. Ibid.

44. Ibid.

CHAPTER 2: THE INTEGRATED CLASSROOM

1. Title IV, Civil Rights Act of 1964, 42 U.S. Code § 2000c–6; Title VI, Civil Rights Act of 1964, 42 U.S. Code § 2000d. The original Elementary and Secondary Education Act appropriated at least $500 million in aid, in 1965 dollars, to public K-12 educational institutions. Elementary and Secondary Education Act, Public Law 89-10 (April 11, 1965), available online at https://deutsch29.files .wordpress.com/2015/12/statute-79-pg27.pdf; Elizabeth Cascio, Nora Gordon, Ethan Lewis, and Sarah Reber, "Paying for Progress: Conditional Grants and the Desegregation of Southern Schools," *Quarterly Journal of Economics* 125, no. 1 (2010): 445–482.

2. Rucker C. Johnson, "Long-Run Impacts of School Desegregation and School Quality on Adult Attainments," NBER Working Paper No. 16664 (revised August 2015), https://doi.org/10.3386/w16664. Desegregation court order timing data obtained by combining American Communities Project data (Brown University, John Logan) assembled by legal scholars with data from Welch/Light on desegregation plan implementation dates in large districts. See Finis Welch and Audrey Light, *New Evidence on School Desegregation* (Washington, DC: US Commission on Civil Rights, 1987). Green v. County School Board of New Kent County, 391 U.S. 430 (1968); James Patterson, *Brown v. Board of Education: A Civil Rights Milestone and Its Troubled Legacy* (New York: Oxford University Press, 2001), 146.

3. Johnson, "Long-Run Impacts of School Desegregation and School Quality." Desegregation court order timing data obtained by combining American Communities Project data, Welch and Light, *New Evidence*, and data compiled by ProPublica: see Yue Qiu and Nikole Hannah-Jones, "A National Survey of School Desegregation Orders," ProPublica, December 23, 2014, https://projects .propublica.org/graphics/desegregation-orders.

4. "Where plaintiffs prove that the school authorities have carried out a systematic program of segregation affecting a substantial portion of the students, schools, teachers, and facilities within the school system, it is only common sense to conclude that there exists a predicate for a finding of the existence of a dual school system." Keyes v. School District No. 1, Denver, 413 U.S. 189, 201 (1973).

5. Milliken v. Bradley, 433 U.S. 267, 281 (1977).

6. In particular, 97 percent of desegregation orders that were ever issued occurred between 1954 and 1977.

7. Andrew Greeley and Paul B. Sheatsley, "Attitudes Toward Desegregation," National Opinion Research Center, December 1971, https://files.eric.ed.gov /fulltext/ED068600.pdf.

8. Quotations in this section from Paul Goren, interview by Rucker Johnson and Alexander Nazaryan, June 20, 2017.

9. Edward McClelland, *Nothin' but Blue Skies: The Heyday, Hard Times, and Hopes of America's Industrial Heartland* (New York: Bloomsbury, 2014).

10. "Encyclopedia of Chicago," Chicago History Museum, accessed April 24, 2018, www.encyclopedia.chicagohistory.org.

11. Quoted in Terry Sullivan, "How Marynook Meets the Negro," *St. Jude*, January 1963.

12. Quotations in this section from Forrest Jones, interview by Rucker Johnson and Alexander Nazaryan, June 24, 2017.

13. Quotations in this section from Paul Goren, interview by Rucker Johnson and Alexander Nazaryan, June 20, 2017.

14. Kamala Harris, Twitter Post, July 9, 2018, 10:02 PM, https://twitter .com/KamalaHarris/status/1016502769493168128.

15. The idiosyncratic nature of court litigation timing documented in the legal history of school desegregation make a prima facie case for treating initial court orders as exogenous shocks that influenced the timing of major desegregation plan implementation and generated changes in school quality from abrupt shifts in racial school segregation. This case is bolstered by the empirical evidence that the bulk of 1962 district characteristics fail to predict the timing of initial court orders. For more information, see Johnson, "Long-Run Impacts of School Desegregation and School Quality." Related evidence is found in Jonathan Guryan, "Desegregation and Black Dropout Rates," *American Economic Review* 94, no. 4, (2004): 919–943.

16. American Communities Project data; Johnson, "Long-Run Impacts of School Desegregation and School Quality."

17. Our models included controls for parental education and occupational status, parental income, mother's marital status at birth, birth weight, child health-insurance coverage, and gender. The adult economic and incarceration outcomes included flexible controls for age (cubic). We also included birth-year fixed effects by region and race and birth-cohort linear trends interacting with various 1960 characteristics of the childhood county (poverty rate, percent black, average education, percent urban, and population size). Other concurrent policy changes were explicitly controlled for (including hospital desegregation in the South and the roll-out and/or expansions of Aid to Families with Dependent Children (AFDC), Medicaid, Food Stamps, Community Health Centers, Title I funding, Head Start, and kindergarten introduction) and do not account for the pattern of results presented here.

18. Our estimates of average educational attainment levels and earnings from the PSID by race correspond closely with national averages reported in Kerwin Charles and Patrick Bayer, "Divergent Paths: A New Perspective on Earnings Differences Between Black and White Men," *Quarterly Journal of Economics* 133, no. 3 (2018): 1459–1501; Thomas J. Kane, "College Entry by Blacks Since 1970: The Role of College Costs, Family Background, and the Returns to Education," *Journal of Political Economy* 102, no. 5 (1994): 878–911; Sandra Black and Amir Sufi, "Who Goes to College? Differential Enrollment by Race and Family Background," NBER Working Paper No. 9310 (2002); William A. Darity Jr. and Samuel L. Myers Jr., *Persistent Disparity: Race and Economic Inequality in the United States Since 1945* (Northampton, MA: Edward Elgar, 1999).

19. The results strongly support a causal interpretation of the effects of school desegregation by uncovering sharp differences in the estimated long-term effects on cohorts born within a fairly narrow window of each other that differ in whether and how long they attended desegregated schools. The effects (1) closely follow the timing of initial court orders (given the evidence showing no preexisting time trends); (2) are geographically confined to the specific school districts in which desegregation court orders were being enacted (given the robustness of the results to the inclusion of cohort-by-race-by-region of birth fixed effects); (3) are constrained only to school-age years of exposure (given the evidence showing no effects for non-school-age years beyond age seventeen); (4) had the largest impacts on blacks in communities where desegregation resulted in the largest changes in school quality inputs; and (5) no negative effects on whites. The results persist even when comparing siblings.

20. Lance Lochner and Enrico Moretti, "The Effect of Education on Crime: Evidence from Prison Inmates, Arrests, and Self-Reports," *American Economic Review* 94, no. 1 (2004):155–189; Rucker C. Johnson and Steven Raphael, "How Much Crime Reduction Does the Marginal Prisoner Buy?" *Journal of Law and Economics* 55, no. 2 (2012): 275–310.

21. As a placebo test, the results demonstrate that timing of unsuccessful court litigation is unrelated to adult attainment outcomes; only the timing of the initial year of successful litigation that led to court-ordered school desegregation is significantly associated with blacks' adult socioeconomic and health attainments. This finding provides additional evidence that the main results are not spurious and helps to rule out confounding influences from changing local demographic characteristics or social policies. If such omitted variables spuriously inflate the estimated effect of desegregation, the placebo coefficient should be significant. It is not.

CHAPTER 3: EQUALITY PROMISED, EQUALITY DENIED

1. School finance cases were founded on the basis that existing local systems of school finance violated the equal protection clause of the Fourteenth Amend-

ment of the US Constitution or the relevant state constitution, as school resources would then be a function of a local community's wealth.

2. Robert Reinhold, "John Serrano Jr., et al., and School Tax Equality," *New York Times*, January 10, 1972, https://www.nytimes.com/1972/01/10/archives/john-serrano-jr-et-al-and-school-tax-equality-serrano-jr-et-al-and.html.

3. Serrano v. Priest, 5 Cal.3d 584 (1971); ibid. at 619 (McComb dissenting) (citing to plaintiff's complaint).

4. Stephen Sugarman and Jack Coons, interview by Rucker Johnson, October 27, 2017.

5. While the California Supreme Court declared, in what is known as *Serrano I*, that the Fourteenth Amendment created a fundamental right to education, the US Supreme Court subsequently held, in *San Antonio Independent School District v. Rodriguez*, that education was not a fundamental right, muddying the California victory. After *Rodriguez*, however, the *Serrano* plaintiffs were able to circumvent this obstacle in *Serrano II* by appealing to the equal protection clause in the California state constitution and arguing that even if education was not a fundamental right *federally*, it was a fundamental right in California. Serrano v. Priest, 18 Cal.3d 728 (1976). To this day, California is among a small group of states in which education is legally deemed a fundamental right—a status education does not enjoy at the federal level.

6. Serrano v. Priest, 5 Cal.3d 584, 619 (1971) (McComb dissenting) (citing to plaintiff's complaint).

7. Serrano v. Priest, 5 Cal.3d 584, 589 (1971).

8. William Celis III, "A Long-Running Saga over Texas Schools," *New York Times*, April 10, 1994, https://www.nytimes.com/1994/04/10/education/a-long-running-saga-over-texas-schools.html.

9. Mark Yudof and Daniel Morgan, "Rodriguez v. San Antonio Independent School District: Gathering the Ayes of Texas—the Politics of School Finance Reform," *Law and Contemporary Problems* 38, no. 3 (Winter/Spring 1974): 383, 392.

10. Rodriguez v. San Antonio Independent School District, 337 F. Supp. 280–282 (1971).

11. Quoted in Evan J. Mandery, *A Wild Justice: The Death and Resurrection of Capital Punishment in America* (New York: W. W. Norton and Company, 2014).

12. San Antonio Independent School District v. Rodriguez, 411 U.S. 1, 2, 28, 32 (1973).

13. Andreas Kluth, ed., "A Lesson in Mediocrity," *Economist*, April 20, 2011, https://www.economist.com/special-report/2011/04/20/a-lesson-in-mediocrity; Dennis Romero, "California Is Home to Some of America's Worst Public Schools," *LA Weekly*, August 2, 2016, www.laweekly.com/news/california-is-home-to-some-of-americas-worst-public-schools-7205447.

14. "What is Proposition 13?" California Tax Data, accessed July 24, 2018, https://www.californiataxdata.com/pdf/Prop13.pdf.

15. Quoted in Clyde Haberman, "The California Ballot Measure That Inspired a Tax Revolt," *New York Times*, October 16, 2016, https://www.nytimes.com/2016/10/17/us/the-california-ballot-measure-that-inspired-a-tax-revolt.html; Conner Friedersdorf, "After 40 Years, Proposition 13's Failures Are Evident," *Los Angeles Times*, June 4, 2018, www.latimes.com/opinion/op-ed/la-oe-friedersdorf-prop-13-20180604-story.html.

16. Haberman, "California Ballot Measure That Inspired a Tax Revolt"; "State Grades on K-12 Education: Map and Rankings," *Education Week*, January 17, 2018, https://www.edweek.org/ew/collections/quality-counts-2018-state-grades/report-card-map-rankings.html.

17. The more nuanced argument posits that increased school spending inevitably leads to waste if not accompanied by a strict school accountability system that dictates how money can be used.

18. James Coleman et al., "Equality of Educational Opportunity," commissioned by the US Department of Health, Education and Welfare, 1966.

19. Eric A. Hanushek, "The Economics of Schooling: Production and Efficiency in Public Schools," *Journal of Economic Literature* 49 (1986): 1141–1177; Eric A. Hanushek, "School Resources and Student Performance," in *Does Money Matter? The Effect of School Resources on Student Achievement and Adult Success*, Gary Burtless, ed. (Washington, DC: Brookings Institution, 1996); Eric A. Hanushek, "Spending on Schools," in *A Primer on American Education*, Terry Moe, ed. (Stanford, CA: Hoover Press, 2001); "The Failure of Input Based Schooling Policies," *Economic Journal* 113 (2003): 65–98; Eric A. Hanushek and Alfred A. Lindseth, "The Effectiveness of Court-Ordered Funding of Schools," *Education Outlook* 6 (May 2009); Rose v. Council for Better Education, 790 S.W.2d 186 (Ky. 1989).

20. Rose v. Council for Better Education, 790 S.W.2d 186 (Ky. 1989).

21. Hanushek and Lindseth, "Effectiveness of Court-Ordered Funding."

22. Ibid.

23. Ibid.

24. Jill Barshay, "U.S. Now Ranks Near the Bottom Among 35 Industrialized Nations in Math," *Hechinger Report*, December 9, 2017, http://hechingerreport.org/u-s-now-ranks-near-bottom-among-35-industrialized-nations-math.

25. C. Kirabo Jackson, Rucker C. Johnson, and Claudia Persico, "The Effects of School Spending on Educational and Economic Outcomes: Evidence from School Finance Reforms," *Quarterly Journal of Economics* 131, no. 1 (2016): 157–218.

26. We then see if "exposed" cohorts (those young enough to have been in school during or after the reforms were passed) have better outcomes relative to "unexposed" cohorts (children who were too old to be affected by reforms at the time of passage) in districts that experienced larger reform-induced spending increases.

27. Rucker C. Johnson, "Ever-Increasing Levels of Parental Incarceration and the Consequences for Children," in *Do Prisons Make Us Safer?*, Steven Raphael and Michael Stoll, eds. (New York: Russell Sage Foundation Press, 2008).

28. Earlier related evidence is found in David Card and A. Abigail Payne, "School Finance Reform, the Distribution of School Spending, and the Distribution of Student Test Scores," *Journal of Public Economics* 83, no. 1 (2002): 49–82; Caroline Hoxby, "All School Finance Equalizations Are Not Created Equal," *Quarterly Journal of Economics* (2001): 1189–1231; Sheila E. Murray, William N. Evans, and Robert M. Schwab, "Education-Finance Reform and the Distribution of Education Resource," *American Economic Review* 88, no. 4 (1998): 798–812.

29. William Penn School District v. Pennsylvania Department of Education, No. 587 (M.D. Pen 2014).

30. Ibid.

31. Emma Brown, "Pa. Schools Are the Nation's Most Inequitable. The New Governor Wants to Fix That," *Washington Post*, April 22, 2015, https:// www.washingtonpost.com/local/education/pa-schools-are-the-nations-most -inequitable-the-new-governor-wants-to-fix-that/2015/04/22/3d2f4e3e-e441 -11e4-81ea-0649268f729e_story.html?utm_term=.72dfb32f904e.

32. "Funding Formulas and Fairness: What Pennsylvania Can Learn from Other States' Education Funding Formulas," *Education Law Center* (February 2013), https://www.elc-pa.org/wp-content/uploads/2013/02/ELC_schoolfundingreport .2013.pdf.

33. Ibid.

34. Jamella Miller and Bryant Miller, "Commentary: Why We Sued over Our Daughter's Education," *Philadelphia Daily News*, September 12, 2016, www .philly.com/philly/opinion/20160912_Commentary__Why_we_sued_over_our _daughter_s_education.html.

35. Quoted in Kayla Lattimore, "DeVos Says More Money Won't Help Schools; Research Says Otherwise," National Public Radio, June 9, 2017, https://www.npr.org/sections/ed/2017/06/09/531908094/devos-says-more -money-wont-help-schools-research-says-otherwise.

36. "Governor Wolf Announces Basic Education Funding Distribution," Governor Tom Wolf, April 5, 2016, https://www.governor.pa.gov/governor-wolf -announces-basic-education-funding-distribution; quoted in Eryn Spanger, "BLOG: Basic Education Fair Funding Formula Signed into Law (Round-up)," Governor Tom Wolf, June 7, 2016, https://www.governor.pa.gov/basic-edu -fair-fund-formula-signed.

37. Avi Wolfman-Arent, "Those Challenging Fairness of Pa. School Funding Will Have Day in Court. Keystone Crossroads: Education," WHYY, October 2, 2017, accessed April 25, 2018, https://whyy.org/articles/challenging -fairness-pa-school-funding-will-day-court.

38. It is important to bear in mind that the *Williams* case is one of a number of active school funding lawsuits that, by design, cannot have more than local

impacts. Their claim is premised on the language in the Pennsylvania state consti-tution. So even if they win, they cannot have a direct impact at the federal level or in any other state. These cases represent more proof that uneven implementation continues, and it is less of a cause for hope for federal school funding change. For federal change, we would need a reinterpretation of the US Constitution or a reauthorization of the Elementary and Secondary Education Act that sub-stantially increases and shifts Title I assistance to require states to spend it to equalize school funding to districts. Neither is in the works, in any meaningful way, anywhere.

39. William Penn School District et al. v. Pennsylvania Department of Educa-tion, J-82-2016 (Pa., September 28, 2017).

CHAPTER 4: GETTING AHEAD WITH HEAD START

1. Darren Walker, interview by Rucker Johnson and Alexander Nazaryan, August 27, 2017.

2. The Economic Opportunity Act of 1964, Pub.L. 88-452, presently en-acted at 42 U.S.C. §§ 9831 to 9852c.

3. Utako Minai, Kathleen M. Gustafson, Robert D. Fiorentino, Allard Jong-man, and J. J. Uriola Sereno, "Fetal Rhythm-Based Language Discrimination: A Biomagnetometry Study," *NeuroReport* 28, no. 10 (July 2017): 561–564.

4. Larissa MacFarquhar, "What Money Can Buy: Darren Walker and the Ford Foundation Set Out to Conquer Inequality," *New Yorker*, January 4, 2016, https://www.newyorker.com/magazine/2016/01/04/what-money-can-buy-profiles-larissa-macfarquhar.

5. Darren Walker, "My Head Start," *Huffington Post* (blog), May 19, 2015, https://m.huffpost.com/us/entry/7310536.

6. Quotations in this section from Darren Walker, interview by Rucker John-son and Alexander Nazaryan, August 27, 2017.

7. *The Economist*, March 30, 1991, cover viewable at https://i.ebayimg.com/thumbs/images/g/wR4AAOxywh1TDnIg/s-l225.jpg.

8. Quoted in "Millions of Lives Transformed: 50 Years of Headstart," Ford Foundation, April 1, 2015, https://www.fordfoundation.org/the-latest/news/millions-of-lives-transformed-50-years-of-head-start/.

9. "Johnson's Remarks on Signing the Elementary and Secondary Educa-tion Act," Johnson City, Texas, April 11, 1965, LBJ Presidential Library, www.lbjlibrary.org/lyndon-baines-johnson/timeline/johnsons-remarks-on-signing-the-elementary-and-secondary-education-act; Jonathan Kozol, *Savage Inequalities: Children in America's Schools* (New York: Broadway Books, 1991).

10. "Lyndon B. Johnson: XXXVI President of the United States, 1963–1969. 603—Remarks at Southwest Texas State College upon Signing the Higher Edu-cation Act of 1965," American Presidency Project, University of California, Santa Barbara, www.presidency.ucsb.edu/ws/?pid=27356.

11. Quoted in Lynn Weiner, *From Working Girl to Working Mother: The Female Labor Force in the United States, 1820–1980* (Chapel Hill: University of North Carolina Press, 1985); Wilma Mankiller, Gwendolyn Mink, Gloria Steinem, Marysa Navarro, and Barbara Smith, eds., *The Reader's Companion to U.S. Women's History* (New York: Houghton Mifflin, 1998), 427; "American Women in World War II," History.com, March 5, 2010, accessed July 23, 2018, https://www.history.com/topics/world-war-ii/american-women-in-world-war-ii; "About 3,000,000 Women Now in War Work," *Science News Letter*, January 16, 1943.

12. Maris Vinovskis, *The Birth of Head Start: Preschool Education Policies in the Kennedy and Johnson Administrations* (Chicago: University of Chicago Press, 2008).

13. Patricia Rosenfield and Rachel Wimpee, "The Ford Foundation: Constant Themes, Historical Variations," Rockefeller Archive Center, 2015, Rockarch.org/publications/ford/overview/FordFoundationHistory1936-2001.pdf; G. William Domhoff, "The Ford Foundation in the Inner City: Forging an Alliance with Neighborhood Activists," September 2005, https://whorulesamerica.ucsc.edu/local/ford_foundation.html.

14. Vinovskis, *Birth of Head Start*.

15. "Lyndon B. Johnson: XXXVI President of the United States, 1963–1969. 259—Remarks on Project Head Start," American Presidency Project, University of California, Santa Barbara, May 18, 1965, www.presidency.ucsb.edu/ws/?pid=26973.

16. Ibid.

17. Ibid.

18. Ibid.

19. Quoted in Vinovskis, *Birth of Head Start*.

20. Edward Zigler and Jeannette Valentine, *Project Head Start: A Legacy of the War on Poverty* (New York: Free Press, 1979), quoted in Vinovskis, *Birth of Head Start*.

21. Shelby County v. Holder, 570 U.S. 2 (2013).

22. "History of Head Start," Office of Head Start in the United States Department of Health and Human Services, last reviewed July 18, 2018, accessed July 23, 2018, https://www.acf.hhs.gov/ohs/about/history-of-head-start; "2016 National Head Start Profile," National Head Start Association, accessed July 23, 2018, https://www.nhsa.org/files/resources/2016-national-head-start-fact-sheet.pdf; David Blau and Janet Currie, "Who's Minding the Kids? Preschool, Day Care, and After School Care," in *The Handbook of Education Economics*, vol. 2, Finis Welch and Eric Hanushek, eds. (New York: North Holland, 2006), 1163–1278.

23. Edward Zigler and Sally J. Styfco, *The Hidden History of Head Start* (Oxford: Oxford University Press, 2010).

24. Joe Klein, "Time to Ax Public Programs That Don't Yield Results," *Time*, July 7, 2011, accessed April 24, 2018, http://content.time.com/time/nation/article/0,8599,2081778,00.html; Matt Mackowiak, "Even Government

Agrees Head Start Is a Failure," *Townhall*, March 23, 2014, accessed April 24, 2018, https://townhall.com/columnists/mattmackowiak/2014/03/23/even-government -agrees-head-start-is-a-failure-n1812639. In contrast, rigorous program evaluations include Avi Feller, Todd Grindal, Luke Miratrix, and Lindsay Page, "Compared to What? Variation in the Impacts of Early Childhood Education by Alternative Care Type," *Annals of Applied Statistics* 110, no. 3 (2016): 1245–1285; Patrick Kline and Christopher R. Walters, "Evaluating Public Programs with Close Substitutes: The Case of Head Start," *Quarterly Journal of Economics* 13, no. 4 (2016): 1795–1848.

25. Lois-Ellin Datta, "A Report on Evaluation Studies of Project Head Start," Office of Economic Opportunity, Washington, DC, 1969, https://files.eric .ed.gov/fulltext/ED037239.pdf; Barbara Bates, "Project Head Start, 1965–67: A Descriptive Report of Programs and Participants," Office of Child Development, US Department of Health, Education, and Welfare, September 1969.

26. *Head Start: Undercover Testing Finds Fraud and Abuse at Selected Head Start Centers*, US Government Accountability Office Report, September, 2010, https://www.gao.gov/assets/320/310200.pdf.

27. Roland Fryer and Steven Levitt, "The Black-White Test Score Gap Through Third Grade," *American Law and Economics Review* 8, no. 2 (July 1, 2006): 249–281, https://doi.org/10.1093/aler/ahl003; Janet Currie and Duncan Thomas, "Does Head Start Make a Difference?" *American Economic Review* 85, no. 3 (June 1995): 344; Jane McLeod and Karen Kaiser, "Childhood Emotional and Behavioral Problems and Educational Attainment," *American Sociological Review* 69, no. 5 (January 2004): 636–658, https://doi.org/10.1177 /000312240406900502; James J. Heckman and Stefano Mosso, "The Economics of Human Development and Social Mobility," *Annual Review of Economics* 6, no. 1 (2014): 689–733, https://doi.org/10.1146/annurev-economics -080213-040753.

28. The majority of counties had their first Head Start center established between 1965 and 1970. We assembled data on county Head Start expenditures from the National Archives Records Administration (NARA, 1965–1980); annual district per-pupil spending data were compiled from US Department of Education, National Center for Education Statistics, Education Finance Statistics Center (EDFIN), https://nces.ed.gov/edfin/state_financing.asp.

29. Our models include controls for parental education and occupational status, parental income, mother's marital status at birth, birth weight, child health-insurance coverage, and gender. The adult economic and incarceration outcomes include flexible controls for age (cubic). We also included birth-year fixed effects by region and race and birth-cohort linear trends interacting with various 1960 characteristics of the childhood county (poverty rate, percent black, average education, percent urban, and population size). Other concurrent policy changes were explicitly controlled for (including school desegregation, hospital desegregation, the roll-out and/or expansions of Aid to Families with Dependent Children (AFDC), Medicaid, Food Stamps, Community Health Centers, Title

I funding, and kindergarten introduction) and do not account for the pattern of results presented here.

30. To validate our models, we show that (1) the identifying variation in Head Start spending is unrelated to family, community, and other policy changes; (2) Head Start spending in a child's county during non–Head Start eligible ages (ages one through three and five through ten) is unrelated to student outcomes conditional on Head Start spending during the target age (age four); and (3) Head Start spending has no effect on non-poor populations that were largely ineligible for the program. We find similar results even when comparing siblings.

31. Related evidence is found in Jens Ludwig and Douglas L. Miller, "Does Head Start Improve Children's Life Chances? Evidence from a Regression Discontinuity Design," *Quarterly Journal of Economics* 122, no. 1 (February 1, 2007): 159–208, https://doi.org/10.1162/qjec.122.1.159; Eliana Garces, Duncan Thomas, and Janet Currie, "Longer-Term Effects of Head Start," *American Economic Review* 92, no. 4 (2002): 999–1012; M. W. Lipsey, D. C. Farran, and K. G. Hofer, "A Randomized Control Trial of the Effects of a Statewide Voluntary Prekindergarten Program on Children's Skills and Behaviors Through Third Grade (Research Report)," Vanderbilt University, Peabody Research Institute, September 2015.

32. Quoted in Vinovskis, *Birth of Head Start.*

33. Zigler and Styfco, *Hidden History of Head Start*; *Project Head Start 1968: The Development of a Program* (Washington, DC: US Department of Health, Education and Welfare, Office of Child Development 1970); *Project Head Start: The Quiet Revolution*, Second Annual Report of the Office of Economic Opportunity (Washington, DC: Government Printing Office, 1967); Rucker C. Johnson, "The Health Returns of Education Policies: From Preschool to High School and Beyond," *American Economic Review* 100, no. 2 (May 2010): 188–194.

34. Julie C. Lumeng, Niko Kaciroti, Julie Sturza, Allison M. Krusky, Alison L. Miller, Karen E. Peterson, Robert Lipton, and Thomas M. Reischl, "Changes in Body Mass Index Associated with Head Start Participation," *Pediatrics*, January 12, 2015, accessed April 24, 2018, http://pediatrics.aappublications.org/content/early/2015/01/07/peds.2014-1725.

35. RaeHyuck Lee, Fuhua Zhai, Wen-Jui Han, Jeanne Brooks-Gunn, and Jane Waldfogel, "Head Start and Children's Nutrition, Weight, and Health Care Receipt," *Early Childhood Research Quarterly* 28, no. 4 (2013): 723–733.

36. "Five Numbers to Remember About Early Childhood Development," Harvard University, Center on the Developing Child, 2009, retrieved from www.developingchild.harvard.edu; Anatole S. Dekaban and Doris Sadowsky, "Changes in Brain Weights During the Span of Human Life: Relation of Brain Weights to Body Heights and Body Weights," *Annals of Neurology* 4, no. 4 (1978): 345–356; Jack P. Shonkoff and Deborah A. Phillips, eds., *From Neurons to Neighborhoods: The Science of Early Childhood Development* (Washington, DC: National Academies Press, 2000); Betty Hart and Todd R. Risley, *Meaningful Differences in the*

Everyday Experience of Young American Children (Baltimore: Paul H. Brookes Publishing, 1995); Steven Pinker, *The Language Instinct* (New York: Harper Perennial Modern Classics, 1994).

37. Jack P. Shonkoff, Andrew S. Garner, Committee on Psychoscocial Aspects of Child and Family Health, Committee on Early Childhood, Adoption, and Dependent Care, Section on Developmental and Behavioral Pediatrics, "The Lifelong Effects of Early Childhood Adversity and Toxic Stress," *Pediatrics* 129, no. 1 (2012): e232–e246; Jack P. Shonkoff and Deborah A. Phillips, eds., *From Neurons to Neighborhoods: The Science of Early Childhood Development* (Washington, DC: National Academies Press, 2000).

38. Shonkoff and Phillips, eds., *From Neurons to Neighborhoods*; James J. Heckman, "The Economics, Technology, and Neuroscience of Human Capability Formation," *Proceedings of the National Academy of Sciences* 104, no. 33 (2007): 13250–13255; Matthew Neidell and Jane Waldfogel, "Cognitive and Non-Cognitive Peer Effects in Early Education," *Review of Economics and Statistics* 92, no. 3 (2010); Greg Duncan and Richard Murnane, eds., *Whither Opportunity? Rising Inequality, Schools, and Children's Life Chances* (New York: Russell Sage Foundation Press, 2011).

39. US Department of Education, Office for Civil Rights, Civil Rights Data Collection, "Data Snapshot: School Discipline," March 2014, https://ocrdata .ed.gov/downloads/crdc-school-discipline-snapshot.pdf; Douglas Almond and Janet Currie, "Human Capital Development Before Age Five," in *Handbook of Labor Economics*, Orley Ashenfelter and David Card, eds. (London: North Holland, 2010); Fryer and Levitt, "Black-White Test Score Gap"; Roland Fryer and Steven Levitt, "Understanding the Black-White Test Score Gap in the First Two Years of School," *Review of Economics and Statistics* 86, no. 2 (2004); Flavio Cunha and James Heckman, "The Technology of Skill Formation," *American Economic Review* 97, no. 2 (May 2007): 31–47.

40. David J. Kelly, Paul C. Quinn, Alan M. Slater, Kang Lee, Alan Gibson, Michael Smith, Liezhong Ge, and Olivier Pascalis, "Three-Month-Olds, But Not Newborns, Prefer Own-Race Faces," *Developmental Science* 8 (2005): F31–F36; Lawrence Hirschfeld, "Children's Understanding of Racial Groups," in *Children's Understanding of Society*, M. Barrett and E. Buchanan-Barrow, eds. (New York: Psychology Press, 2005), 199–221; Phyllis Katz and Jennifer Kofkin, "Race, Gender, and Young Children," in *Developmental Psychopathology: Perspectives on Adjustment, Risk, and Disorder*, S. S. Luthar, J. A. Burack, D. Cicchetti, and J. R. Weisz, eds. (New York: Cambridge University Press), 51–74; Frances E. Aboud, "The Development of Prejudice in Childhood and Adolescence," in *On the Nature of Prejudice: Fifty Years After Allport*, J. F. Dovidio, P. Glick, and L. A. Rudman, eds. (Malden: Blackwell, 2005), 310–326; Kristin Shutts, Katherine D. Kinzler, Rachel C. Katz, Colin Tredoux, and Elizabeth S. Spelke, "Race Preferences in Children: Insights from South Africa," *Developmental Science* 14 (2011): 1283–1291; Yarrow Dunham, Andrew Baron, and Mahzahrin Banaji, "The De-

velopment of Implicit Intergroup Cognition," *Trends in Cognitive Sciences* 12 (2008): 248–253.

41. For example, "They're Not Too Young to Talk About Race!" Children's Community School, February 2018.

42. Clive R. Belfield, Milagros Nores, W. Steven Barnett, and Lawrence Schweinhart, "The High/Scope Perry Preschool Program Cost-Benefit Analysis Using Data from the Age-40 Follow-up," *Journal of Human Resources* 41, no. 1 (2006): 162–190, https://highscope.org/perrypreschoolstudy; James J. Heckman, Rodrigo Pinto, and Peter Savelyev, "Understanding the Mechanisms Through Which an Influential Early Childhood Program Boosted Adult Outcomes," *American Economic Review* 103, no. 6 (2013): 2052–2086; W. Steven Barnett and Leonard N. Masse, "Comparative Benefit-Cost Analysis of the Abecedarian Program and Its Policy Implications," *Economics of Education Review* 26, no. 1 (2007): 113–125. Rigorous evaluations of these programs demonstrated substantial return on investment, ranging from $4 to $16 for every dollar invested in the program.

43. Quoted in Joe Heim, "Head Start Is Underfunded and Unequal, According to a New Study," *Washington Post*, December 14, 2016; "The State(s) of Head Start," National Institute for Early Education Research Report, 2016, http://nieer.org/headstart.

44. "State(s) of Head Start."

45. David L. Kirp, "How New York Made Pre-K a Success," *New York Times*, February 13, 2016.

46. Will Dobbie and Roland G. Fryer, "Are High-Quality Schools Enough to Increase Achievement Among the Poor? Evidence from the Harlem Children's Zone," *American Economic Journal: Applied Economics* 3, no. 3 (July 2011): 158–187.

CHAPTER 5: PUTTING THE PIECES TOGETHER

1. David Shipler, *The Working Poor: Invisible in America* (New York: Vintage, 2004).

2. Harriet Lipman Sepinwall, "The New Jersey Constitution and the 1875 'Thorough and Efficient' Education Amendment," *Journal of the Rutgers University Libraries* 59 (2001): 57–72.

3. Ibid.

4. Ibid.

5. N.J. Const. Art. VIII § IV. Italics mine.

6. Homer Bigart, "Newark Riot Deaths at 21 as Negro Sniping Widens; Hughes May Seek U.S. Aid," *New York Times*, July 16, 1967, https://archive.nytimes.com/www.nytimes.com/library/national/race/071667race-ra.html. Amount in 2018 dollars. The riots cost $10 million in 1967 dollars: Jessica Mazzola and Karen Yi, "50 Years Ago Newark Burned," NJ.com, July 13, 2017,

https://www.nj.com/essex/index.ssf/2017/07/what_you_need_to_know_about
_the_1967_newark_riots.html.

7. Stephen M. Gillon, *Separate and Unequal: The Kerner Commission and the Unraveling of American Liberalism* (New York: Basic Books, 2018).

8. National Advisory Commission on Civil Disorders, *The Report of the National Advisory Commission on Civil Disorders,* June 27, 1967, available at https://www.ncjrs.gov/pdffiles1/Digitization/8073NCJRS.pdf.

9. Ibid.

10. Ibid.

11. Robinson v. Cahill, 118 N.J. Super. 223 (1972), aff'd Robinson v. Cahill, 62 N.J. 473 (1973); Robinson v. Cahill, 62 N.J. 473, 481 (1973).

12. "Public School Education Act of 1975," N.J. Sen. Bill 1516, presently enacted at N.J. Rev. Stat. § 18A:7F-44 (2017), available at https://repo.njstatelib.org/bitstream/handle/10929.1/5995/L1975c212.pdf?sequence=1&isAllowed=y.

13. Abbott v. Burke, 100 N.J. 269, 278 (1985) (describing plaintiff's argument).

14. Abbott v. Burke, 100 N.J. 269, 296 (1985).

15. Abbott v. Burke, No. EDU 5581-88 (OAL 1988); "Eighth Annual State of the State Message to the State Legislature," Governor Thomas H. Kean, January 9, 1990, Center on the American Governor at Rutgers University, accessed July 29, 2018, http://governors.rutgers.edu/testing/wp-content/uploads/2014/01/kean_speech_1990-01-09_Sos.pdf.

16. Abbott v. Burke, 119 N.J. 287, 295 (1990).

17. Ibid.

18. Gary Stein, interview by Rucker Johnson, October 2017.

19. Ibid.

20. Today, there are thirty-one Abbott districts. The New Jersey commissioner of education, William Librera, and the New Jersey legislature so certified Plainfield, Neptune, and Salem City in a subsequent administrative decision and statute. William Librera, "Designation of Abbott Districts Criteria and Process," New Jersey Department of Education, June 15, 2015, https://www.state.nj.us/education/archive/abbotts/regs/criteria/criteria2.htm; "History of Funding Equity," New Jersey Department of Education, accessed July 30, 2018, https://www.state.nj.us/education/archive/abbotts/chrono; Peter Kerr, "Senate Passes Changes in Aid in Florio Plan," *New York Times*, March 8, 1991, https://www.nytimes.com/1991/03/08/nyregion/senate-passes-changes-in-aid-in-florio-plan.html; Comprehensive Educational Improvement and Financing Act, codified at N.J.S.A. 18A:7F-1 to -34; Abbott v. Burke, 149 N.J. 145, 444, 451 (1997).

21. The court specifically "direct[ed] that the Commissioner implement whole-school reform; implement full-day kindergarten and a half-day preschool program for three- and four-year olds as expeditiously as possible; implement the technology, alternative school, accountability, and school-to-work and college-transition programs; prescribe procedures and standards to enable

individual schools to adopt additional or extended supplemental programs and to seek and obtain the funds necessary to implement those programs for which they have demonstrated a particularized need; implement the facilities plan and timetable . . . proposed; secure funds to cover the complete cost of remediating identified life-cycle and infrastructure deficiencies in Abbott school buildings as well as the cost of providing the space necessary to house Abbott students adequately; and promptly initiate effective managerial responsibility over school construction, including necessary funding measures and fiscal reforms, such as may be achieved through amendment of the Educational Facilities Act." Abbott v. Burke, 149 N.J. 145, 444, 451 (1997).

22. Deborah Poritz, interview by Rucker Johnson, October 20, 2017.

23. Rucker C. Johnson, "Follow the Money: School Spending from Title I to Adult Earnings," in David Gamson, Kathryn McDermott, and Douglas Reed, eds., *The Elementary and Secondary Education Act at 50, RSF: The Russell Sage Foundation Journal of the Social Sciences* 1, no. 3 (2015): 50–76; Rucker C. Johnson, "Can Schools Level the Intergenerational Playing Field? Lessons from Equal Educational Opportunity Policies," in *Economic Mobility: Research and Ideas on Strengthening Families, Communities, and the Economy*, Federal Reserve Bank of St. Louis and the Board of Governors of the Federal Reserve System, eds. (Washington, DC: Federal Reserve Bank of St. Louis and the Board of Governors of the Federal Reserve System, 2015), 289–324.

24. Julien Lafortune, Jesse Rothstein, and Diane Whitmore Schanzenbach, "School Finance Reform and the Distribution of Student Achievement," *American Economic Journal: Applied Economics* 10, no. 2 (2018): 1–26, https://pubs .aeaweb.org/doi/pdfplus/10.1257/app.20160567. The paper reported average effects using data across all states. From a research design perspective, this comparison between New Jersey and Pennsylvania is reminiscent of a famous study on the impacts of the minimum wage in these two states by the economists David Card and Alan Krueger: "Minimum Wages and Employment: A Case Study of the Fast-Food Industry in New Jersey and Pennsylvania," *American Economic Review* 84, no. 4 (1992): 772–793.

25. Lafortune et al., "School Finance Reform and the Distribution of Student Achievement."

26. Gary Stein, interview by Rucker Johnson, October 2017; Gary Orfield, Jongyeon Ee, and Ryan Coughlan, "New Jersey's Segregated Schools: Trends and Paths Forward," Civil Rights Project, November 2017, https://www.civilrights project.ucla.edu/research/k-12-education/integration-and-diversity/new-jerseys -segregated-schools-trends-and-paths-forward/New-Jersey-report-final-110917 .pdf.

27. Martin Luther King Jr., speech in Chicago to the second convention of the Medical Committee for Human Rights, March 25, 1966; Simkins v. Moses H. Cone Memorial Hospital, 323 F.2d 959 (4th Cir. 1963); Civil Rights Act of 1964, Title VI, 42 U.S.C. § 2000d et seq.; Social Security Amendments of 1965, Pub. L. 89-97.

28. I used the American Hospital Association's Annual Survey of Hospitals along with the Centers for Medicare and Medicaid Services Provider of Services data files to identify the precise date on which a Medicare-certified hospital was established in each county of the United States, an accurate marker for hospital desegregation compliance. Amy Finkelstein, "Aggregate Effects of Health Insurance: Evidence from the Introduction of Medicare," *Quarterly Journal of Economics* 122, no. 1 (2007): 1–37; Douglas Almond, Kenneth Chay, and Michael Greenstone, "The Civil Rights Act of 1964, Hospital Desegregation and Black Infant Mortality in Mississippi," NBER Working Paper JEL No. J15, I18, I11, I38, N32 (March 2008), http://s3.amazonaws.com/zanran_storage/qed.econ .queensu.ca/ContentPages/52986132.pdf; Kenneth Chay, Jonathan Guryan, and Bhashkar Mazumder, "Birth Cohort and the Black-White Achievement Gap: The Roles of Access and Health Soon After Birth," Federal Reserve Bank of Chicago, June 2009, https://files.eric.ed.gov/fulltext/ED505624.pdf.

29. Rucker C. Johnson and Robert F. Schoeni, "The Influence of Early-Life Events on Human Capital, Health Status, and Labor Market Outcomes over the Life Course," *B.E. Journal of Economic Analysis and Policy: Advances* 11, no. 3, article 3 (2011), www.bepress.com/bejeap/vol11/iss3/art3.

30. Rucker C. Johnson and C. Kirabo Jackson, "Reducing Inequality Through Dynamic Complementarity: Evidence from Head Start and Public School Spending," NBER Working Paper No. 23489 (forthcoming).

31. Crawford v. Los Angeles Board of Education, 458 U.S. 527 (1982) (describing the student reassignment aspect of LAUSD's desegregation plan, as it stood in the 1970s and early 1980s); ibid. (describing Proposition 1). In 1978, *Crawford v. Board of Education of Los Angeles* led to a desegregation plan (which still exists today) whereby schools with a minority student population of more than 70 percent would receive compensatory funding to (1) hire more teachers to reduce class size; (2) establish a priority staffing program to help fill teacher vacancies; (3) provide access to a pre-K School Readiness Language Development Program; (4) offer a Medical Counseling, Organizing and Recruiting (Med-COR program)—which provides extra support for high school students enrolled in the medical magnet schools; and (5) provide additional parent-teacher conferences and parent education classes to better support parental involvement. Because of the sheer size and sprawling layout of the city, integration via busing quickly became defunct. Thus, LAUSD employed a multifaceted approach to address the disparities born from segregation that involved substantial resource increases that were *not* tied to integration. The city therefore provides a lens into how important an ingredient integration is as we seek synergistic solutions.

32. "Compliance Review, Los Angeles Unified School District," United States Department of Education, Office for Civil Rights, Region IX, October 11, 2011, accessed July 30, 2018, https://www2.ed.gov/about/offices/list/ocr/docs /investigations/09105001-a.html.

33. At one end of the spectrum were districts like those in Louisiana wherein school spending for minority children increased dramatically and was leveled up to that of white children via a greater state infusion of funds to desegregating districts. At the other end were districts like the Los Angeles Unified School District that infused compensatory funds across five different school-related platforms. Sarah Reber, "From Separate and Unequal to Integrated and Equal? School Desegregation and School Finance in Louisiana," *Review of Economics and Statistics* 93, no. 2 (May 2011): 404–415.

34. The amount of desegregation achieved by the courts varied from district to district, as did the resulting change in access to school-quality inputs received by minority children. This was in part because desegregation was achieved in a variety of ways across school districts and applied in many different initial school environments based on the form of racial segregation—de jure in the South and de facto in other regions of the country. To further explore potential mechanisms, for every district we isolated the desegregation-induced change in per-pupil spending and racial school integration, respectively, which are net of time-invariant school district characteristics, district-specific trends, and a host of other coincident policy changes. We then exploited the variations in the scope of desegregation court orders in addition to quasi-random variations in the timing to assess whether there was evidence of a dose-response effect of school quality improvements on subsequent education, economic, and health attainment outcomes among blacks. This methodology can be viewed as a triple-difference strategy that compares the difference in outcomes between treated and untreated cohorts within districts (variation in exposure) and across districts with larger or smaller changes in school spending due to desegregation (variation in intensity). Importantly, we find no evidence that districts that underwent larger changes in school spending resulting from desegregation exhibited differential trends in outcomes preceding the enactment of court orders, which provides additional support for the identification strategy. We find that court-ordered desegregation that led to larger improvements in school quality resulted in more beneficial educational, economic, and health outcomes in adulthood for blacks who grew up in those court-ordered desegregation districts.

35. Rucker C. Johnson and Sean Tanner, "Money and Freedom: The Impact of California's School Finance Reform on Academic Achievement and the Composition of District Funding," Getting Down to Facts II, 2018, http:// gettingdowntofacts.com/publications/money-and-freedom-impact-californias -school-finance-reform-academic-achievement-and; Rucker C. Johnson and Sean Tanner, "Money and Freedom: The Impact of California's School Finance Reform," Learning Policy Institute Research Brief, 2018, https://learningpolicyinstitute .org/sites/default/files/product-files/Money_Freedom_CA_School_Finance _Reform_BRIEF.pdf.

36. See, for example, Lafortune et al., "School Finance Reform and the Distribution of Student Achievement." These extend earlier studies by David

Card and Alan B. Krueger, "Does School Quality Matter? Returns to Education and the Characteristics of Public Schools in the United States," *Journal of Political Economy* 100 (1992): 1–40. See also David Card and Abigail A. Payne, "School Finance Reform, the Distribution of School Spending, and the Distribution of Student Test Scores," *Journal of Public Economics* 83 (2002): 49–82; Sheila E. Murray, William N. Evans, and Robert M. Schwab, "Education-Finance Reform and the Distribution of Education Resources," *American Economic Review* 88 (1998): 798–812; Caroline M. Hoxby, "All School Finance Equalizations Are Not Created Equal," *Quarterly Journal of Economics* 116 (2001): 1189–1231.

37. Matthew M. Chingos, "How Progressive Is School Funding in the United States?" Brookings Institution, June 15, 2017, https://www.brookings.edu /research/how-progressive-is-school-funding-in-the-united-states.

38. "SFRA Funding Summary," Education Law Center, accessed July 30, 2018, www.edlawcenter.org/research/school-funding-data.html.

39. Gary Stein, interview by Rucker Johnson, October 2017.

40. Winnie Hu and David Chen, "Corzine Is Set to Revamp School Aid Formula," *New York Times*, November 30, 2017, https://www.nytimes.com/2007 /11/30/nyregion/30jersey.html.

41. Ibid.

CHAPTER 6: BUSING IN BOSTON: "WE WON'T GO TO SCHOOL WITH N—RS"

1. "The Boston Busing Crisis Story (1974–1975)," YouTube, December 14, 2016, accessed April 26, 2018, https://www.youtube.com/watch?v=ZgM9sX7deOs.

2. "Eyes on the Prize Interviews: Interview with Jean McGuire," Henry Hampton Collection, Film and Media Archive, Washington University Digital Gateway, accessed April 15, 2018, http://digital.wustl.edu/cgi/t/text/text-idx?c =eop;cc=eop;rgn=div2;view=text;idno=mcg5427.0507.112;node=mcg5427.0507 .112%3A1.4.

3. Matthew Delmont, *Why Busing Failed: Race, Media, and the National Resistance to School Desegregation* (Berkeley: University of California Press, 2016).

4. Morgan v. Hennigan, 379 F. Supp. 410 (D. Mass. 1974).

5. Delmont, *Why Busing Failed*.

6. "Lyndon B. Johnson: XXXVI President of the United States, 1963–1969. 357—Remarks at the University of Michigan, May 22, 1964," American Presidency Project, University of California, Santa Barbara, www.presidency.ucsb.edu /ws/?pid=26262.

7. Milliken v. Bradley, 418 U.S. 717 (1974).

8. Quoted in Richard Rothstein, *The Color of Law: A Forgotten History of How Our Government Segregated America* (New York: Liveright, 2017).

9. Beryl Satter, *Family Properties: Race, Real Estate, and the Exploitation of Black Urban America* (New York: Picador, 2010); William Julius Wilson, *The*

Truly Disadvantaged: The Inner City, the Underclass, and Public Policy (Chicago: University of Chicago Press, 1987).

10. C. Gerald Fraser, "P.S. Super OK's N.Y. Segregation: Says Best Teachers in Harlem," *New York Amsterdam News* June 5, 1954, accessed April 15, 2018, https://search-proquest-com.libproxy.berkeley.edu/docview/225723582 /550FDEFA574A44FDPQ/1?accountid=14496.

11. Kenneth Clark, "Segregation and Desegregation in Our Schools," in Algernon Black, Kenneth Clark, and James Dumpson, *Ethical Frontiers: The City's Children and the Challenge of Racial Discrimination* (New York: Society for Ethical Culture, 1958), 15.

12. Public Education Association, assisted by the New York University Research Center for Human Relations, "The Status of the Public School Education of Negro and Puerto Rican Children in New York City," October 1955.

13. Peter Bart, "School Migration," *Wall Street Journal*, January 29, 1957.

14. Quoted in Adina Back, "Up South in New York: The 1950s School Desegregation Struggles" (PhD diss., New York University, September 1997), 231.

15. Delmont, *Why Busing Failed*.

16. "A Boycott Solves Nothing," *New York Times*, January 31, 1964, accessed April 15, 2018, https://search-proquest-com.libproxy.berkeley.edu /docview/115667231/AAD757EB95354418PQ/1?accountid=14496.

17. Delmont, *Why Busing Failed*; Matt Delmont, "NBC—NY Antibusing Mother," Critical Commons, www.criticalcommons.org/Members/mattdelmont /clips/nbc-ny-antibusing-mother-speaking/view.

18. Delmont, *Why Busing Failed*; "De Facto School Segregation," US Congress, House of Representatives, Special Subcommittee of the Committee on Education and Labor, 89th Cong., 1st sess., July 27–28, 1965, 151, 162, accessed April 15, 2018, https://babel-hathitrust-org.libproxy.berkeley.edu/cgi /pt?id=uc1.$b655386;view=1up;seq=5; "'Willis Wagons' was the pejorative term for portable school classrooms used by critics of Superintendent of Schools Benjamin C. Willis (1953–1966) when protesting school overcrowding and segregation in black neighborhoods from 1962 to 1966." "Willis Wagons," *Encyclopedia of Chicago*, accessed August 6, 2018, www.encyclopedia.chicagohistory .org/pages/1357.html.

19. "Chicago School Boycott," National Archives, accessed August 6, 2018, https://www.archives.gov/education/lessons/desegregation/chicago.html.

20. Delmont, *Why Busing Failed*.

21. "Pucinski Hits Halt to Aid as Arbitrary," *Chicago Tribune*, October 2, 1965; Delmont, *Why Busing Failed*.

22. NPR Staff, "Life After Iconic 1976 Photo: The American Flag's Role in Racial Protest," National Public Radio, September 18, 2016, accessed April 27, 2018, https://www.npr.org/2016/09/18/494442131/life-after-iconic -photo-todays-parallels-of-american-flags-role-in-racial-protes.

23. Roberts v. City of Boston, 59 Mass. 198 (1850).

24. NPR Staff, "Life After Iconic 1976 Photo"; Massachusetts Advisory Committee on Racial Imbalance and Education, "Because It Is Right—Educationally," Massachusetts State Board of Education, 1964, https://repository .library.northeastern.edu/downloads/neu:m039wk782?datastream_id=content.

25. "Because It Is Right—Educationally."

26. Ibid.

27. Jeffrey A. Raffel, *Historical Dictionary of School Segregation and Desegregation: The American Experience* (Westport, CT: Greenwood Press, 1998).

28. "METCO," Massachusetts Department of Education, accessed August 6, 2018, www.doe.mass.edu/metco; "School Enrollment in the Boston Area," *Statistical Atlas*, accessed August 6, 2018, https://statisticalatlas.com/metro-area /Massachusetts/Boston/School-Enrollment; Joshua Angrist and Kevin Lang, "Does School Integration Generate Peer Effects? Evidence from Boston's Metco Program," *American Economic Review* 94, no. 5 (December 2004): 1613–1634.

29. Raffel, *Historical Dictionary of School Segregation and Desegregation*.

30. Quoted in J. Anthony Lukas, *Common Ground: A Turbulent Decade in the Lives of Three American Families* (New York: Alfred A. Knopf, 1985).

31. Ibid., 123.

32. Delmont, *Why Busing Failed*.

33. Quoted in Lukas, *Common Ground*.

34. Katie Zezima, "Louise Day Hicks Dies at 87; Led Fight on Busing in Boston," *New York Times*, October 23, 2003, accessed April 15, 2018, https:// www.nytimes.com/2003/10/23/us/louise-day-hicks-dies-at-87-led-fight-on -busing-in-boston.html.

35. Morgan v. Hennigan, 379 F. Supp. 410 (D. Mass. 1974).

36. Lukas, *Common Ground*.

37. Morgan v. Hennigan, 379 F. Supp. 410 (D. Mass. 1974).

38. Lukas, *Common Ground*.

39. Quoted in ibid.

40. Quoted in ibid.

41. Quoted in Kathleen Banks Nutter, "'Militant Mothers': Boston, Busing, and the Bicentennial of 1976," *Historical Journal of Massachusetts* 38, no. 2 (September 22, 2010): 52.

42. Jeremy Wolff, "A Timeline of Boston School Desegregation, 1961–1985," Civil Rights and Restorative Justice Project, n.d., accessed August 6, 2018, www .racialequitytools.org/resourcefiles/Boston%20Desegregation%20Timeline.pdf.

43. Quoted in Ronald Formisano, *Boston Against Busing: Race, Class, and Ethnicity in the 1960s and 1970s* (Chapel Hill: University of North Carolina Press, 2004), 76.

44. Wolff, "Timeline of Boston School Desegregation"; quoted in Bruce Gellerman, "'It Was Like a War Zone': Busing in Boston," National Public Radio, Boston, WBER, September 5, 2014, www.wbur.org/news/2014/09/05/boston -busing-anniversary.

45. Quoted in Wolff, "Timeline of Boston School Desegregation."

46. Thomas H. O'Connor, *South Boston, My Home Town: The History of an Ethnic Neighborhood* (Boston: Northeastern University Press, 1994), 220.

47. Lukas, *Common Ground.*

48. Morgan v. Nucci, 831 F.2d 313 (1st Cir. 1987); Jim Rattray, "Boston Schools Declared Desegregated," United Press International, September 29, 1987.

49. Ibid.

50. Quoted in "4 Decades After Clashes, Boston Again Debates School Busing," *New York Times*, October 4, 2012.

51. National Association for the Advancement of Colored People, Legal Defense and Educational Fund, *It's Not the Distance, It's the Niggers: Comments on the Controversy over School Busing* (New York: NAACP, 1972).

CHAPTER 7: HOW CHARLOTTE (BRIEFLY) GOT IT RIGHT

1. Pamela Grundy, *Color and Character: West Charlotte High and the American Struggle over Educational Equality* (Chapel Hill: University of North Carolina Press, 2017). For further reading, see also Roslyn Arlin Mickelson, Stephen Samuel Smith, and Amy Hawn Nelson, eds., *Yesterday, Today, and Tomorrow: School Desegregation and Resegregation in Charlotte* (Cambridge, MA: Harvard Education Press, 2015).

2. Don Sturkey's story and photograph are reproduced at Tommy Tomlinson, "Dorothy Counts at Harding High: A Story of Pride, Prejudice," *Charlotte Observer*, September 4, 1957, https://www.charlotteobserver.com/news/local/article66900492.html.

3. Quoted in Elisabeth Arriero, "Charlotte Integration Pioneer Dorothy Counts-Scoggins: 'I Was Ahead of My Time,'" *Charlotte Observer*, February 15, 2015.

4. "History of CMS," *Charlotte-Mecklenburg Schools*, accessed August 17, 2018, www.cms.k12.nc.us/mediaroom/aboutus/Pages/History.aspx.

5. James Ferguson II, interview by Rucker Johnson and Alexander Nazaryan, November 2017.

6. James T. Patterson, *Brown v. Board of Education: A Civil Rights Milestone and Its Troubled Legacy* (New York: Oxford University Press, 2001); "Thurgood Marshall—an American Hero," Los Angeles Public Library blog, February 26, 2017, accessed April 15, 2018, https://www.lapl.org/collections-resources/blogs/lapl/thurgood-marshall-american-hero; Patterson, *Brown v. Board*, 155.

7. Mark Price, "Charlotte Civil Rights Battle Earns Place in History with Julius Chambers Statue," *Charlotte Observer*, November 23, 2016; Swann v. Charlotte-Mecklenburg Board of Education, 402 U.S. 1 (1971).

8. Swann v. Charlotte-Mecklenburg Board of Education, 311 F. Supp. 265 (W.D.N.C. 1970).

9. Ibid.

10. Ibid.

11. Simon Hall, *American Patriotism, American Protest: Social Movements Since the Sixties* (Philadelphia: University of Pennsylvania Press, 2011); Ben A. Franklin, "Impact of White Boycott Unclear as Charlotte Schools Begin Busing Program," *New York Times*, September 10, 1970, accessed April 15, 2018, https://www.nytimes.com/1970/09/10/archives/impact-of-white-boycott-unclear-as-charlotte-schools-begin-busing.html.

12. "Richard Nixon: XXXVII President of the United States, 1969–1974. 91—Statement About Desegregation of Elementary and Secondary Schools," March 24, 1970, American Presidency Project, University of California, Santa Barbara, www.presidency.ucsb.edu/ws/?pid=2923.

13. Swann v. Charlotte-Mecklenburg Board of Education, 402 U.S. 1 (1971).

14. Ibid.

15. Quoted in Grundy, *Color and Character*.

16. Ibid.

17. Quoted in ibid.

18. Quoted in ibid.

19. Quoted in ibid.

20. Ibid.

21. "An Imperfect Revolution: Voices from the Desegregation Era," American Radio Works, n.d., accessed August 19, 2018, http://americanradioworks.publicradio.org/features/deseg/b1.html.

22. Peter Applebome, "Busing Is Abandoned Even in Charlotte," *New York Times*, April 15, 1992, accessed April 15, 2018, https://www.nytimes.com/1992/04/15/education/busing-is-abandoned-even-in-charlotte.html.

23. Editorial, "You Were Wrong, Mr. President," *Charlotte Observer*, October 9, 1984.

24. Grundy, *Color and Character*.

25. Arthur S. Hayes, "Against the Odds: As Others Scale Back on School Integration, Charlotte Presses On; Parents Have Helped Create a Model Busing Program; Harmony Aids Economy; Test Scores Remain a Problem," *Wall Street Journal*, May 8, 1991.

26. Kaycee Hailey, "How I Pursue Change at My Segregated CMS School," *Charlotte Observer*, November 19, 2017.

27. James Ferguson II, interview by Rucker Johnson and Alexander Nazaryan, November 20, 2017; Grundy, *Color and Character*.

28. Quoted in David Francis, "Anatomy of a Boomtown: The Real Story Behind the Rise of Charlotte," City Lab, September 4, 2012.

29. Vicki Bott, *1987 to Today: More Mecklenburg Growth Than Ever Before*, 2008 State of the Environment Report, Mecklenburg County, accessed April 2018, https://www.mecknc.gov/LUESA/Documents/EnviroReport08Land.pdf.

30. Quoted in Grundy, *Color and Character*.

31. Steven Holmes, "Whites' Bias Lawsuit Could Upset Desegregation Efforts," *New York Times*, April 25, 1999.

32. Ross v. Houston Independent School District, 583 F. 2d 712 (1983); Riddick v. The School Board of the City of Norfolk, 784 F. 2d 521 (1986); Board of Education of Oklahoma City v. Dowell, 498 U.S. 237 (1991).

33. Capacchione v. Charlotte-Mecklenburg Schools, 57 F. Supp. 2d 228 (W.D.N.C. 1999).

34. Ibid.

35. Ibid. It is worth noting that Potter hedged slightly, holding that race-based student reassignment would only be deemed unconstitutional "to the extent that [it] would violate the commands of the Equal Protection Clause absent a remedial purpose." Ibid. However, his opinion made clear that combatting resegregation stemming from the actions of citizens, rather than school officials, would not constitute a sufficient "remedial purpose" to warrant race-based student reassignment.

36. Belk v. Charlotte Mecklenburg Board of Education, 269 F.3d 305 (4th Cir. 2001), available at https://www.leagle.com/decision/2001574269f3d3051547. Reagan nominated James Wilkinson III, William Walter Wilkins, and Paul V. Niemeyer. Richard Nixon nominated Hiram Emory Widener Jr. George H. W. Bush nominated John M. Luttig, Karen Williams, and William Traxler. All seven were the only judges on the US Court of Appeals for the Fourth Circuit who voted in favor of affirming the district court's determination that Charlotte had achieved unitary status.

37. Justin Perry, interview by Rucker Johnson and Alexander Nazaryan, November 20, 2017.

38. Ibid.; Johanne Boisjoly, Greg J. Duncan, Michael Kremer, Dan M. Levy, and Jacque Eccles, "Empathy or Antipathy? The Impact of Diversity," *American Economic Review* 96, no. 5 (2006): 1890–1905; Rupert Brown and Miles Hewstone, "An Integrative Theory of Intergroup Contact," *Advances in Experimental Social Psychology* 37 (2005): 255–343.

39. Reprinted in Sam Fulwood III, "Commentary: Charlotte, an Odd Mixture of Progress and Retreat," *Charlotte Observer*, September 5, 2015, https://www.charlotteobserver.com/article34097949.html.

40. Ann Doss Helms, "Racial Breakdowns Highlight School Differences and CMS Challenges," *Charlotte Observer*, November 18, 2015; Kris Nordstrom, "Stymied by Segregation: How Integration Can Transform North Carolina Schools and the Lives of Its Students," North Carolina Justice Center Education and Law Project, 2018, www.ncjustice.org/sites/default/files/STYMIED%20BY%20SEGREGATION%20-%20Integration%20can%20Transform%20NC—FINAL-web.pdf.

41. Raj Chetty, Nathaniel Hendren, and Emmanuel Saez, "Where Is the Land of Opportunity? The Geography of Intergenerational Mobility in the United States," *Quarterly Journal of Economics* 129, no. 4 (2014): 1553–1623.

42. Public School Forum of North Carolina, 2018, https://www.ncforum.org/.

43. Milliken v. Bradley, 418 U.S. 717 (1974); "Fast Facts," Charlotte-Mecklenburg Schools, December 2015, www.cms.k12.nc.us/mediaroom/aboutus/Documents/CMS%20Fast%20Facts%20Sheet%202015-2016.pdf; quoted in Anders Walker, *The Burning House: Jim Crow and the Making of Modern America* (New Haven, CT: Yale University Press, 2018), 183.

44. Belk v. Charlotte Mecklenburg Board of Education, 269 F.3d 305 (4th Cir. 2001), available at https://www.leagle.com/decision/2001574269f3d3051547.

45. Capacchione v. Charlotte-Mecklenburg Schools, 57 F. Supp. 2d 228 (W.D.N.C. 1999).

46. Gene Johnson, "Appeals Court Upholds Seattle's Use of Race in School Admissions," *Seattle Times*, October 20, 2005, accessed April 15, 2018, https://www.seattletimes.com/seattle-news/education/appeals-court-upholds-seattles-use-of-race-in-school-admissions.

47. Parents Involved in Community Schools v. Seattle School District No. 1, 551 U.S. (2007) 701, 742 (Nos. 05-908 and 05-915).

48. Kris Nordstrom, "With HB 514, Legislature Unambiguously Embraces School Segregation," North Carolina Policy Watch, May 31, 2018.

49. Mark Dorosin and Elizabeth Haddix, "NC Bill Would Foster Racial Segregation of Mecklenburg County Schools," *News & Observer*, June 1, 2018.

50. Hugh Macartney and John D. Singleton, "School Boards and Student Segregation," NBER Working Paper No. 23619 (July 2017).

51. Elizabeth Harris, "De Blasio Won't Call New York Schools 'Segregated' but Defends His Diversity Plan," *New York Times*, June 8, 2017.

52. Quoted in Grundy, *Color and Character*; Swann v. Charlotte-Mecklenburg Board of Education, 311 F. Supp. 265 (W.D.N.C. 1970); Hailey, "How I Pursue Change."

53. Sean P. Corcoran, William N. Evans, and Robert M. Schwab, "Changing Labor-Market Opportunities for Women and the Quality of Teachers, 1957–2000," *American Economic Review* 94, no. 2 (May 2004): 230–235; David J. Deming, "Better Schools, Less Crime?" *Quarterly Journal of Economics* 126, no. 4 (2011): 2063–2115.

54. Thomas S. Dee, "Teachers, Race, and Student Achievement in a Randomized Experiment," *Review of Economics and Statistics* 86 no. 1 (2004): 195–210, https://www.mitpressjournals.org/doi/10.1162/003465304323023750; Thomas S. Dee, "A Teacher Like Me: Does Race, Ethnicity, or Gender Matter?" *American Economic Review* 95, no. 2 (2005): 158–165, https://doi.org/10.1257/000282805774670446; Seth Gershenson, Cassandra M.D. Hart, Constance A. Lindsay, and Nicholas W. Papageorge, "The Long-Run Impacts of Same-Race Teachers," IZA Institute of Labor Economics, Discussion Paper Series, ISA DP No. 10630, March 2017, http://ftp.iza.org/dp10630.pdf. The Student Teacher Achievement Ratio, otherwise known as Project Star, was a four-year longitudinal

class-size reduction research project funded by the Tennessee General Assembly and conducted by the State Department of Education.

55. Seth Gershenson, Steven B. Holt, and Nicholas W. Papageorge, "Who Believes in Me? The Effect of Student-Teacher Demographic Match on Teacher Expectations," *Economics of Education Review* 52 (June 2016): 209–224.

56. Jason Grissom and Christopher Redding, "Discretion and Disproportionality: Explaining the Underrepresentation of High-Achieving Students of Color in Gifted Programs," *AERA Open* 2, no. 1 (2016).

57. David Card and Laura Giuliano, "Universal Screening for Gifted Education," *Proceedings of the National Academy of Sciences* 113, no. 48 (November 2016): 13678–13683, https://doi.org/10.1073/pnas.1605043113; Alan A. Aja, William A. Darity Jr., and Darrick Hamilton, "Segregated Education in Desegregated Schools: Why We Should Eliminate 'Tracking' with 'Gifted and Talented' for All," *Huffington Post*, August 2013, https://www.huffingtonpost.com/alan-a-aja/segregated-education-in-d_b_3443865.html.

58. Quotations in this section from Anthony Foxx, interview by Rucker Johnson, January 5, 2018.

59. James Ford, interview by Rucker Johnson, November 2017.

CHAPTER 8: THE BATTLE OF JEFFERSON COUNTY

1. Stout v. Jefferson Cty. Bd. of Educ. (Stout I), 448 F.2d 403, 404 (5th Cir. 1971).

2. Alexander Nazaryan, "Whites Only: School Segregation Is Back, from Birmingham to San Francisco," *Newsweek*, May 7, 2017, https://www.newsweek.com/race-schools-592637.

3. *Fractured: The Breakdown of America's School Districts*, EdBuild, June 2017, https://edbuild.org/content/fractured/fractured-full-report.pdf, citing Ala. Code § 16-8-8; Ala. Code § 16-13-199; Ala. Code § 11-41; Ala. Code § 11-47.

4. Milliken v. Bradley, 418 U.S. 717 (1974).

5. Rebecca Sibilia, interview by Alexander Nazaryan, Spring 2017.

6. Erica Frankenberg, "Splintering School Districts: Understanding the Link Between Segregation and Fragmentation," *Law and Social Inquiry* 34, no. 4 (Fall 2009): 869–909; "Quick Facts: Jefferson County, Alabama: Population Estimates, July 1, 2017, (V2017)," US Census Bureau, n.d., accessed August 22, 2018, https://www.census.gov/quickfacts/fact/table/jeffersoncountyalabama/PST045217; "Alabama School District Rankings," *School Digger*, n.d., accessed August 22, 2018, https://www.schooldigger.com/go/AL/districtrank.aspx; Trisha Powel Crain, "Wealthier Communities Still Spend More on Alabama Students, Data Shows," Alabama.com, October 24, 2017.

7. Frankenberg, "Splintering School Districts."

8. *Fault Lines: America's Most Segregating School District Borders*, EdBuild, August 23, 2016, https://s3.amazonaws.com/edbuild-public-data/data/fault+lines /EdBuild-Fault-Lines-2016.pdf.

9. *Fractured: The Breakdown of America's School Districts*; Joyce Tsai, "Northgate Community Seeks Split from Mt. Diablo School District," *East Bay Times*, January 7, 2017.

10. Tsai, "Northgate Community Seeks Split."

11. John Yun, Michigan State University, expert testimony of research evidence, US District Court for the Northern District of Alabama, Southern Division, Linda Stout et al. v. Jefferson County Board of Education and Gardendale City Board of Education, filed August 26, 2016.

12. Stout v. Jefferson, 882 F.3d 988 (2018).

13. Original data compiled by Sean Reardon, updated with information from American Communities Project data (Brown University) and ProPublica data on status of desegregation court cases (Yue Qiu and Nikole Hannah-Jones, "A National Survey of School Desegregation Orders," ProPublica, December 23, 2014, https://projects.propublica.org/graphics/desegregation-orders); Sean F. Reardon, Elena Tej Grewal, Demetra Kalogrides, and Erica Greenberg, "Brown Fades: The End of Court-Ordered School Desegregation and the Resegregation of American Public Schools," *Journal of Policy Analysis and Management* 31, no. 4 (2012): 876–904; Byron Lutz, "The End of Court-Ordered Desegregation," *American Economic Journal: Economic Policy* 3, no. 2 (2011): 130–168, https://doi.org /10.1257/pol.3.2.130; "The Integration Report," Civil Rights Project, University of California, Los Angeles, 2011.

14. C. Kirabo Jackson, "Student Demographics, Teacher Sorting, and Teacher Quality: Evidence from the End of School Desegregation," *Journal of Labor Economics* 27, no. 2, (2009): 213–256.

15. Rucker C. Johnson, "The Consequences of the End of Court-Ordered Desegregation," University of California, Berkeley, and National Bureau of Economic Research, 2018; David J. Deming, "The Growing Importance of Social Skills in the Labor Market," *Quarterly Journal of Economics* 132, no. 4 (2017): 1593–1640.

16. Martin Luther King, Jr., "Advice for living," *Ebony* 13, no. 7 (May 1958): 112, retrieved from MasterFILE Premier, 48347474; Will Dobbie and Roland G. Fryer Jr., "The Impact of Voluntary Youth Service on Future Outcomes: Evidence from Teach for America," *B.E. Journal of Economic Analysis and Policy* 15, no. 3 (2015): 1031–1065; Johanne Boisjoly, Greg J. Duncan, Michael Kremer, Dan M. Levy, and Jacque Eccles, "Empathy or Antipathy? The Impact of Diversity," *American Economic Review* 96, no. 5 (2006): 1890–1905; Rupert Brown and Miles Hewstone, "An Integrative Theory of Intergroup Contact," *Advances in Experimental Social Psychology* 37 (2005): 255–343; Thomas F. Pettigrew and Linda R. Tropp, "A Meta-Analytic Test of Intergroup Contact Theory," *Journal of Personality and Social Psychology* 90, no. 5 (2006): 751–783.

17. Tracy E. K'Meyer, "The Busing Crisis," in *Civil Rights in the Gateway to the South: Louisville, Kentucky, 1945–1980* (Lexington: University Press of Kentucky, 2011).

18. "40 Years After Desegregation, a Look Back at Busing in Louisville," Wave3 News, February 8, 2016, accessed February 19, 2018, www.wave3 .com/story/31170091/on-a-journeybusing-a-look-back; K'Meyer, "Busing Crisis"; Alfonso A. Narvaez, "Judge James Gordon Dies at 71; Imposed a Landmark Busing Plan," *New York Times*, February 13, 1990, accessed September 28, 2018, https://www.nytimes.com/1990/02/13/obituaries/judge-james-gordon-dies -at-71-imposed-a-landmark-busing-plan.html; Harvey Sloane, "Busing Left Slow-Healing Scar," *Courier-Journal*, August 30, 2015, accessed February 19, 2018, www.courier-journal.com/story/opinion/contributors/2015/08/30 /harvey-sloane-busing-left-slow-healingscar/32276003; Edith Nelson Yarbrough, phone interview by Rebecca Damante, August 28, 2016; William Griffin, "Two Cities Await Day of the Buses," *Chicago Tribune*, September 8, 1975, accessed July 18, 2016, http://archives.chicagotribune.com/1975/09/08/page/1/article /louisville; "10,000 Rampage in Louisville Busing Fight," *Chicago Tribune*, September 6, 1975.

19. Reed Karaim, "Are U.S. Schools Becoming Resegregated?" *CQ Researcher* 24, no. 31 (September 5, 2014), http://library.cqpress.com/cqresearcher /document.php?id=cqresrre2014090500.

20. Parents Involved in Community Schools v. Seattle School District No. 1., 551 U.S. (2007) 701, 742 (Nos. 05-908 and 05-915).

21. Quotations in this section from Sheldon Berman, interview by Rucker Johnson and Alex Nazaryan, August 10, 2017; "Courageous Acts: Personal Tales," School Superintendents Association, n.d., accessed September 29, 2018, www.aasa.org/SchoolAdministratorArticle.aspx?id=19996.

22. Holly Holland, "Schools Worried by Clusters of Poverty," *Louisville Courier Journal*, December 11, 1993.

23. Karaim, "Are U.S. Schools Becoming Resegregated?"; Dawn Gee, "Forced Busing: Was It Worth It?" Wave3 News, February 10, 2016, www .wave3.com/story/31191208/forced-busing-was-it-worth-it; Alana Semuels, "The City That Believed in Desegregation," *Atlantic*, March 27, 2015, accessed July 18, 2016, www.theatlantic.com/business/archive/2015/03/the-city-that-believed -in-desegregation/388532.

24. Genevieve Siegel-Hawley, *When the Fences Come Down: Twenty-First-Century Lessons from Metropolitan School Desegregation* (Chapel Hill: University of North Carolina Press, 2016).

25. Kimberly Quick and Rebecca Damante, "Louisville, Kentucky: A Reflection on School Integration," Century Foundation Report (September 15, 2016), https://s3-us-west-2.amazonaws.com/production.tcf.org/app/uploads/2016 /09/03193859/louisville-kentucky-a-reflection-on-school-integration.pdf.

26. Sheldon Berman, excerpt included courtesy of Dr. Berman.

27. Carolyn Phenicie, "Interview: Arne Duncan Grades Himself," The 74, February 7, 2016, https://www.the74million.org/article/the-74-interview-arne-duncan-grades-himself-and-sees-failures-on-pre-k-safety-desegregation.

28. Gary Orfield and Erica Frankenberg, "Experiencing Integration in Louisville: How Parents and Students See the Gains and Challenges," Civil Rights Project, University of California, Los Angeles, January 2011, accessed February 19, 2018, https://civilrightsproject.ucla.edu/research/k-12-education/integration-and-diversity/experiencing-integration-in-louisvillehow-parents-and-students-see-the-gains-and-challenges/LOUISVILLE_finalV3_12711.pdf; Semuels, "The City That Believed."

CHAPTER 9: MEMPHIS CITY SCHOOL BLUES

1. Jennifer Pignolet, "A Shelby County School Went Nearly a Year Without a Chemistry Teacher—and No Students Passed the Test," *Commercial Appeal*, October 15, 2017.

2. Barack Obama, "Commencement Address at Booker T. Washington High School," *Time*, May 16, 2011, http://time.com/4340922/obama-commencement-speech-transcript-booker-t-washington-high-school.

3. Dwania Kyles, interview by Rucker Johnson and Alexander Nazaryan, November 2017.

4. Daniel Kiel, "Exploded Dream: Desegregation in Memphis City Schools," *Law and Inequality* 26, no. 2 (2008): 270.

5. *The Memphis 13* (documentary), directed by Daniel Kiel, October 3, 2011, https://thememphis13.com.

6. Linda Moore, "The First Steps—Satchels, Big Hopes Weighed Heavy on 13 First-Graders as They Made History 50 Years Ago Integrating Memphis Schools," *Commercial Appeal*, October 2, 2011.

7. Claude Armour, "The Other South," *Time*, May 7, 1965, quoted in Ben Kamen, *Room 306: The National Story of the Lorraine Motel* (East Lansing: Michigan State University Press, 2012).

8. W. E. B. Du Bois, *The Souls of Black Folk* (New York: Dover, 1903).

9. Ernest Withers, "First Day of Memphis Integration, TN," Collection of the Smithsonian National Museum of African American History and Culture, 1961; Kiel, "Exploded Dream," 273.

10. Northcross v. Board of Education, 302 F.2d 818, 824 (6th Cir. 1962); Kiel, "Exploded Dream," 273.

11. Martin Luther King Jr., "I've Been to the Mountain Top," speech, April 3, 1968, King Papers, Stanford University, https://kinginstitute.stanford.edu/king-papers/documents/ive-been-mountaintop-address-delivered-bishop-charles-mason-temple.

12. Sam Roberts, "Rev. Samuel Billy Kyles Was a Witness to Martin Luther King's Last Moments," *The Bulletin*, May 1, 2016, https://www.bendbulletin.com/home/4272195-151/rev-samuel-billy-kyles-was-a-witness-to.

13. *Newsweek*, October 27, 1969.

14. Northcross v. Board of Education 341 F. Supp. at 592 (6th Cir. 1972); Marcus D. Pohlmann, *Opportunity Lost: Race and Poverty in the Memphis City Schools* (Knoxville: University of Tennessee Press, 2010).

15. Kiel, "Exploded Dream," 273, 295; *Fractured: The Breakdown of America's School Districts*, EdBuild, June 2017, https://edbuild.org/content/fractured/fractured-full-report.pdf.

16. Tenn. Code Ann. § 49-2-501 (2010); Tenn. Code Ann. § 6-58-112 (2010).

17. "Booker T. Washington High School Wins Race to the Top Commencement Challenge," US Department of Education, May 10, 2011.

18. Dan Balz, "The GOP Takeover in the States," *Washington Post*, November 13, 2010, www.washingtonpost.com/wp-dyn/content/article/2010/11/13/AR2010111302389.html?sid=ST2010111400091&noredirect=on.

19. "2010 Election Results: Tennessee," *New York Times*, 2010, https://www.nytimes.com/elections/2010/results/tennessee.html.

20. *Fractured: The Breakdown of America's School Districts*.

21. Ibid.

22. Tenn. Code Ann. § 49-2-501 (2010); Tenn. Code Ann. § 6-58-112 (2010).

23. Bill Dries, "Emotions Bared over School Charter Fight," *Memphis Daily News*, December 22, 2010, https://www.memphisdailynews.com/news/2010/dec/22/emotions-bared-over-school-charter-fight.

24. Ibid.

25. Campbell Robertson, "Memphis to Vote on Transferring School System to County," *New York Times*, January 27, 2011.

26. Board of Education of Shelby County v. Memphis City Board of Education, No. 11-2101 (D. Ct. W.D. Tenn., August 8, 2011).

27. Sam Dillon, "Merger of Memphis and County School Districts Revives Race and Class Challenges," *New York Times*, November 5, 2011.

28. "State Report Card," Tennessee Department of Education, n.d., accessed August 28, 2018, https://www.tn.gov/education/data/report-card.html. The Tennessee Department of Education website allows users to review demographic profiles for each of the state's school districts in any of the four most recent academic years.

29. Kontji Anthony, "All Six Municipalities Choose to Form School Districts," WMC Action News 5, July 16, 2013; Erica Frankenberg, conversation with Rucker Johnson, March 2018.

30. *Fractured: The Breakdown of America's School Districts*.

31. Clay Bailey, "About Time for Suburbs to Chant 'Told You So' to Doubters of Municipal School Districts," *Commercial Appeal*, August 3, 2017.

32. *Fractured: The Breakdown of America's School Districts.*

33. Rucker C. Johnson, "The Grandchildren of Brown: The Long Legacy of School Desegregation," University of California, Berkeley, and National Bureau of Economic Research, 2018. For the "Grandchildren of Brown" intergenerational analysis, we examined the educational outcomes of cohorts born since 1980. The comparisons are between children whose parents had grown up in the same district and were otherwise similar, but where some parents had been exposed to desegregated schools during childhood and some had not (i.e., they had been eighteen or older at the time of the initial court orders); we also compared those whose parents had been exposed for only a portion of their school-age years (i.e., the court orders occurred during their middle school or high school years) to those whose parents had been exposed throughout their school-age years (i.e., the court orders occurred prior to school entry). We accounted for other coincident policies (food stamps, safety net policies, Medicaid, Head Start) and an extensive set of parental family and neighborhood factors in order to isolate the school reform effects.

34. David Card, Alexandre Mas, and Jesse Rothstein, "Tipping and the Dynamics of Segregation," *Quarterly Journal of Economics* 123, no. 1 (2008): 177–218.

35. William E. Schmidt, "Some Whites Are Returning to Memphis Schools," *New York Times*, May 25, 1985, https://www.nytimes.com/1985/05/25/us/some-whites-are-returning-to-memphis-schools.html.

36. Quotations in this section from Willie Herenton, interview by Rucker Johnson and Alexander Nazaryan, November 2017.

37. William H. Frey, "Black Flight to the Suburbs on the Rise," Brookings Institution, July 31, 2015, https://www.brookings.edu/blog/the-avenue/2015/07/31/black-flight-to-the-suburbs-on-the-rise.

38. Nick Anderson and Bill Turque, "Obama Says D.C. Schools Not on Par with Sidwell," *Washington Post*, September 28, 2010, www.washingtonpost.com/wp-dyn/content/article/2010/09/27/AR2010092706887.html.

39. David Card and Laura Giuliano, "Universal Screening for Gifted Education," *Proceedings of the National Academy of Sciences* 113, no. 48 (November 2016): 13678–13683, https://doi.org/10.1073/pnas.1605043113; Jason Grissom and Christopher Redding, "Discretion and Disproportionality: Explaining the Underrepresentation of High-Achieving Students of Color in Gifted Programs," *AERA Open* 2, no. 1 (2016): 1–25.

40. Claude M. Steele and Joshua Aronson, "How Stereotypes Influence the Standardized Test Performance of Talented African American Students," in *The Black-White Test Score Gap*, Christopher Jencks and Meredith Phillips, eds. (Washington, DC: Brookings Institution Press, 1998), 401–427.

CONCLUSION: COMING UP TOGETHER

1. The analyses we have conducted have focused primarily on black-white differences mainly because data limitations in the PSID reduce the sample sizes of other racial or ethnic groups that have been followed from birth to adulthood.

2. Richard Rothstein, *The Color of Law: A Forgotten History of How Our Government Segregated America* (New York: Liveright, 2017).

3. Tim Henderson, "How Some Cities Reverse Segregation," *Governing*, October 5, 2015.

4. Mimi Kirki, "How Economically Diverse Neighborhoods Give Poor Black and Latino Youth a Leg Up," CityLab, March 10, 2017, accessed April 30, 2018, https://www.citylab.com/equity/2017/03/economically-diverse-neighborhoods -give-poor-black-and-latinx-youth-a-leg-up/519171. See also Raj Chetty, Na-thaniel Hendren, and Lawrence F. Katz, "The Effects of Exposure to Better Neighborhoods on Children: New Evidence from the Moving to Opportunity Experiment," *American Economic Review* 106, no. 4 (April 2016): 855–902.

5. Sara Mead, "Happy Birthday, Head Start," *U.S. News & World Report*, May 18, 2017, accessed April 30, 2018, https://www.usnews.com/opinion /knowledge-bank/articles/2017-05-18/after-52-years-head-start-still-helps-families -and-children.

6. David Kirp, "Opinion: How New York Made Pre-K a Success," *New York Times*, January 19, 2018, accessed April 30, 2018, https://www.nytimes .com/2016/02/14/opinion/sunday/how-new-york-made-pre-k-a-success.html.

7. Ibid.

8. Phillip B. Levine and Diane Whitmore Schanzenbach, "The Impact of Children's Public Health Insurance Expansions on Educational Outcomes," NBER Working Paper No. 14671 (January 2009), www.nber.org/papers/w14671.

9. C. Kirabo Jackson, Rucker C. Johnson, and Claudia Persico, "The Effects of School Spending on Educational and Economic Outcomes: Evidence from School Finance Reforms," *Quarterly Journal of Economics* 131, no. 1 (2015): 157–218.

10. Jackie Mader, "How One Mississippi District Made Integration Work," *Huffington Post*, April 19, 2016, accessed April 30, 2018, https://www.huffington post.com/entry/mississippi-integration_us_57151ff2e4b0060ccda3df7c; "2019 Best School Districts in Mississippi," Niche, accessed September 9, 2018, https:// www.niche.com/k12/search/best-school-districts/s/mississippi.

11. For "Most Livable Cities," see "Retirement," Clinton, https://www .clintonms.org/residents/relocation/retirement. Other data from US census, 2010.

12. Mader, "How One Mississippi District Made Integration Work."

13. Ibid.

14. Danielle Elliot, "Restoring the Promise of Public Education," *Atlantic*, n.d., accessed April 30, 2018, https://www.theatlantic.com/sponsored/allstate -2017/restoring-the-promise-of-public-education/1181.

15. Mader, "How One Mississippi District Made Integration Work."

16. Ibid.

17. Ibid.

18. Quotations from Linda Brown Thompson in this section are from "Linda Brown Thompson at the Brown v. Board of Education Anniversary," C-SPAN, June 28, 2017, accessed April 30, 2018, https://www.c-span.org/video /?c4675164/linda-brown-thompson-brown-v-board-education-anniversary.

INDEX

RUCKER JOHNSON is an associate professor in the Goldman School of Public Policy at the University of California, Berkeley, and faculty research associate at the National Bureau of Economic Research. He lives in Oakland, California.